A Complete User-Friendly Guide

by

Tom Rohrer, Ph.D., M.F.T.

Thriving Beyond Addiction™: A Complete User-Friendly Guide

ISBN: 978-1-941713-42-6

ANDREW BENZIE BOOKS
andrewbenziebooks.com

Other books and products by Tom Rohrer

Thriving Beyond Addiction™ Workbook, (In Revision) 2016
www.thrivingbeyondaddiction.com

Harmonious Passion™ (Due out) 2017
www.harmoniouspassion.com

Affirming Stage II Recovery Audio MP3 © 1988, 2013

ACKNOWLEDGMENTS

First, I want to thank the many thousands of recovering individuals who contributed over the years to this book, however indirectly, by choosing to be in recovery with me one-on-one or at a treatment center where I worked or consulted. I want to acknowledge John "J" Bird, Maureen Rookwood, and Chuck Dutchman for their support at the beginning of this journey.

I want to thank Sharyn Abbott, Janet Green, Jeannine Jones, Robin Ramsey, Diana Sangston, Stephanie Scott, Rachel Zohn, my mother Gladys and my brother Fred for their support, and Linda Saker for her significant work and perseverance with the difficult graphics and layout of this book.

I am grateful for the professional feedback from John Kerbs, PhD; Joan Zweben, PhD; Hilding Ohrstrom, LCPC, CCS; Chesley Swanson, LCSW, and Casey Brodhead, PhD; and the staff of the Haight Ashbury Free Clinic Counseling Services, especially John Patton; Dennis Doland; and Daryl Inaba, PharmD for their feedback and support. I would also like to recognize the hundreds of clients who have used the information in this book and who have worked with me individually and in research groups at Haight Ashbury Free Clinic Counseling Services, Diablo Valley Ranch, Frederic Ozanam Center, and at other treatment programs.

A very special thanks to Ann Schiebert, PsyD, whose support and feedback has been invaluable and very appreciated.

DEDICATION

This book is dedicated to everyone who has ever been affected by addiction. Addiction is a constant struggle, but there are answers and options. If you choose to open up and grow, you will become happier, healthier, and more successful, possibly a lot more than you are now. Others in your life may not join you, only time will tell if they do, but there are reasons for you to have hope and even faith that you and your family will do what it takes to recover and thrive!

This book is also dedicated to all of the professionals, from Dr. William Silkworth forward, who have for many decades attempted to help people struggling with addictive disorders to recover.

It is my hope that, for everyone who takes the time to read or skim this book, they will find value in the words written, enough to help motivate them to take the first steps to addiction recovery.

INTRODUCTION

I'm a curious person who loves to learn. Over the decades, I've explored many approaches to healing, and I've worked in a wide range of addiction treatment programs. **Thriving Beyond Addiction** is my attempt to share what I have learned.

It's the people who can look outside of the box who will incite change for themselves and others. My observation is that many addiction treatment providers and those involved in self-help recovery still think very much inside of the box, bound by old, limited practices. I hope this book will cause every reader to think or at least peek outside of their own box, to be inspired by new, creative, and effective methods of addiction recovery.

Thriving Beyond Addiction pairs the tried and true methods of addiction recovery with thinking that is outside of the box. Its goal is to help you to thrive beyond your active addiction by introducing you to all of the resources, information, tools, strategies, and encouragement you'll need to successfully deal with your addiction and create the life you want.

Knowledge of how to achieve and maintain successful recovery from addiction has grown over the years, but much of this knowledge has yet to reach the many people struggling with the terrible issues that are packaged with addiction – the people who need the knowledge the most.

Unfortunately, to describe in detail every experience, fact, strategy, and tool in one book, **Thriving Beyond Addiction** would have to be so big, or the print would have to be so small, that few would be willing to read it. To limit the size of the book for the benefit of readers, ideas and topics discussed within have been optimized for easy readability. I've also narrowed the length of the examples and stories used, prioritizing quality over quantity. In future books, I will expand on some of the ideas presented in this book that require further depth.

To be clear, most of the ideas and approaches in this book are not new. They came from many sources. I thank all of the professionals in the field of addiction recovery for their wonderful resources. Some acknowledgment is given by way of listing their books. (See APPENDIX 10.)

This book and workbook will help you clarify what you want **Your Recovering Future™** to be. You will realize that recovery is not about what you are giving up; it's about what you are gaining. Yet, this book is not meant to be your only resource; you must go out into the world and develop a meaningful life, using a program that engages real people and real emotional experiences.

Nutritional-based addiction treatment is not accepted by most professionals in the traditional or medical addiction treatment fields, but I believe in its validity. In April of 2009, I took a nutritional compound I thought would help my moderate-level, situational depression. Two hours later, the situation was still depressing, but I was not depressed. I don't need research to validate my experience. Since then, I've shared with many recovering addicts my experience of amino acids and proper nutrition in sustaining recovery. Most of those who've tried amino acid supplements have been happy with the results. I believe that nutrition-based addiction treatment must be a top priority in everyone's recovery.

This book will forever be a work in progress. I hope that you, the reader, will help me to continue to improve it by sending me your feedback to <drtom@tomrohrer.com>. Thank you in advance.

Note: My goal in writing this book is to share information. It can't replace medical, psychological, or other treatments used by healing professionals. Before you stop using any medication or service, start to exercise, significantly change your nutritional intake, consult your MD or appropriate professional, and get professional feedback. Unfortunately, most MDs don't understand nutritional supplements or other alternative approaches. If you are detoxifying from drugs or sugar, don't assume the transition will be smooth, especially in the first few days.

Disclaimer: The information in this book is for educational purposes only. Any suggestions should not be taken as expert advice, and everyone's specific situation must be evaluated individually. If you have been diagnosed with mental or physical symptoms of a medical or psychiatric condition, you need to consult a qualified health care professional before following any suggestions in this book. Please find and use the mental and emotional support necessary to deal with your specific situation regarding addiction recovery.

So let's get started!

Thriving Beyond Addiction™
Table of Contents

Chapter 1

First Things First

Chapter 1: First Things First
Table of Contents

FIRST THINGS FIRST

Welcome and congratulations! Your decision to read this book as part of your recovery program will be rewarding. Congratulate yourself for taking an important first step.

CONGRATULATIONS!

The goal of **Thriving Beyond Addiction™** is to offer you facts, resources, and wisdom about recovery in a user-friendly way. This information will help you to move through the recovery maze and onto better days. The process will be stimulating. Your beliefs will affect whether your experience will feel scary, sad, and limited, or happy, joyous, and free. If you accept that what you're leaving behind is a destructive addiction, you'll be more likely to embrace recovery.

A Defining Moment

I'm assuming you've had your moment-of-truth and that you've accepted that you are an addict. Hopefully, your *Defining Moment* brought you the clarity that it was time to accept the challenge of recovery. If not, ask yourself, why not? You may need to take a deeper look at your addiction, motivations, or goals. Read APPENDIX 1 and take the Addiction Evaluation. Explore your answers for their accuracy and then make a decision. Do you want to recover?

If you're reading this book to help a loved one who suffers

with an addiction, educate yourself so that you can be helpful when they're ready to change; consider intervening as described in APPENDIX 1.

Recovering Intelligence

To help your loved one, be ready, be educated!

Breathe! – You'll Be Okay

If you're feeling down because you're an addict, and if in your mind you're using words like "loser" or "stupid," stop

now. Give yourself a break! As Billy Joel sang in *Second Wind*, "You're only human, you're supposed to make mistakes." The reality is that addiction is a human issue; many struggle with it to some degree. Amongst those who suffer from it, some struggle with addiction their whole life, while others are able to let go and embrace recovery.

It's vital to know that you're not responsible for your addiction, but you are responsible for your recovery. The family, genetic, nutritional, social, or spiritual issues that contributed to your addiction need to be managed, neutralized, or eliminated. You didn't start out using alcohol, placing a bet, or super-sizing your meal with the goal of becoming an addict. Yet, if you've had major life problems due to using and are not in recovery, you're choosing to be ill. This is your *Defining Moment*! Please choose health!

Recovering Intelligence

You're not responsible for your addiction. You are responsible for your recovery!

THRIVING BEYOND ADDICTION™

There is an extra emphasis on drug addiction in this book, but it will be a useful guide for those recovering from any addiction because:

1. The process of addiction (See APPENDIX 2.) and recovery is similar for all addictions.
2. Most addicts deal with two or more addictions. Recovery from all of them is best done at the same time, showing your total commitment to recovery.

Though recovery is similar for all addictions, there are some behavioral differences that may arise when recovering from individual addictions, such as:

- An anorexic's voice saying, "You're fat."
- Intense shame for a female sex addict.
- The constant need to "look good" for someone who is a codependent partner.
- Physical damage from consumed substances.
- Food addicts who are overweight.
- Reward-seeking for the success and fame addict.

By understanding exactly what recovery is, it's more likely you will embrace it. Recovery isn't a one-time event. There are some addictions in which you can't be totally abstinent from, such as food for the food addict and shopping for the shopaholic. Therefore, recover is a lifelong process of observing your behavior while adapting and moving toward a more positive and healthier lifestyle. To succeed, you'll

need to change some of your beliefs, thoughts, and behaviors. You are intelligent; you just need to learn about the tools and strategies for successful recovery. In recovery, you'll learn to be happier and healthier. Not entering recovery is a decision to walk the path of self-destruction. Make a commitment to do whatever it takes. This will make it much easier to live your best life, for the rest of your life.

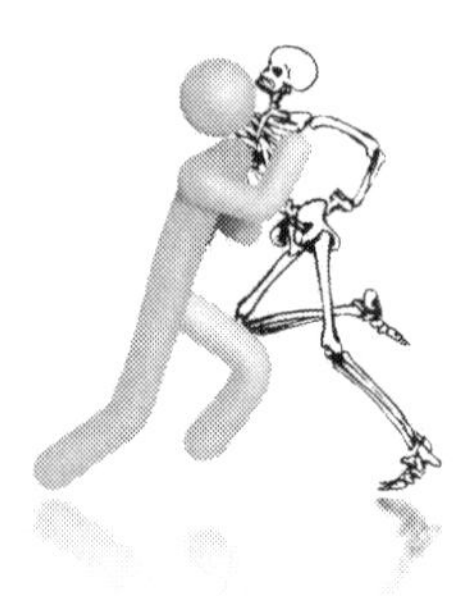

Taking Action

At a basic level, there are two things you need to do:

1. Choose to be abstinent or abuse. Consult your MD before you stop using physically addictive drugs.
    - Your body will naturally detoxify from drugs and sugar, but work with your medical doctor to ensure no damage is done to your body during the detox process.
2. Connect with yourself, others, and The Source.
    - Yourself: Connect with your thoughts, emotions and sensations, needs, motivations, and goals.
    - Others: Find supportive, knowledgeable, and objective people.
    - The Source: Find a spiritual guide or participate in a spiritual or religious practice.

It's frustrating and even overwhelming to start a new life journey without knowing the rules. ***Don't Allow Yourself to Get Overwhelmed!*** Start by taking a few deep breaths and honestly acknowledging your current situation. YOU

NEED TO CHANGE! To do this, you'll have many tasks ahead of you, but you have the rest of your life to work on them, one day at a time, or even one minute at a time. Recovery will move you forward and help you to create new life goals. The key is to do whatever it takes to get started and to keep moving until you are successful.

Recovering Intelligence

You must stop abusive behaviors & connect with yourself & supportive others!

The pilot of an airplane must go full throttle to get the plane off the ground. Once the plane is flying, the power can be reduced and the plane will stay in the air. It may take a major effort to get your recovery off of the ground, but once you've leveled off, it will be easier. In addition, your life will start to change in many positive ways.

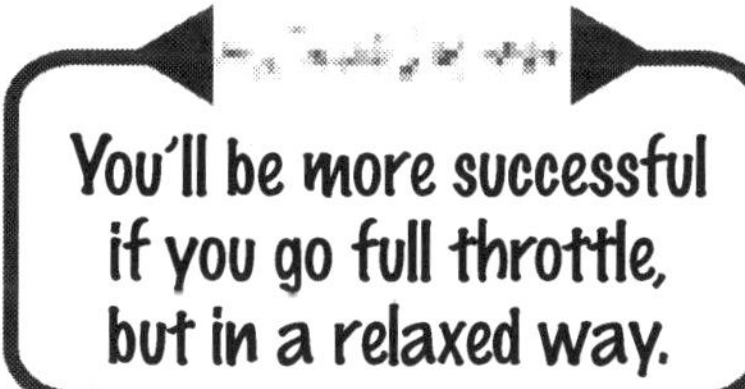

Take a desirable action right now, this very moment, because action breaks up the negative emotions that keep you stuck, unhappy, and in your addiction.

IMPORTANT THINGS

There are several important things you need to know as you start your recovery:

1. This book offers an ideal model. Strive for it, but

feel okay with something less than ideal.

2. You probably have many questions. As you read this book, they'll be answered. Relax, breathe, get out of your own way, and engage in a recovery process that tens of thousands of people before you have successfully followed.
3. This book offers many resources to help you clarify and find answers for the who, what, when, where, why, and how of recovery. It introduces you to traditional and cutting-edge recovery options. It helps you in adapting a program to meet your needs.
4. The best approach for you is the one that fits or intuitively matches you, because you're more likely to follow it. If you interpret this to mean an easy, simple, or limited approach, it's doubtful that it will be effective. At the start, an excellent strategy is to embrace a universal, time-tested structure until you and your recovery support group members agree on how to improve your program. If you do change how you're going to handle your recovery, stay active in your current approach until you are engaged in the new one.

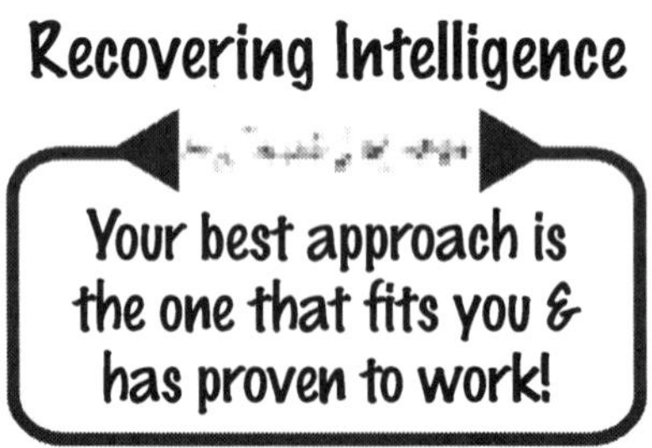

5. There may be some undesirable consequences in your decision to deal with your addiction. Examples are: you may need to let go of a true friend who's still using, or your family might become upset because

recovery is taking up a lot of your time.

6. In your approach, you may need to let go of old beliefs, fears, and strategies that have guided your life thus far. This can be difficult; commit to new changes for a few weeks, and it'll get easier. Your best approach will be a holistic one that includes:
   - **Bio-Nutritional**
   - **Mental-Emotional**
   - **Learning-Growing**
   - **Relational-Social**
   - **Spiritual-Quantum Physics**
7. Whatever approach you choose, you must open up, become involved, and evolve. You may have to move out of your comfort zone. You don't have to be enthusiastic or even like it, but you must be willing to go through the process. You may question whether you are changing and whether these changes will be permanent. Expect that others will have the same questions. Those closest to you will notice your behavioral and emotional changes, especially if you consistently follow your program to the best of your ability. A benefit of this book and the workbook is that they provide you with an opportunity to be totally honest with yourself. Ask yourself the tough questions. Listen for the answers. Sharing your journey with other people will help make it real.

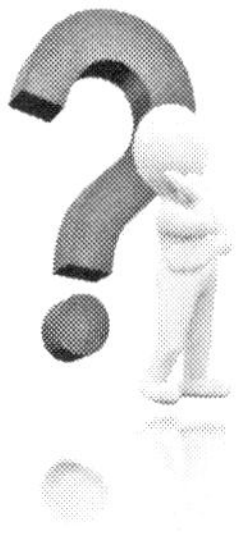

THE FORMAT OF THIS BOOK

This book will be an introduction, reference guide, and road map for your recovery. It's a brief, basic, yet complete introduction to what you'll need to do to be successful. It expands on many important areas in the APPENDIXES. You can easily find terms and concepts using the Index or Table of Contents.

Highlight Boxes

Highlight boxes summarize and point out key ideas, and can be used as an additional resource in overviewing and reviewing important information as you are reading. To help you become familiarized with the book, I've included tips below on how you can use these boxes as you read and what kind of information they offer.

Image of video controls for the vision that you want to create.

Your Recovering Future

INTRODUCING THE RED DOT REMINDER CHECK-IN SYSTEM

Red Dot Reminder Check-In System - Like a red stoplight or a hand signal at a crosswalk, these highlight boxes offer reminders of recovery skills, tools, and strategies.

When you see a Red Dot Reminder, it's a cue for you to stop and focus on your recovery by:

- Remembering to breathe and relax.
- Observing yourself and your situation.
- Reminding yourself what's most important to your recovery.
- Remind yourself that doing this check-in is helpful.

The Red Dot Reminders help you stay aware that there are forces within yourself that may undermine your recovery. Your own instincts, emotions and past behavioral patterns can thwart your desire for recovery. You have compelling reasons you seek recovery – the Red Dot Reminders help you remain aware of those reasons even when your past behavioral patterns try and reemerge.

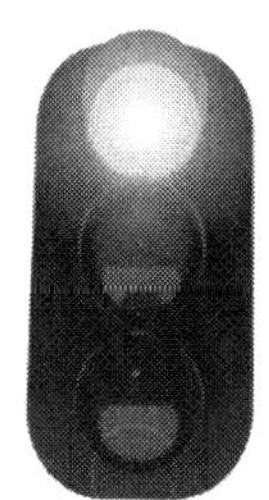

Red Dot Reminder highlight boxes serve to keep you on track and remind you why you want a healthy recovering lifestyle. Examples are:

- I need to feel proud of myself, to see a look of pride in my (family's) face!
- I want to live a spiritual driven life!
- I want to be a good parent and a role model!
- I want the best life I can have!

- I want to live happy, joyous and free!
- I never want to experience the negative consequences of addiction!
- I'm sick and tired of being sick and tired!

Each time you check in with yourself, it's a chance to consciously refocus. In time, the new behavior will sink into your unconscious mind and will become the new you!

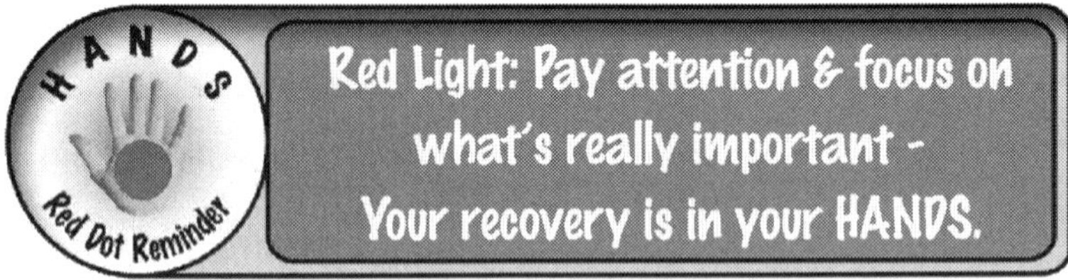

INTRODUCING RECOVERING INTELLIGENCE™

Recovering Intelligence™ - These highlight boxes focus on intelligent recovery options for building and maintaining your recovery.

Recovering Intelligence™ boxes remind you how to think, feel, and behave in order to create and maintain successful recovery. RI boxes help you to review what has worked and what hasn't worked in your life; and to then build on what worked by adding knowledge, tools, strategies, and positive experiences to it.

Recovering Intelligence

This image is of a neurotransmitter conveying information.

To develop a high level of **RI**, you must do the following:

- Accept and embrace self-awareness.
- Develop the ability to observe yourself and your situation accurately.
- Understand how to set up, work, and live an effective personal recovery program.
- Learn the Seven Intelligences of Recovery. Develop and use them until they become part of who you are. (See list below.)
- Understand how your past behavior, roles, strategies, situations, and decisions helped form the values, attitudes, and beliefs you have today.
- Develop a basic understanding of who you are – your issues, your addict and sober personality, and the strengths that worked well for you in the past.
- Understand self-development and actively engage in your personal growth.
- Learn how to achieve your tasks, goals, and dreams and build **Your Recovering Future™**.

The Seven Intelligences of Recovery

These intelligences can overlap. They are:

Emotional Intelligence: The ability to know your feelings and how to effectively deal with them.

Growth and Healing Intelligence: The ability to evaluate, learn, and grow; and to apologize, forgive, and heal from life injuries.

Intimacy Intelligence: The ability to open up, to trust, and to bond with important people in your life.

Resiliency Intelligence: The ability to bounce back from life's setbacks and live a full life.

Social Intelligence: The ability or desire to know someone's feelings and how to relate to them.

Spiritual Intelligence: The willingness and ability to open up to your Higher Power.

Success Intelligence: The ability to clarify what you need and want, then find and use the best resources to achieve your goals and dreams.

As **Recovering Intelligence™** becomes your personal reminder of the kind of life and recovery you want, you'll use it to build the vehicle that will carry you into your quality recovering lifestyle. **Your Recovering Intelligence™** will give you the ability to create **Your Recovering Future™**.

INTRODUCING
YOUR RECOVERING FUTURE™

Your Recovering Future™ - These highlight boxes assist you in creating a vision of your recovery in the future, to see how your life will change and to begin to feel the benefits of being in recovery. **Your Recovering Future™** is a powerful, positive image of your ideal recovery. Make this imagined recovering future so desirable that you're compelled, in the present, to do whatever it takes to create it and keep it. The **YRF** image that you see, hear, feel, taste,

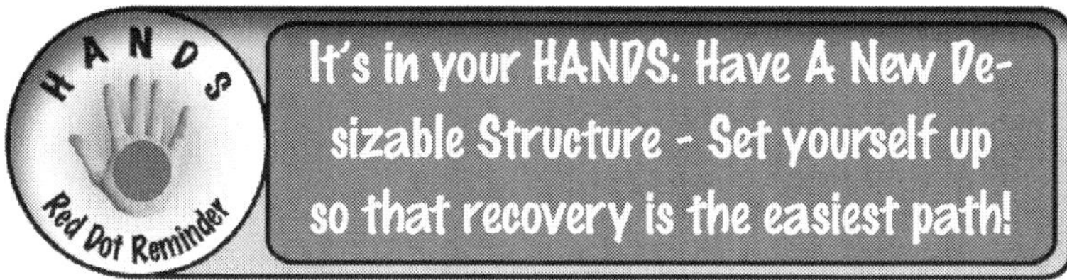

and smell needs to be realistic and obtainable. A recovery program with a structure has to be at the heart of **YRF**. You'll use that structure to help set yourself up for success. You'll be molding and managing your recovery daily and reviewing it weekly, monthly, and yearly. The **YRF** model has three important aspects:

Structure: Set yourself up for success with a structure that makes it easier to stay on your recovery path than it is to get off of it. If, on both sides of your recovery road, there are recovery reminders, supportive people, and a solid program, you'll be aware when you're sliding off – just like how you would know if you were running over speed bumps, hitting orange construction cones, or going up a steep embankment. Your structure makes it easier for you to go straight down your recovery track.

Vision: Visualize the completion of your next positive recovering event or milestone, such as celebrating your next recovery chip, completing a step or a page in a recovery workbook, or attending a family event. Like a motion picture playing in your mind's eye, imagine your future with all five senses – take a few minutes to do this every morning and at night. Make your vision as detailed an image as you can – or start with a simple snapshot that you can build on.

Your Recovering Future™ is the image of your ideal recovery that you feel you must create.

Your Recovering Future

Acknowledge the total truth of what's happening today in relationship to **Your Recovering Future™.** For example:

- "I'm having a bad day. I want to use, but I have three days of clean time that I don't want to throw away. My goal is to get 30 days clean. I'm not going to use because I want to feel proud of myself in My Recovering Future."
- "I'm excited, confused, and scared about starting my new recovering life, even though I hope it will be wonderful."

Keep all negative beliefs and attitudes out of your speech and thoughts. It's difficult to do this when, chances are, negative thoughts and emotions triggered you to engage in your addiction. Once you start thinking or saying, "I can't do it," or "It's too hard," or "F___ it – it's not worth it," RUN to the nearest phone and call someone in your recovery support group.

Action: Setting yourself up for success is about taking action now. For example, if you need to do something next week that you know will trigger your addiction, right now, while you are thinking of it, arrange to be accompanied by a recovering friend(s) who can support and remind you to stay on task.

Remember to live your recovery one step at a time – but don't lose the vision of your future. That way, your unconscious will adopt these new visions and assist you with creating **Your Recovering Future**™.

Additional Resources

You will come across "See..." or "Find..." at the end of some paragraphs. These references direct you to additional information in an APPENDIX, or in the Definitions or Index sections at the back of the book. An expanded Table of Contents is included at the beginning of each chapter to outline the material covered in that chapter.

Chapter Summaries

At the end of all seven chapters, you'll find a summary, which will summarize the important information in that chapter. There, you will find a list of key ideas and insights.

Chapter Two – Immediate Recovery discusses some of the major components of recovery, types of addictions, treatment options, stages of recovery, how to begin recovery, and general and specialized treatment issues and options.

Chapter Three – Early Recovery introduces how to build a recovery program and incorporates information about recovery challenges and development.

Chapter Four – Continuing Recovery – Strategies & Tools offers many valuable resources, from affirmations to mental imagery to writing.

Chapter Five – Continuing Recovery – Personal Issues introduces you to recovery issues such as behavioral changes, emotional development, interpersonal challenges, mental health complications, and spiritual evolvement.

Chapter Six – Continuing Recovery – Personal Growth discusses the mental, emotional, personal, social, spiritual, and structural solutions for creating a healthy recovering lifestyle.

Chapter Seven – Continuing Recovery – Relapse teaches you how to avoid mental-emotional relapse and offers approaches and solutions to handle triggers, cravings, and symptoms when they appear.

Chapter Eight – Marriage & Family Recovery briefly introduces you to addiction and recovery-related relationship and family challenges.

Appendixes

You will find additional in-depth information about recovery in the APPENDIXES. The APPENDIXES provide more detailed information on select topics.

APPENDIX 1 – Before Recovery Can Start
APPENDIX 2 – Addictions: Causes & Types
APPENDIX 3 – Nutrition
APPENDIX 4 – Definitions – Use as a dictionary.
APPENDIX 5 – Social-Emotional Intelligence
APPENDIX 6 – Developing Your Recovering Future™
APPENDIX 7 – "In My Experience... Things You Don't Want."
APPENDIX 8 – The Top 21 Thinking Errors
APPENDIX 9 – Introduction To Group Process
APPENDIX 10 – Recovery Resources

Index

At the back of the book, you'll find all the main topics listed in alphabetical order.

AN OVERVIEW: THE 7 TASK AREAS OF YOUR RECOVERING FUTURE™ MODEL

In early recovery, it's generally best to follow a program that has worked for others. There's no one approach that's best for everyone. Today, you should have several options available to choose from. In early recovery, select a program that is easy and simple for you to follow. Your first program doesn't need to be complicated or intense.

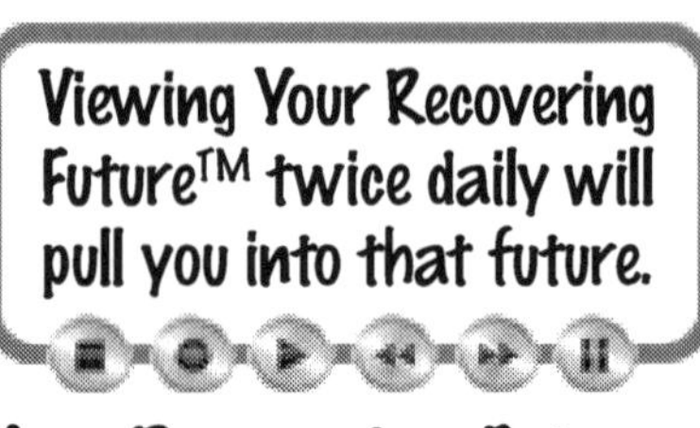

Your Recovering Future

A thriving life demands an adaptable, flexible, and expandable style. The order of the following task areas are only a suggestion; however, all seven are important.

1. Your Approach: *Learning and Using Effective Resources* – How you enter and think about recovery highly affects your outcome.
   - Find: Support, guidance, modeling.
   - Develop: Recovery and spiritual practices.
2. Your Recovery Skills: *Foundation* – Follow a path that has proven its value. Set up your recovery plan for primary and secondary addictions, create a relapse prevention plan, learn tools and strategies, and use reminders to remember to practice and to employ these tools and strategies often.
3. Your Awareness: *Opportunity* – Use each opportunity to learn about yourself, recovery and relapse issues, tools and strategies, and faith; take responsibility, make clearer and better choices. Without awareness you have no chance to succeed.
4. Managing Your Life: *Responsibility* – Managing change: Take care of yourself by developing your mental, emotional, nutritional, physical, social, and spiritual health, as well as your recovery and relationships. Find a recovery guide (someone who has already done this) to help you.
5. Your Personal Work: *Resolving and Managing Issues*

– Problem solving model: Examine addictions, family history, problem solving and conflict resolution styles; deal with emotions, physical and relationship issues, relapse triggers and symptoms, and Post Acute Withdrawal Symptoms (PAWS).

6. Your Personal Growth: *Expanding, Engaging, and Living Fully* – Observe, assess, and evolve; pursue social, emotional, physical, and spiritual growth; engage in the purposeful life that you want.
7. Your Mental Shifts: *Expanding Perception and Focus* – Major mental and emotional (paradigm) shifts will happen when you gain significant knowledge and perspective about yourself. Your attitudes, beliefs, emotions, identity, self-esteem, recovery, and spirituality will all be affected and change.

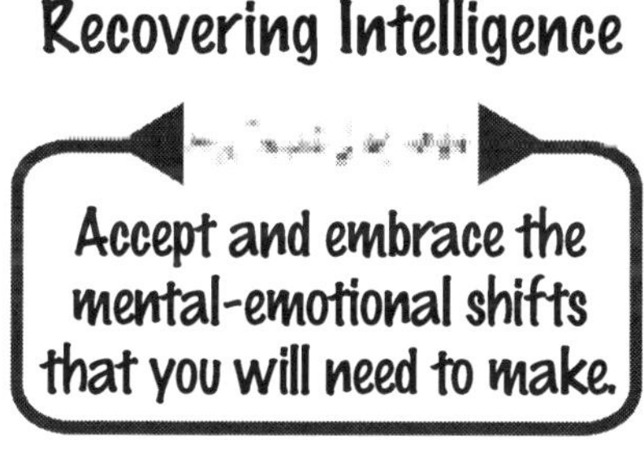

Terms

Below are some common terms you will see throughout the book:

- *Approach*, *program*, and *structure* will be used to mean the same thing.
- *Addict* will refer to someone actively involved with any physical addictions or

Recovering Intelligence

The 1, 2, 3 approach is simple & desirable, yet limited; more is needed.

addictive behaviors, or at least has not yet embraced recovery.

- *Clean* and *sober* will mean abstinence from mind-altering addictive drugs or addictive behaviors.
- *Drugs* will include alcohol, caffeine, nicotine, over-the-counter and prescription medications, and processed food, especially (processed) sugar, sugar substitutes, and processed carbohydrates.
- *Feelings* will mean emotional feelings and body sensations.
- *Higher Power*, *spirit*, *spiritual*, *Source,* and *The Source* are used to mean the same thing.
- *Mental* and *emotional* or *mental-emotional* are used to mean the same thing as psychological.
- *Recovery* and *recovering* are used to describe an addict who is clean, or sustaining a maintenance addiction, and actively involved in a recovery program and personal growth.
- *Triggers* and *cues* mean the same thing.
- *Using* or *use* mean active involvement in any addiction or addictive behavior.

(See APPENDIX 4: Definitions.)

Understand that, like every other addict, you can only stay clean by choosing to turn away from the darkness of your addiction and towards the light of recovery – one moment, one breath, one step, one day at a time. Know that every day, even every hour, that you are clean is a success for you. Your experience, knowledge, and confidence will build day by day.

Thriving Beyond Addiction™ offers you the knowledge that can enable you to have a second chance at a first-class life. And it's yours if you choose it. Breathe slowly and deeply!

Feel your joy, love, & excitement!

Chapter 2

Immediate Recovery

Chapter 2: Immediate Recovery
Table of Contents

A NEW BEGINNING: INTRODUCTION INTO RECOVERY

Welcome to recovery. I bet it took you a long time to get here. Breathe. Your life is about to change for the better – if you stay on your recovery road. You may experience some hard bumps along the way, but it is worth the effort to work through and smooth them out. If you don't return to using, you WILL realize many positive changes in your life. Until you start recovery, you are stuck in "Nowhere Land," with your mind confused and your heart caught between two worlds. Treatment professionals call this the pre-treatment stage. During the pre-treatment stage, your addict self falsely believes using is the answer to all your problems, while the dopamine in your brain, altered by your addiction, incorrectly sends you the message that you need to use to survive. At the same time, you know you need to change your lifestyle. What a struggle!

Recovering Intelligence

Breathe Deeply & Slowly!

It takes courage to start recovery, courage you have shown even by picking up this book to learn how to change your life for the better. By using your inner and outer resources, you can keep traveling along your recovery road, and be successful, no matter what is thrown your way. Stay courageous! You can do it!

Recovering Intelligence

Recovery begins as you commit to and are active on your path of recovery.

To Get a Good Start:

- Contact your physician! Have a check-up! Be honest! Follow all medical advice.
- Practice abstinence from all addictive substances and behaviors.
- Join a recovery program. Sit there, listen, and take it all in. You do not have to do a thing. Magic can happen if you just keep going back.

- Accept recovery into your life. It takes work, but consider whatever event that got you into recovery as a blessing. Do whatever it takes to stay the course. As you progress along your path, acknowledge, nurture, and reward yourself.

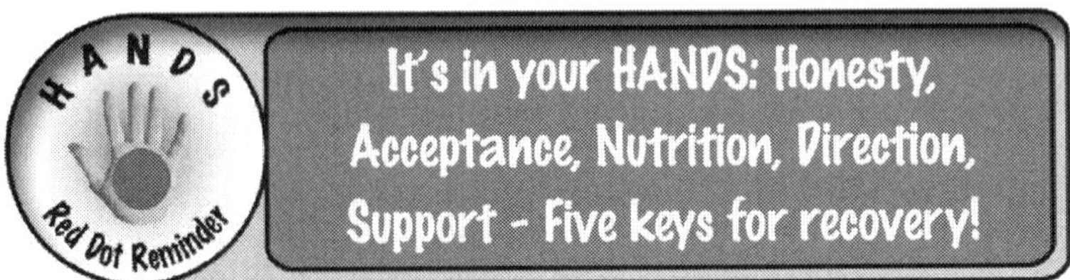

- Learn about the PINK CLOUD that is experienced in early recovery. You may not consciously want to use, the abstinence may feel wonderful, but when this "pink cloud" collapses (and it will), your fall to earthly reality will be much easier if you have begun building your recovery structure.

If you want to start your recovery, don't allow your

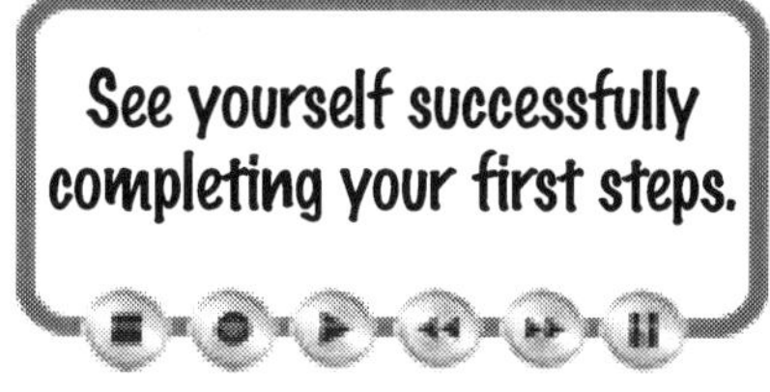

addict self to sabotage what you want by indulging in, "I'll do it soon," or "I'll be okay," type of thinking. If you truly cannot begin now, set yourself up for success by taking action to ensure that you will follow through ASAP. Examples of taking action are: contacting a referral center and asking for help; making an appointment with a counselor for the first possible appointment time; going to a self-help support group meeting; or signing a clear and specific, time-limited contract with yourself and putting it in a visible place. Whatever you decide to do, commit, take whatever action you can, and follow through.

READY? GREAT! LET'S GET STARTED!

GETTING STARTED

As you read this chapter, take appropriate action. Plan, build support for, or start a treatment program! You will benefit from reading the complete book when you have the time, but reading it without taking action only gives you facts, not results. Recovery is an emotional experience. You'll need to open up and recognize your feelings, and allow them to guide you. Once you understand what you need to do, take action as soon as possible.

IMMEDIATE TASKS

Finding Support

Every recovering addict needs help and encouragement. Even if you decide to use only this book as the basis for your recovery (not recommended), you'll want an active core support group. Consider friends and family as part of your support group, ideally who are in recovery and can relate, but only accept help from those who'll give you quality support and good direction, who'll be there for you in the hard times. Trust those you have chosen to work with, unless you discover you shouldn't.

See your support and feel your excitement as you start your journey into Your Recovering Future™

Your Recovering Future

Eliminating Cravings and Neutralizing Triggers

Addictions occur because of excessive behavior, like the abuse of substances, that overstimulates the neuropathways in the brain, causing cravings that can be difficult to suppress. Cravings do not go away overnight. All addicts in recovery have cravings, which can cause a range of issues, from occasional discomfort to an addict's return to using. Though cravings can develop on their own, they are also caused by triggers, environmental cues that initiate the rapid fire of neuropathways, such as when a smoker sees a cigarette. To be successful in recovery, it is mandatory to minimize or eliminate these triggers.

There are effective techniques for neutralizing triggers. (See Professional Therapeutic Styles in the Index.) Cravings can also be reduced or eliminated with options such as: awareness of your desire for recovery (called Your Heart Trigger); distractions like fun and humor, nutritional supplements (Vitamin D, Omega 3, and L-glutamine), and a high-quality diet. Always check with your M.D.

Recovering Intelligence

Reduce cravings with amino acids & learn to neutralize triggers.

Stress is a major cause of triggering. Reducing stress will neutralize triggers or at least lower the likelihood of being triggered and succumbing to relapse.

Other methods to deter cravings include acupuncture, meditation, progressive relaxation, and sleep. (See APPENDIX 3.)

Medical Exam

A physical examination by a medical doctor is highly recommended, especially when abstaining from drug and food addictions. Be honest with your MD about your situation and issues. For instance, sex addicts need to get tested for STDs. Ask about vitamin, mineral, amino acid, and nutritional supplements. Medication for relief of physical withdrawal symptoms may be necessary. If possible, work with a physician who specializes in addiction medicine (or at least one who understands addictions) and who will consult with an addiction nutrition specialist. Ask for a referral through the association ASAM. (See APPENDIX 10.)

DETOXIFICATION

The period of physical withdrawal from all substances – drugs, medications, and sugars – is called detoxification, or detox for short. If you have been putting an addictive substance into your body on a daily or reoccurring basis, abstaining from that substance will cause some level of physical withdrawal symptoms to occur.

Your body (mainly your liver, lungs, and skin) will detox you naturally. Toxins leave the body at varying rates of speed, and depending on the type of toxin, can cause a range of physical complications. Commonly during a hard detox, symptoms vary from mild physical discomfort to those similar to a severe flu. It's best to be under a physician's care when detoxing, especially when abstaining from drugs like alcohol, barbiturates, opiates, and benzodiazepines, which due to their chemical properties, require monitoring by a medically trained professional. Detoxing is a necessary stage of recovery, but be careful to follow medical guidelines, especially if you've had a history of seizures, cardiac issues, or other complications related to detoxification. Get evaluated for conditions such as hyperglycemia, hypoglycemia, diabetes, and high blood pressure.

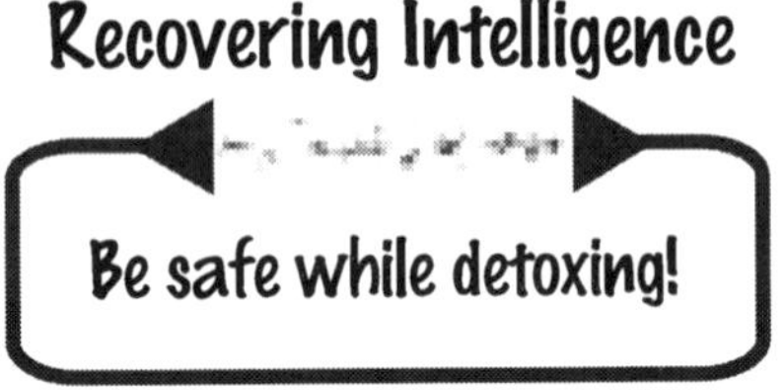

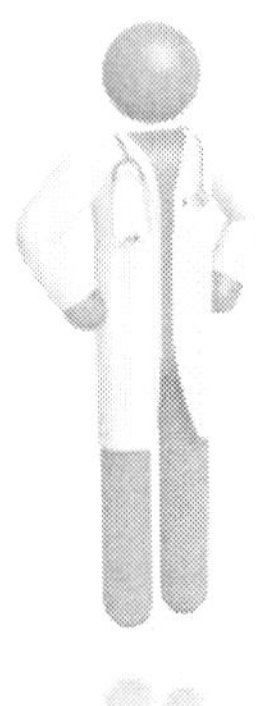

Most people detox at home or in a hospital. There

are private programs or publicly funded detox centers that have medical backup. Contact your physician, local treatment program or hospital, or look for "Addiction..." "Alcoholism..." or "Drug Abuse..." in your phone book or on the Internet.

Note: It can be dangerous to refrain from all drugs, especially if you're on medications for a severe mental illness or a physical condition. Ask for advice from respected and informed professionals and follow it during early recovery.

Relief of Withdrawal Symptoms

All methods discussed below are effective in relieving physical withdrawal symptoms in the detox recovery stage. Each method can be used alone or together with other options.

Not all withdrawal symptoms are physical. There are also emotional withdrawal symptoms. Addicts build an attachment, or affection, to a particular substance or behavior. Letting go of the substance or behavior can prompt a sense of loss, causing emotional pain. Both emotional pain and physical withdrawal symptoms can be alleviated through the methods below.

Nutrition

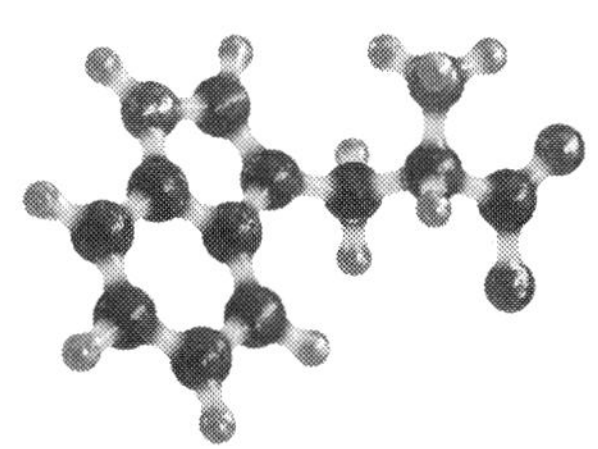

Nutritional supplements are a prime option for relieving physical withdrawal symptoms due to their immediate and effective results, minimal side effects, and no potential for abuse. For optimal results, it's best to work with a nutritionist, whose knowledge will be helpful and sometimes necessary. Many physicians do not have an extensive knowledge of nutritional supplements. If possible, talk to your physician regarding your desire to try alternative approaches, or at least keep him or her informed of the alternative approaches that you are taking.

Recovering Intelligence

Support your detoxing with amino acids, they are safe and effective!

Most people can experience powerful symptom relief from basic amino acid supplements. An amino nutrient blend is even more effective, but costs more. Amino acids can relieve physical and emotional pain, and they can reduce or stop cravings, anxiety, and depression. They also stabilize blood sugar and promote the rebuilding of your brain and body to a healthier state. Amino acid supplements are sold over-the-counter; the higher the purity (in the mid 90% range), the better. But ensure your source for nutritional supplements are from a reliable supplier! (See APPENDIX 3.)

When it comes to the dosage, be cautious. Test with 1/4 of the suggested dose and wait 30 minutes to see how you feel. The only way of knowing the exact amount you need is with a blood test, which is expensive, trial and error should also work well to help you decide what dosage works best for you. The body's response to amino acid supplements is rapid. Some people claim to have taken higher than recommended dosages of amino acids with no serious side effects, but to begin, do not exceed the recommended dosages listed on the package. Powdered Vitamin C can eliminate side effects. (See APPENDIX 3.)

An intravenous amino acid drip is known to be effective for extreme withdrawal of difficult substances, but at this time, there is limited documentation and availability of the procedure in the US. (See APPENDIX 3.)

Alternative Methods

These additional tools are useful, of which a search can be conducted online:

- Acupuncture appears to be helpful in treating the withdrawal symptoms of some addictions, especially when relaxation is needed, but the benefits of acupuncture only last a day. It is theorized that bigger needles are more effective.
- The Cranial Electrical Stimulant (CES) unit is believed to be good for calming pain and other symptoms.
- Hyperbaric Oxygen Therapy is expensive but is known to be very effective for detoxing and rejuvenating the brain and body.
- A sauna aids in the detoxification of fat soluble drugs, such as marijuana or PCP, from the body.

Medical Model

The medical model is the use of medical drugs as a means of recovery. Medical drugs can also be used for detoxification, as prescribed by a physician. Ask for specific information from the physician regarding the type of medical drugs available. For health and legal reasons, you must be in the care of a MD to use the medical model.

<u>Medications</u>: Some medications directly reduce negative symptoms, while others lower the potential of returning to your addiction. Ask about the addictive properties of these medications, which should only be taken when needed. Some people consider these medications to be just another crutch. That's true only if you don't really need them.

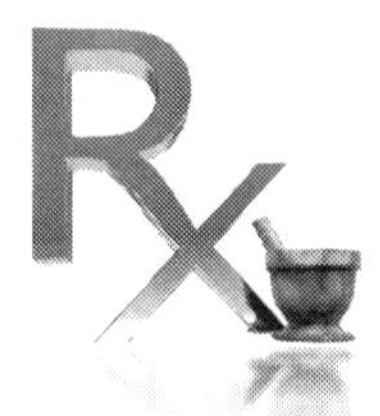

If, during drug detoxification, your physical symptoms become significant or prolonged, get medical help immediately. Seniors need to be extra careful.

When using medications that stimulate neurotransmitters, your nutritional intake must be good for them to work.

Detox Medications

The following medications will help stop withdrawal symptoms and reduce cravings. They are also used to treat chronic pain. Yet, it can be very difficult to stop taking them if they are used for more than a few months.

- *Benzodiazepines* are commonly used in detoxification; they are effective but very addictive.
- *Methadone* is the purest, most addicting opiate. It should only be used for a brief detox from other opiates.
- *Suboxone* is a highly praised detox medication, but

it contains an opiate that's pure and very addicting.

Support Medications

- *Antabuse* blocks the digestion of alcohol after it's in an acid state, but it causes a lot of stomach pain.
- *Baclofen* appears to reduce the brain's "Go" response from being activated by triggers.
- *Campral* is known to reduce the craving for alcohol.
- *Naltrexone* blocks any "high" from opioids and alcohol that is above normal.
- *Vivatrol*, an injection, is an extended release naltrexone.
- *Zyban* (*Wellbutrin*) reduces the desire for nicotine.

Medications for Emotional Withdrawal Symptoms

- Anxiety: Non-addicting anti-anxiety and anti-depressant medications can help suppress racing thoughts. Benzodiazepines, also used as a detox medication, are potent, making them both effective and very addicting. The newer, shorter acting benzos are harder to get off than the older, longer acting formulas.
- Depression: There are several groups of anti-depressants. Most increase the level of the neurotransmitters serotonin, dopamine, and norepinephrine in the brain, but none work as well as promoted. They work for the long-term about one-third of the time, with minimal side effects, but the withdrawal symptoms from some can be severe,

- Physical and emotional pain: Benzodiazepines and opiates are effective, but very addicting. There are several non-addictive medicines for physical and emotional pain, but all medications have toxicity.

Note: Some research questions the benefits of anti-depressant medication and Tryptophan. Abuse of over-the-counter and prescription medications is common, monitor your use.

MAINTENANCE & ABSTINENCE ADDICTIONS

There are two categories of addictions:
(See APPENDIX 2):

1. Maintenance Addictions: those behaviors that are necessary to sustain and enjoy life but have led to compulsions and obsessions. These can include food, relationship, and sex addictions.
   - The best approach to recover from maintenance addictions is to learn to engage in these behaviors without allowing them to become excessive.
2. Abstinence Addictions: those behaviors that are life-hindering and not sustainable, such as drugs, gambling, dieting, tanning, etc.
   - The proven recovery method from life-hindering addictions is to abstain from all related substances and activities.

Both maintenance and abstinence addictions can cause

physical cravings that are combined with rituals and other obsessive-compulsive behaviors. Knowing whether recovery from an addiction requires maintenance or abstinence is only the starting point. It isn't recovery in itself.

Maintenance Addictions

Maintaining control of how often you engage in potentially addictive behaviors can be a struggle, especially when what you desire is unavoidable. For some of your life needs, like eating, intimacy, or working, abstinence is unrealistic. Therefore, you may need a lot of structure and support in controlling your cravings. If you're unable to achieve moderation, find additional support and structure, and disengage from the behavior when possible. A good structure for moderation is:

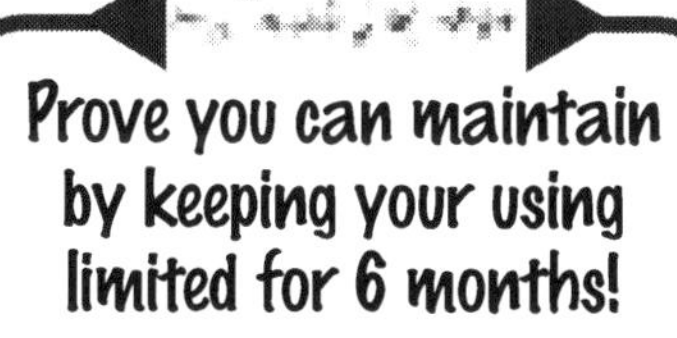

- A moderate level is one that is normal and healthy. Discover what a moderate level is for eating, shopping, sex, etc. Practice maintaining this moderate level with balance and consistency.
- Just before you use, take a breath and ask yourself:
  - » "What am I feeling?"
  - » "What need am I trying to meet?"
- Count and chart your daily use, and discuss any issues and your progress with your support group.
- Continue practicing moderation until it feels really easy, usually after six months. Restart if you relapse.

Maintenance strategies do not only pertain to maintenance addictions. They can also be used in recovery from abstinence addictions.

Harm Reduction is a medical model maintenance strategy where the goal is to reduce the harm of using until abstinence is achieved. Relapse and even regular using is acceptable, yet total abstinence is the desired goal. This is a viable approach if you can't, don't want to, or won't abstain – a decision that true addicts will usually regret.

Participation in an addiction moderation program for unnecessary addictions like alcohol is very questionable. Yet, if a person is rejecting recovery, moderation is better than full-scale use. However, harm reduction is not recovery, only a step towards it. (See APPENDIX 10.)

Abstinence Addictions

Abstinence is a no tolerance, black and white approach to addiction recovery and the easiest one for most people to achieve. Abstinence means giving up all undesirable or harmful substances and behaviors. In the beginning, this may be threatening and difficult for an addict, at least for the first six months. Avoid white knuckling it (toughing it out). You have support to help you through it. Use your resources to go after what you need and want.

Recovering Intelligence

Abstinence/Maintenance is necessary to recover, but it isn't recovery.

A big benefit of abstinence from all addictive substances

and behaviors is you stop chasing a reward that will never be satisfied (high, pleasure, energy, relaxation, relief, etc.). Remember, like maintenance, abstinence is necessary for recovery, but it isn't recovery in its entirety.

IMMEDIATE RECOVERY WORK

After initiating recovery by addressing urgent issues, like detoxification and beginning abstinence, focus on the next level of tasks. As you move into each task, you'll gradually relax, gain balance, and feel stronger. Remember to breathe!

The Void

When you refrain from the behaviors you practiced in your addiction, a natural void will be created. To fill this void, load your life with positive experiences, like new people, places, situations, and activities. Don't leave your voids empty, or it'll fill up with whatever comes along, good or bad. Positive experiences will override the negative ones. Happy people need 3 positive experiences to every one negative one. Stay away from the negative, embrace the positive!

Recovering Intelligence

Recovery creates a void; fill it with positives!

Your Approach

First, breathe and pay attention to your thoughts, feelings, and behavior, and what's going on around you.

Second, keeping breathing and ask "Are my thoughts and behaviors supporting my recovery? What are my most important needs and how can I meet them?"

The effectiveness of your approach to recovery will be greatly affected by three factors:

- Your beliefs about yourself, life, and recovery.
- The level of your motivation and commitment.
- The structure and strength of your approach.

Your awareness will help you build and strengthen your approach. Are your beliefs and thoughts about recovery accurate, healthy, and helpful? Are you connected with your motivation and commitment for recovery?

Recovery Contract

A contract is your commitment to do what is needed to be successful in your recovery and to rebuild your life. Signing a contract with yourself can finalize your motivation and commitment to starting and pursuing your recovery. Make your contract (tasks, goals, or milestones) clear, specific, measurable, and dated (start and end). Sign it in front of a support person. Keep it visible!

Consistent Recovery Focus

Throughout the day you need to remain focused on your personal reasons for recovery and on the positive aspects of life in recovery. This is vital to get you through triggers and cravings. (Find *Options Card* in the Index.)

A reminder strategy, such as the Red DOT Reminder Check-In System, can be quite useful in overriding negative triggers with positive cues to refocus on your recovery.

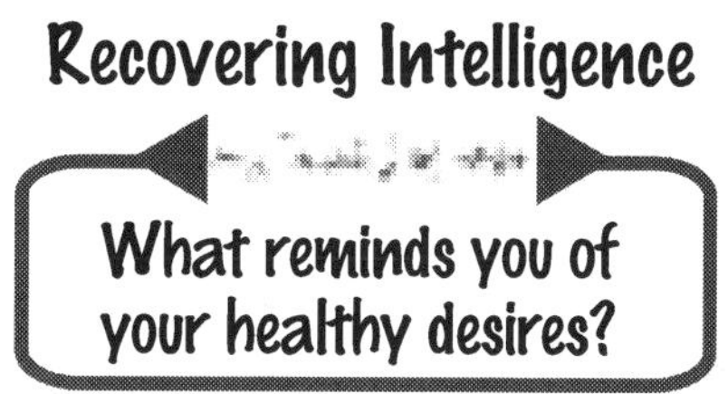

Daily Recovery Activity

From the moment you wake up each day, you want to visualize and act on your desire to build the quality life that you want, which is **Your Recovering Future™**. A daily recovery activity keeps you occupied and on track with your goals. Daily recovery activities include spending quality time with healthy family and friends, church, classes, sober dances, conferences focused on health and growth, and any other positive experience that offers you support in your recovery. Your daily recovery activity gives you a clear reason to stay clean. Plan a week in advance and don't go to bed without having your next daily recovery activity confirmed.

Support Groups

At first, you'll be in a state of neediness and find the support of your core group of friends and family invaluable. Along with normal needs, you will have new recovery needs. Assume your using acquaintances and even using friends will disappear.

Seven is a good number of people for a core support group. It's good to be in contact with at least one person every day. Early recovery is a time to affirm current positive friendships and renew old ones, especially people who understand recovery and with whom you can share feelings and talk through difficult situations. Very likely, during addiction, substances and behaviors replaced people, numbing your needs in an attempt to overcome personal pain. Now you will want to have supportive people around you to meet your emotional, social, and physical needs.

Recovering Intelligence

Your support group is a life line; stay in close, daily contact!

Accountability Partner: You and your accountability partner will support, encourage, and carefront (a loving type of confronting) each other about achieving tasks and goals. Your accountability partner may be the only one you can rely on for the truth. You both must be totally honest with each other.

Connecting With Others: In recovery, you will need to replace the friends with whom you practiced your addiction. With new friendships that support your recovery, you can begin to heal and learn how to be emotionally available. You'll want to listen and open your heart to the needs, wants, and experiences of others. Ask questions, listen, and have a dialogue. Show your interest, understanding, and empathy through your response to them. Then share your experiences

See yourself in the future, engaging with your closest friends.

Your Recovering Future

and pay attention to their feedback. Do they show interest and match your deep level of sharing?

Observe how people relate to each other. You may want to adopt some of their relational styles. If you still have trouble with relationships, pay attention to how you interact with others. Ask yourself why you shy away from relationships, and listen for the answers. It might be your fear of being embarrassed, ridiculed, or rejected. Choose to move past your negative feelings and take positive action.

Emotional Support: Recovery is about change, which takes emotional energy. Feelings will need to be felt, understood, and dealt with. It's important that you have friends who are understanding of your ups and downs, as emotional support is vital to your healthy development.

Buddy System: A buddy system is when a pact is made between addicts to help each other through recovery. This can be very valuable, but it can also be destructive. If using the buddy system, team up with a motivated person(s) you are connected to (non-sexually) in a personal or emotionally way. Be clear with each other about expectations and limits. Set up specific agreements for dealing with and responding to difficult situations, such as style differences, personal issues, and the possibility of relapsing.

Social Support: You'll benefit from a support group or fellowship to motivate you and provide you with healthy activities, especially when you're easily triggered. Recovering communities (12-Step, your treatment program, a professional support group, or an Internet group) are some of the best social networking resources available to help you work through general and practical issues of addiction recovery. For example, you can take a person from a support group with you when you must attend an activity where triggers are expected, such as a food addict going to a restaurant or a drug addict visiting a neighborhood where drugs are easily available.

Going Crazy

Change can make you feel as if you're going crazy. It's more likely you're just very stressed out, fearful, or need better structure. If you're working a quality program, things will get better, day-by-day. These negative feelings will go away within a few months. If not, seek additional help.

Mentor Role

A mentor, sponsor, or coach is a guide who has experienced a similar journey to the one you need to go through or has a lot of knowledge about how to successfully approach recovery. They'll be there for you in hard times, ready to answer any questions you have. This approach can develop into a solid friendship, but at the first hint of sexual or romantic interest, immediately get a new mentor, as your relationship with your mentor should be undiluted. This shouldn't be an issue with a professional, due to ethics. Choose a mentor you can trust, but feel free to re-evaluate their efforts month-by-month to confirm they are well-suited for you. When

Recovering Intelligence

A mentor-type person brings vital knowledge, intelligence, & support.

re-evaluating your relationship, ensure you are basing your assessment on actual conduct, and not your own fears or biases.

Reality Testing

Your internal map is your image of outer reality. Although it's true you create your own reality, there are some limitations. A table is a table, no matter what you choose to believe. Develop and use your observing self. (Find *Observing Self* in the Index.)

To ensure your internal map is in-line with actual outer reality, check your internal map against the internal maps of trusted others. Ask for their feedback regarding their perceived outer realities, and compare it with your own. Get a second or a third opinion. This will give you valuable perspectives regarding reality that may be difficult to develop on your own.

Spiritual reality testing can come from praying, meditating, and talking with your Higher Power. Trust your spiritual experiences and allow yourself to follow the guidance that comes from them, but reality test all important decisions.

Recovering Intelligence

Check your reality with your inner map, outer reality, & core group.

Note: Be careful of extreme people and extreme beliefs. This is a difficult part of life, but in general, go with moderation. Extremes tend to cause more problems than they solve, and sometimes they cause big problems. It's difficult to have perspective in extreme situations. Instead, ask several trusted, emotionally uninvolved others for feedback.

Thriving Beyond Addiction™ Workbook

The companion to this book, the **Thriving Beyond Addiction™ Workbook**, gives you an opportunity to explore yourself, your addictions, and your issues in-depth. Use it to

develop strategies and tools for recovery and to help clarify what **Your Recovering Future™** will be. The worksheets cover most aspects of recovery. Using the workbook is a positive commitment. It'll help you work through problems, clarify goals, and set up a solid foundation. The quality of your recovery will be equal to the amount of effort you make. The people that achieve and maintain quality recovery do whatever it takes, for as long as it takes, to achieve it.

PHASES OF RECOVERY

Recovery does not happen at once. It occurs in phases. There are many theories regarding the correct number of phases and their length. Each theory is an opinion and is meant to act as a guideline. In general, the length of time

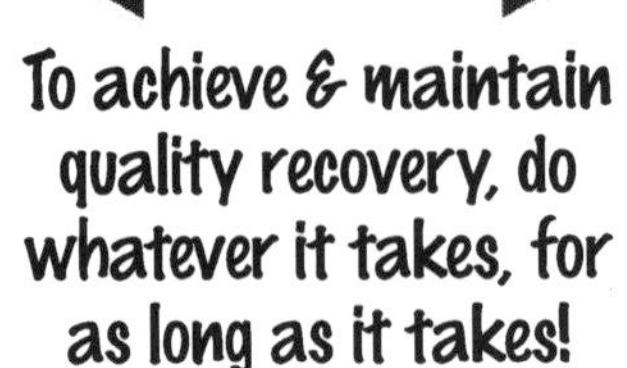

it takes to complete each phase is mostly based on your efforts. Completing specific tasks doesn't necessarily end a phase. Recovery can't just be computed. It also has to be felt. Rather than completing tasks like a robot, attempt to sincerely connect with your full emotional experience and the spirit of recovery. This approach will give you a greater chance of success.

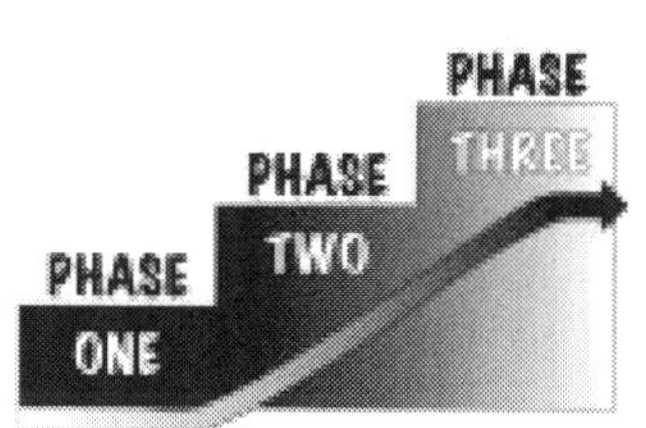

Phase One: Primary Recovery

Phase One, the primary recovery phase, starts the day you commit to your recovery and extends for about six to twelve months. The goal of Phase One is to develop the foundation you need to be successful in recovery. In this early recovery period, it's vital to open up your mind and build a support team. Listen to trusted others, work with a mentor, and, if required, seek the advice of a MD. Work within a recovery structure, completing needed tasks and goals.

Withdrawal from drugs and sugar occurs during the beginning of the primary recovery phase. Your initial treatment program is completed during this phase. The supportive treatment that follows primary care, is usually called continuing care or aftercare. This aftercare is very valuable. Make use of it!

Recovering Intelligence

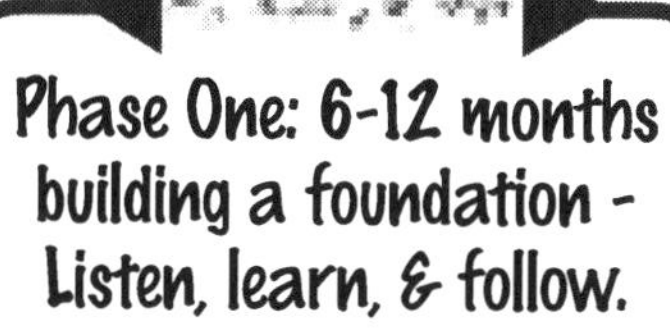

It's essential that you stay actively involved in your

recovery throughout Phase One and beyond. It is widely believed that you should maintain a solid recovery structure for at least two years; however, you need to be involved in your recovery for as long as is necessary to be successful. Many people stop participating early and relapse.

The Three Major Stages of Primary Recovery are:

- Withdrawal: During the initial period of physical and emotional withdrawal, you need to focus on taking care of yourself. Consume quality nutrition, drink water, and exercise; be around supportive people and attempt to do small but positive and productive tasks. Stay focused on necessary and immediate needs and issues you can do something about. Initial drug withdrawal will take between a few days to a few weeks (six or more for marijuana). For some medications, it takes years for full withdrawal.

Recovering Intelligence

High-quality nutrition reduces withdrawal symptoms & cravings.

- Honeymoon: As you start to become healthier, you may feel overly happy with your newfound recovery. The return of your health, energy, and brain chemistry may make you feel ready to go. You may have thoughts of ending treatment. Be very careful! This sense of wellbeing isn't entirely whole. You aren't healthy yet. It takes time to heal, so don't take on things that are unnecessary. Focus on building your recovery. Usually, this honeymoon feeling will last about three months, but it varies according to the person and the addiction.

- Facing Reality: The truth of your reality at this point may be more about the wreckage than the rewards, and that's hard to deal with. You'll come down from the honeymoon period and remember that parts of recovery are hard, not just positive and happy. This becomes a risky period. At times, you may feel like going back to old, familiar situations that provided a false sense (even briefly) of happiness. Because early using memories may be pleasant, they can easily be romanced. Remember, this is a relapse symptom. Breathe and face reality. It is the only way you can move past the wreckage.

Recovering Intelligence

Always remember your negative using history! Especially if early recovery is easy!

During Phase One, many people will feel better quicker than expected. This may lead them to question if they were as sick as they thought. Always remember your past. Your recovery process should follow a proven approach that works for you, and then add personal aspects to meet your unique needs.

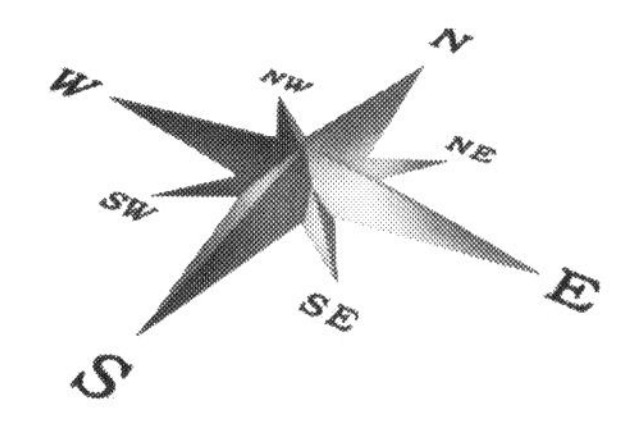

Phase Two: Intermediate Recovery

Intermediate recovery starts after the building of your

foundation has begun and takes at least one to two years. The goal of Phase Two is to adjust to living in recovery and facing life on life's terms, all while completing your foundation and becoming comfortable. This includes finishing all tasks, goals, and milestones; dealing with all current issues; and developing and using important tools and strategies.

During Phase Two, you'll settle into your new recovery patterns, experiences, and relationships, and they will become familiar to you, even easy. But your past temptations are not that far behind you, and you must stay aware of this. Your concerns about maintaining a positive attitude, stability, and inner strength during early recovery gradually lessen and become only occasional concerns.

Phase Three: Continuing Recovery

Phase Three, continuing recovery, will begin after you've built a solid, quality foundation; consistently dealt with immediate issues; started processing your deeper personal issues; and established a period (6 months minimum) of crisis-free, stable recovery. This will likely take at least one to three years beyond intermediate recovery to complete, extending through your fifth year of recovery. During this phase, childhood, adult, and other major life issues at your deeper core will begin to be fully explored, addressed, and hopefully (at least partially) resolved. These issues are ongoing, so don't get discouraged! You have all the

> **Recovering Intelligence**
>
> The quality of your program shapes the pace of your recovery.

time you need to deal with them! Just do your best.

Let Go ~ Apologize ~ Forgive
You can move past your history,
live fully, & thrive in the present!

TREATMENT PATHS

Treatment is a term used when working with an experienced addiction recovery professional – individually or as part of a program. With quality support, your journey will be easier and quicker, and your results will likely be stronger, deeper, and last longer. Look for and use the resources in your community. No matter the resources available, if you are committed to your recovery, you can be successful.

Those in treatment are more likely to stop abusing, engage in personal growth activities, and develop a healthy, happy, and successful life. But many addicts try to recover on their own and fail. If you decline treatment, set goals and be very honest with yourself. Consistently and frequently re-evaluate your

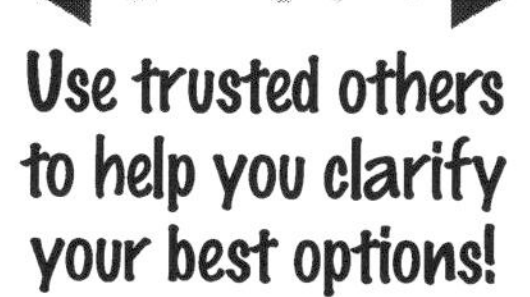

progress! If you fail, or even fall short, choose to go into some type of treatment. (See APPENDIX 10.)

Types of addiction treatment include:

- Private work: Coach, counselor, or therapist
  - » Individual and group
- Inpatient: Professional (in or outside your area)
  - » Hospital: Up to 28 days
  - » Residential: 28 days, 3 months, or longer
- Outpatient: Professional
  - » Day treatment
  - » Evening and weekend programs
- Clean & Sober Living/Sober Living Environment
- Self-help programs: In person or online

Investigate different addiction treatment options until you are certain that you've found a workable one. Recovery options need to allow you to determine the pace and direction of your recovery. A careful evaluation with a competent, impartial mentor is a good approach. When you and your mentor have selected your best options, act immediately; do not wait for even an hour!

Recovering Intelligence

Your best approach is the one that you'll accept & meets your needs.

If you believe that you do not need a hospital, residential setting, or even an outpatient program, consider starting with a less intense approach. First, try one session or more a week in a group, a self-help meeting, or with a professional.

Along the way, review your progress with the help of your

mentor or professional support. It's essential to accept more intensive treatment if you're progressing poorly. Notice your mental-emotional signs of relapsing, such as negative attitudes, emotions, and behaviors. Ask your support group for feedback and for help if needed.

Treatment Orientation

Historically, the most accepted treatment approaches have been the medical model and the 12-Step model. However, the poor success rates of each, along with the high cost of treatment with the traditional medical model, has incited many treatment professionals to explore additional options.

Options to the more traditional models show promise. These recovery approaches, including tools and strategies, are just as effective and are being integrated into a vast selection of treatment programs. Most treatment programs are a mixture of different approaches. These approaches will be explored throughout the book. This is good news for you as it means a greater chance at success by finding an approach that fits your needs. The bad news is that it's more difficult to clarify which approach, or combination of approaches, is your best option.

Most programs are heavy on group counseling, meaning you deal with personal issues in a group setting. A big debate amongst professionals is whether you can (or should) deal with all of your personal issues in a room full of people who may be strangers to you. Many believe a group setting probably isn't the best place to talk about deep core issues, definitely not if you feel emotionally fragile. Yet, group counseling has been the model of choice for many treatment programs.

The biggest division in treatment is:

- Addiction Model: You are an addict, and you must deal with that first. After a year or longer of being clean and stable, you can begin to deal with your deeper issues.
- Psychological Model: You are a person with negative patterns and core issues that must be dealt with, or you will continue to choose your negative behaviors. (See APPENDIX 2.)

Group counseling is considered an effective approach due to:

- Peer carefrontation, growing together, and bonding
- Learning from watching others work through their process
- Cost effectiveness

Quality programs offer a complete, balanced, and holistic approach – behavioral, cognitive, educational, emotional, medical, nutritional, physical, psychological, social, and spiritual. They encourage and expect the participation of spouses and families, and they provide aftercare for at least one year after the basic program.

When choosing a treatment program, some questions to ask yourself are:

- What are my immediate needs and how can I meet

them right now?

- How will I stay away from my addiction today?
- How will I deal with cravings, moods, and other personal issues?
- What practical support do I need for my medical, emotional, and personal needs?
- Can I succeed at home or do I need to get away?
- Can or should I get away from the pressures of life to focus on recovery for a month or longer?
- What recovery education do I and my family need?
- What are my most important recovery needs and which treatment approach meets them?
- What will be my overall approach and structure?

Realize that most people want to choose the easiest option, that which requires the least amount of involvement, no matter what is most beneficial for them. The best answers to the questions above are the brutally honest ones. This is your life; make the best choices for you, not the easiest ones.

Recovering Intelligence

Make the best treatment choice, not the easiest one.

Confidentiality: In all professional treatment situations, the law protects your privacy. Without your written consent, a program and their staff cannot disclose any personal information about you, not even that you are in treatment. This doesn't apply to the other members of the program, who by the nature of your presence will know you're in treatment. But don't worry. As you move through your recovery and build acceptance of your situation, you will become more comfortable with other people knowing.

Recovery Structure

Live within the recovery structure that you have chosen, built, and maintained. Look at your life daily and add things you need for your recovery; subtract the things you don't. Even if it doesn't feel right in the beginning, do it anyway, because it's the best thing for you.

Structure is crucial to recovery; it provides you with the constant reminders necessary to stay focused on your recovery rather than allowing you to go on autopilot and mindlessly respond to whatever comes along, such as the environmental cues that trigger your cravings. You will need to develop a personal structure that will set you up to be successful. Every day (or maybe every hour), have a healthy place to go, supportive people to see, and desirable things to do. Use your reminders to stay focused and move forward. Most successful recovering people started their recovery within the structure of an established program.

Recovering Intelligence

Your personal structure will highly influence the ease of achieving & keeping your recovery.

The need for extensive structure will continue for many months or even years into your recovery. If you are in a treatment program, as it approaches its end, start preparing to leave that structure and join another program and/or develop your own structure.

Consider: **"In my experience, you don't want... inadequate structure or to use your structure inconsistently."**
(See APPENDIX 7.)

Professional Help

Professionals are a valuable resource for recovery work:

- Licensed counselors and psychotherapists for deep, personal, relationship, and family work.
- Coaches for initial recovery and behavioral work.
- Physicians for medical issues.
- Health practitioners for nutritional, physical, spiritual, and health issues and development.
- Body workers, chiropractors, masseuses, personal trainers, and physical therapists for physical help.

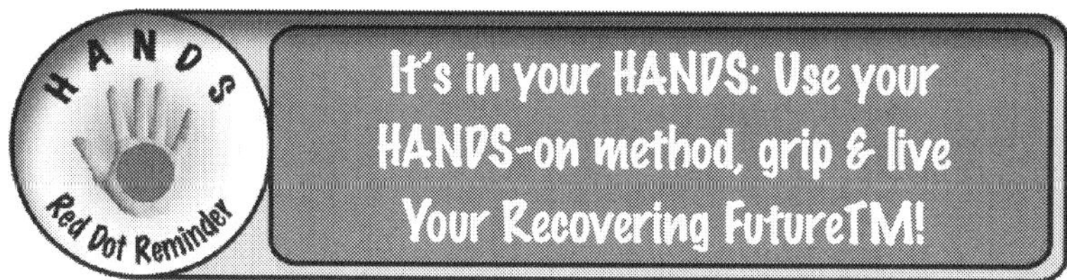

The initial focus should be on your:

- Thinking and behavior
- Pressing problems
- Goal achievement

The mind has a limited amount of energy it can use at once. In early recovery, brief work may be needed to address relationship or family issues, but other core issues, no matter how troubling – like childhood, family, and trauma issues – should be addressed after you've stabilized your recovery so that you can focus on more immediate recovery goals.

Selecting A Professional: Not all professionals know about effective addiction recovery, have good skills, or will work well with you. For instance, a professional with solid experience may have good skills but may not be up-to-date with current resources, which a newly trained person has learned. This can also be true of treatment program staff. Ask the person you're considering working with about her or his addiction recovery experience and approach to working with clients. A competent professional will answer your questions thoroughly.

Recovering Intelligence

Personal work is very desirable, but contain & postpone deeper work!

You want to work with someone who you respect and feel is competent. Ask a friend (minister, teacher, or another professional) for a recommendation or to help you sort out and pick the best person for you. Make a choice and then work with that person for a while.

Many addicts wonder if they should work with a male or female. The gender of a counselor shouldn't be a big concern unless you have personal issues that make one or the other preferable.

Working With A Professional: While it's important to be secure with the professional you select, general anxiety and fear regarding the recovery process may cause you to feel uncomfortable at first. Give a qualified professional a fair chance, unless you have

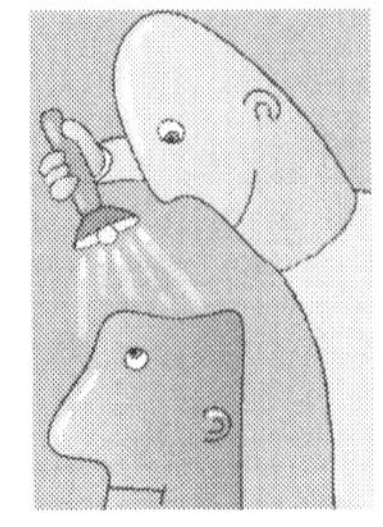

a very negative reaction. This person is supposed to be healthy and competent. If you're truly trying your best, you should expect the professional to work with your negative attitudes, feelings, issues, and behaviors. Any feeling or topic should be acceptable, even the unusual. However, they should not tolerate dishonesty, extreme negative attitudes (as opposed to minor issues), or a half-hearted effort.

Recovering Intelligence

It's vital that you believe that you're getting the help you need to recover.

If you feel you have not gotten any real help within ten sessions, but you believe you've made a strong effort to be open and honest, and you've done what has been asked of you, then you have a valid reason to be concerned. These concerns need to be resolved. Try a few more sessions, but share your concerns with a trusted other. If you still aren't satisfied after you've tried a few more sessions, find someone else to work with before ending the relationship.

Recovering Intelligence

Expect quality help, measurable results, & professional behavior!

All professionals must have boundaries. If you think the professional is being improper in any way, take action. It is never okay for a professional to display sexual intimacy or other boundary violations. Immediately find someone new to work with. Furthermore, the professional in question should be reported to his or her certifying organization or state licensing board.

Professional Recovery Coaches

Professional recovery coaching is a new field where coaches attend private coaching programs and are certified by private coaching organizations, not the government. A professional recovery coach will focus on your goals and solutions, not on your history – how or why you became an addict. This may be a good option for addicts who have already been in more traditional therapy and have worked through their deeper issues, like those pertaining to childhood, family, and trauma. Professional recovery coaches can also be helpful to those who are in early stages of recovery and trying to focus on immediate goals.

Psychotherapists

Licensed psychologists, licensed clinical social workers, licensed marriage and family therapists, board certified psychiatrists, and licensed mental health counselors can legally practice psychotherapy. They are qualified to work on all general human issues, such as deep, childhood, and core issues, and any specific areas for which they are trained. This is said to be in their "scope of practice." Understanding the different certifications, licenses, and other credentials is not necessary to begin recovery, but interview the

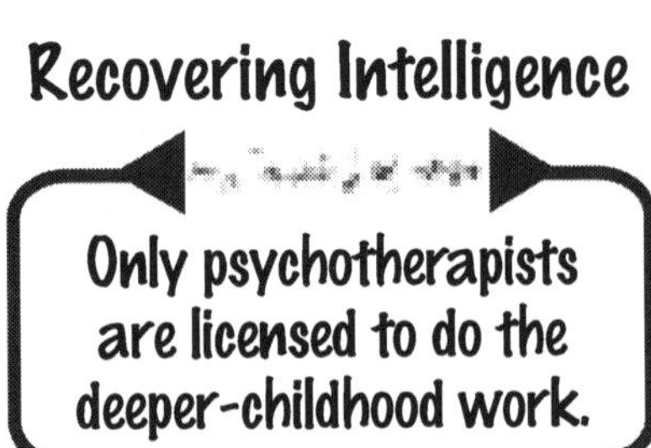

person you're considering taking on as your psychotherapist about their background, approaches, and experience to confirm they are a right match for you.

Professional Therapeutic Styles

Therapeutic styles – how recovery is approached – differ between counselors, coaches, therapists, and other treatment professionals. Well-trained professionals will often use a style that combines several approaches. In early recovery, the best approach is a straightforward one.

It's vital that you receive quality treatment and that you are comfortable within your professional relationships, especially when you reach a stage of planning deeper, long-term work, the type only a licensed psychotherapist can provide. To help ensure your recovery is successful, you must be on the same wavelength with the people you work with in terms of the therapeutic style that is best for you. This may not happen overnight. Give the relationship you have with a professional time to develop, but immediately talk to the person about any concerns that may arise.

Recovering Intelligence

Professionals should offer an effective approach, a nurturing relationship, & a healing environment.

Results-Oriented Psychotherapy

- Behavioral: Both negative and positive behaviors are observed and tracked. Positive behaviors are supported and encouraged; negative behaviors are discouraged. Techniques like the Red Dot Reminder Check-In System are used regularly.

- Biofeedback: Instruments are used to retrieve physical feedback of your body (pulse, temperature, etc.) so you can learn how to control your ability to relax, alleviate pain, and reduce your stress levels, benefiting your health and performance in recovery.
  - » Neurofeedback (NFB): A type of biofeedback that uses real time electroencephalography (EEG) to illustrate brain activity to control the central nervous system.
- Body therapies: There are several types of body therapies and all have a physical focus and style; movement and somatic therapies are examples.
- Cognitive Therapy: Thoughts and language, and the feelings and behaviors that result, are examined, assessed, and changed to ensure they are accurate and useful. There is special attention placed on mental perceptions, with the intention of inspiring positive feelings and behaviors.
  - » T.E.A.M. Therapy: Testing, Empathy, Agenda Setting, & Methods; provides an individualized framework for conducting evidence-based cognitive therapy. It is known for producing fast results.
- Emotional Freedom Techniques (EFT): Purports to manipulate the body's energy field by tapping on acupuncture points; some think it's controversial.
- Exposure: Intentional contact with a hot trigger in

a controlled environment. This results in a gradual lessening of the effects of the specific trigger. After each session, it's important to totally disconnect from the trigger and reconnect with the present. There are several types of exposure therapies, including EMDR.

- Eye Movement Desensitization & Reprocessing (EMDR): Uses cross-hemisphere brain stimulation technology, quickly neutralizing the intensity of triggers; it is used along with other therapy approaches.
- Hypnotherapy: Hypnosis is used as part of the therapeutic process to modify the unconscious mind's negative thoughts and behaviors, such as habits, physical pain, or stress-related issues.
- Motivational Interviewing: Focuses on motivation to resolve a conflict (use vs. recovery); it examines and clarifies the best decision to make (recovery).
- Neuro-Linguistic Programming (NLP): In NLP, the focus is on language and behavior re-patterning. It emphasizes techniques for personal, relationship, and professional development.
- Psycho-Spiritual Approaches: A specific religious or spiritual path, or a general spiritual approach, is brought into the work. Many professionals avoid psycho-spiritual approaches.
- Re-patterning: Approaches that shift negative patterns to healthier ones. Examples are NLP and Resonance Re-patterning.

- Reality Therapy: A straight-talking, problem solving approach that looks at issues, feelings, and solutions realistically.
- Other Approaches: There are many other psychological, psycho-physical, and psycho-spiritual approaches that could be helpful, but there are far too many to describe.

Deeper Focused Psychotherapy

- Insight, in general, focuses on identifying issues, especially unconscious conflicts, from your personal history. Deep psychotherapy is based on the belief that having knowledge of what is wrong (cause) and the means to fix it will result in a decision to fix it (effect). This is a big assumption. Though promoted often, insight gained through deep psychotherapy doesn't always help treat an addiction. Some examples of deep psychotherapy:
  - » Client Centered Therapy: A flexible, indirect method, which aids the client in finding their own solutions to their issues; widely adapted and used in many approaches.
  - » Narrative Therapy: Therapeutic focus on the client's dominant story; explores harmful perceptions you have and how they came about.
  - » Psychoanalysis: A psycho-dynamic approach which raises your awareness of hidden conflicts from childhood, the root causes of feelings and expectations, and how they affect you today;

examples include Ego Psychology and Jungian Psychology.

- » Transactional Analysis: Uses parent, child, and adult ego states to explain how we live out our childhood life script.
- » Other Approaches: There are many others, but again, too many to list here.

Training Treatment Professionals

The counseling staff in treatment programs will have a range of training. Since most programs treat drug and alcohol addiction, a majority of addiction training is D&A focused. There are many training resources available to those involved in addiction treatment; they include university degrees, various addiction certification programs (through schools and independent groups), professional societies, community workshops, in-house training, and public seminars. Scholastic achievement is important, but it doesn't include much hands-on experience. Therefore, competent professionals keep evolving through a variety of training opportunities.

Some counseling staff will be in recovery from their own addictions. Personal recovery gives one valuable, personal, but limited experience. Having undergone recovery doesn't necessarily give the staff member the complete knowledge, techniques, and experiences that a professional needs to help his or her clients. When working with counseling staff, question, listen, and clarify as you get to know them so that you acquire some sense of their training.

Recovering Intelligence

The current staff affects the quality of today's program, even good ones!

For entry level positions, the addiction treatment field requires counseling staff to be in recovery for at least two years. Other positions may require three to five years. Overall, the years of experience for any one staff member can vary, including high positions like clinical directors. Sometimes, an organization will advertise the combined years of experience of the entire history of their staff, earning them a desirable reputation. The reality could be different. The present staff may have far less experience; therefore, the organization's reputation may not be justified.

Addictive patterns appear in most individuals. Counseling staff who know their own addictive patterns are more likely to have empathy and to fully understand the experience of addiction and recovery. Every professional has something to offer. Take what you can from all the staff.

Professionally Run Groups

Most professionally run groups treat drug and alcohol addiction or codependency, but thanks to awareness and online communication, more groups than ever have arisen that focus on other types of addiction. But many more options are needed.

Sharing personal issues and information in front of other people can feel uncomfortable, even scary. Yet, many people will benefit more from a group than from individual work.

A professionally run group can cost $15 to $60 per hour. Groups ran by interns or through a nonprofit agency may cost less. Most meet weekly for one to two hours.

Recovering Intelligence

Many people will benefit from group work & from individual work.

Professionally run groups have several important advantages over peer run groups, including:

- They are more consistent.
- They are less likely to have interpersonal issues.
- They have a wider range of resources.
- They are more likely to provide members with emotional help to resolve issues and move on.

There are several types and styles of professional groups. Common ones are:

- Educational: Informational, held for a few weeks.
- Psycho-Educational/Coaching: Informational, goal setting, solution finding, emotional and practical support; either time-limited or ongoing.
- Therapeutic: The support and guidance to explore, gain insight, grow, and resolve deeper emotional issues; usually on-going time line.

Working with a Group: Those who feel guilty, shy, or vulnerable, or those who want to go deeper into their issues and grow quicker, may benefit from individual work before they take on group work, but they should remain aware that support and carefrontation of peers

can be very effective in breaking down defenses (especially denial and minimization) and dealing with the many issues of recovery. In mainstream treatment, clients are challenged by carefrontation, but never attacked, emotionally broken down, or morally judged. Most groups meet at least once a week for between one and two hours. (See APPENDIX 10.)

Codependent recovery support groups offer the support to focus on yourself, not others. This isn't easy for most co's, who usually have strong defenses regarding their addiction to be needed by others. Expect to be carefronted until you're truly able to focus on yourself.

Adult Child of Alcoholics or dysfunctional families (ACA/ACOA) groups are helpful for support and carefronting of childhood issues. Because of the deep emotional intensity of such old issues, personal psychotherapy can also be very beneficial. The individual work involved in psychotherapy gives you personal time, a safe environment, and the guidance of a therapist.

The style and cost for codependent recovery groups and ACA/ACOA groups are similar to other recovering support groups. They have their unique focus.

Professional Outpatient Treatment Programs

Outpatient programs (OPTs) are a good choice for people with a primary or secondary addiction to drugs and alcohol. This is especially true if you have no medical complications, it's your first treatment, you must stay working, or if you want to stay close to home because of certain obligations.

Though most OPTs are centered around alcohol and drug

addiction, with a bit of research, hopefully you can find a local OPT program that focuses on your addiction.

Professionally run outpatient programs, such as those that are 12-Step or self-help based, offer a treatment system and are educational and personal-growth oriented, giving you a chance to deal with the issues behind your addiction. Limited individual and family counseling is often included in these programs, offering you a basic foundation for recovery. Added counseling is often needed.

Recovering Intelligence

Outpatient programs are a good choice for most people.

Intense Day Treatment: Sessions start in the morning and go through late afternoon, usually five to six days a week. They offer basically the same program that inpatient programs offer but for fewer hours a week and at a much lower cost, which varies widely.

Outpatient Treatment: Sessions last two to three hours each day, three to six times per week, for six months to a year. They usually include brief to long-term continuing support of up to several years and are primarily held in the evening. They provide much of the same program structure that inpatient programs offer, but over a longer period of time. Therefore, they are less intense and cost much less. Again, the cost ranges widely.

Professional Inpatient Treatment

Although there are exceptions, like outpatient programs, most inpatient treatment programs are also centered around alcohol and drug addiction, but some programs treat other addictions at the same time. A handful of programs are available for other primary additions, like codependency food, sex, or gambling.

Inpatient programs are good for people who need to get away from their environment, who want or need an intense introduction to recovery, or who want to build a close recovery community. Inpatient programs are mostly group-oriented, offering education, treatment structure, and a treatment process. They also include at least some individual or family counseling. The style used commonly involves a multidisciplinary team evaluation with an extensive medical-psycho-social history, and may also include a nutritional approach.

Recovering Intelligence

Inpatient programs are intense and helpful if you need to get away.

When treatment is finished, many inpatient programs also provide support for re-entry into the community for at least one year. The intense inpatient treatment approach is only a good first step. Begin planning and using your own structure before you leave the program.

The inpatient experience can be intense, working towards your recovery for eight to twelve hours daily, six days each week, with a partial day on Sunday. Breaks are taken throughout the day for relaxation and exercise. Some programs are completely 12-Step based, while others hold 12-Step or other self-help meetings as part of their program. Visitors are usually allowed after the first week or so.

Out Of Your Area/Rural Residential Programs can be expensive. Luxury ones can cost over $70,000 per month. You're separated from negative influences, and the physical distance encourages residents to stay. Yet, rural residential programs can be difficult for your family to participate in.

Inpatient hospital programs are the most intensive and the most restrictive programs, but they are only moderately expensive. They are ideal for people who have physical and medical issues. A multidisciplinary medical team of several professionals together is usually employed – a counselor, psychiatrist, nurse, social worker, recreational therapist, etc. Along with the medical model, some will also use non-medical approaches. The basic cost for a 30-day hospital-based program is typically $15,000 and up. It's common for an inpatient to only stay through the toughest part of the detoxification period (three to 21 days), and then move on to an outpatient program.

Social Model programs have a homelike setting. They rely mostly on recovering staff and peer leadership, not professional staff. They are non-medical and often 12-Step oriented. The cost is usually the least expensive. They offer structure through their rules, activities, and mutual support.

Therapeutic Communities (TCs) require participation within a group-based recovery approach. In general, they are for individuals who have had a long history of addiction and need in-depth, long-term intense treatment. They can be excellent for people who need a family setting where the total person can be helped. In some TCs, members work within and for the community.

TCs had a history of using attack therapy to attempt to breakdown new members' defenses, and "games" to help them grow, rebuild, and re-socialize. This process can take years and is growing obsolete. Successful TCs have become more user-friendly and offer a lifelong community.

The TC's democratic, family orientation and intense, long-term treatment plan have proven moderately successful for people who need such a level of work. These include those with a long and severe history of drug abuse, severe personality disorders, and other mental health issues.

Recovery Homes

Recovery homes are valuable for people who don't have a healthy home environment or who want the additional support and security of a built-in recovery community. As the cost may not be significantly more than normal living expenses, they are a very good option for many people.

Clean & Sober Living (CSL) or a Sober Living Environment (SLE) are homes where you may choose to live on a month-to-month basis, usually in shared bedrooms. The amount of structure and services that are provided and the quality of the facility and its location will vary. Costs are adjusted accordingly.

Recovering Intelligence

Clean & Sober Living offers low cost, a family feel, & some structure.

The requirements of a CSL or SLE program range

from none to mandatory daily house meetings or recovery activities outside the program such as self-help meetings. Some are well supervised and some are not. Sober Living is an excellent option for many, especially single people.

Codependency Treatment

There are very few inpatient codependency treatment programs even though dependency is a common co-symptom with other addictions, it's usually covered in those programs. They are run similarly to other treatment programs; yet, they are unique to their own model. They include identifying emotions, harmful patterns, childhood issues, and trauma. Codependency can be difficult to treat because the addiction of helping others appears to be so positive. The reward of codependency treatment is realizing that you are a good person with a misguided motivation, and you learn to focus on you.

Recovering Intelligence

Codependents often deny they need help, but they do!

Relapse Prevention Treatment

All addicts need relapse prevention education, especially chronic relapsers. A specific relapse track is needed if you have already gone through a primary treatment program at least once. Chronic relapsers particularly need to have an aspect of their recovery focused on relapse prevention. If you have a history of relapsing, you might want to consider a relapse prevention treatment program. There are a few, most of which are focused on alcohol and drug addiction.

Success Rates

Success rates are more of a selling tool than a reality. Outcome studies are expensive and often biased. For instance, the current staff of a program advertising a high success rate may not have been working at the program when the statistics were gathered. It does appear that nutritionally-based programs have a higher success rate (claims of 80%) than other programs. Your success depends on you. When you start your recovery early in your addiction, you'll suffer less and you're more likely to be successful, with the exception of young adults. If you choose a quality approach, you're also likely to be successful.

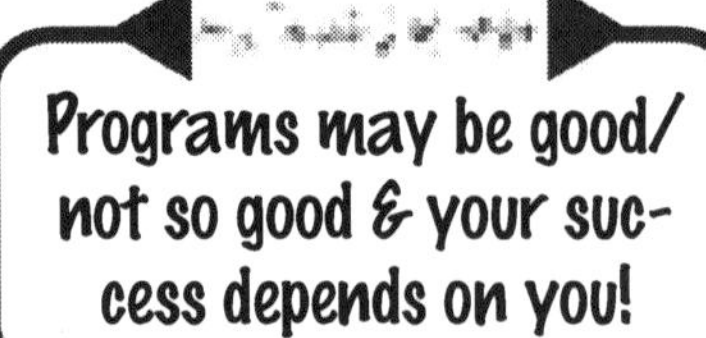

The most important factors for your success are:

- Your belief that your approach can be effective for you and you can do it!
- Your commitment that you will do your best.

PAYING FOR TREATMENT

Costs

The hourly rates of private professionals vary greatly, partly due to geographic location. Some professionals offer sliding scale rates, blocks of time, or packaged plans at a lower rate. Many licensed professionals take managed care insurance. The approximate range for hourly services, usually paid in cash (fee for service), is:

- Addiction Counselor: Work mostly for programs
- Board Certified Psychiatrist: $150 to $350
- Coach (Uncert/Certified): $30 to $250
- Certified/Licensed Counselors: $50 to $150
- Licensed Psychotherapist (Clinical Social Worker, Mental Health Counselor, Marriage & Family Therapist, Clinical Psychologist): $50 to $200
- Private Interventionist: $50 to $150; often free if the intervention is being run by a program's staff where the client is expected to go into treatment, usually immediately after the intervention.
- Practitioners (Educator, Hypnotherapist, Behavioral Practitioner, etc.): $50 to $150.

Paying more may mean you end up working with a more competent professional, but not necessarily. Licensed (board certified) psychiatrists are medical doctors who have had some psychological training and can prescribe medication. Like many psychotherapists, psychiatrists usually broaden their knowledge with additional training. For all the reasons listed above, they are at the higher end of the cost scale.

Addiction counselors or therapy interns will be available at lower fees or sliding scale rates, especially at nonprofit clinics, churches, or graduate schools. Interns must be supervised by a licensed or certified professional.

There is another group of professionals that, although are often unlicensed and uncertified, offer valuable services. They work under titles such as consultant, hypnotherapist, interventionist, practitioner, educator, etc. Their scope of practice is limited to specific disciplines like behavior, education, evaluation, etc.

Third Party Payments

Unless you're paying out-of-pocket for your professional treatment, you'll need to involve a third party – your medical insurance company.

Managed care companies oversee (hold down the cost of) your addiction treatment and mental health benefits. This means treatment providers receive less money, so many psychotherapists don't participate in managed care work.

If the services of an Employee Assistance Program (EAP) is available to you, it could be very helpful in assisting you with your treatment needs and communicating vital information with management at your place of employment. The EAP is supposed to keep your treatment confidential, but your employer will likely already know you have a problem of some sort.

Client Evaluation: If you are going to use third party medical insurance to help pay for your treatment, they'll want a professional to diagnose your condition. They'll use a code from the American Psychiatric Association's DSM V (Diagnostic and Statistical Manual of Mental Disorders). Parity diagnoses, such as depression and chemical dependency, fall under the Mental Health Parity Law, which gives you the right for coverage. Some medical insurance providers will pay less or nothing for a non-parity diagnosis. You or the professional you plan to work with should check your benefits and get preauthorization before you agree to treatment.

Inexpensive Treatment Options

Most publicly funded programs have a waiting list and limited staff and funding, and yet they are worthwhile. It's possible to find inexpensive treatment programs or to combine parts of several low-cost programs to fit your needs.

AGE, GENDER, AND OTHER AREAS

Addictions and addictive behaviors are a problem for everyone. The biggest group of addicts is middle-aged Americans, but adolescents also suffer from addictions. Adults are role models for kids, including how they chose to deal with their addictions.

Adolescence

Youth has been described as a form of insanity. With limited perspective, overridden by arrogance, adolescence can be difficult. This means teens are more prone to addiction, especially when they cope with issues like parental addictions, social pressure, poor diet, and availability of substances. Important development occurs during adolescence, but addictions can interfere with the emotional growth of teenagers, including how they mature. They can become emotionally stuck at the age when their addiction started.

Teens develop symptoms of addiction within a few years, quicker than adults, but they struggle with accepting their addictions because they believe they are not old enough or have not used long enough.

Friends, and sometimes even parents, can soften the consequences of adolescents using by enabling them and promoting continued use. Making teens face consequences of their use can be the quickest way to wake them up and encourage them to stop.

Recovering Intelligence

In adolescence, lack of experience, insight, maturity, & perspective makes recovery harder.

Recovering adolescents have unique issues, such as:

- Lack of major consequences
- Peer pressure
- Identity: Lack of, searching for
- Boundaries: Pushing to understand, experience, and to learn about reality and their place in it
- The adolescent stage of life:
    - » Arrogance, curiosity, no established identity, being easily influenced, and lack of perspective

- » Blocked emotional growth due to addiction
- » They are younger than their age

A teen treatment group needs to include at least one peer who is actively recovering to be a positive role model (better if they have social status) by offering identification, support, and encouragement. Support for recovery must be strong enough to combat the social pressure of peers that use and the desire of the addict self to continue to use.

If there are adolescents within a recovery group who are more experienced in using, have more social importance, and who aren't invested in their recovery, they can influence younger peers who have a lower status or are less experienced, escalating the likelihood of continued or increased using. This situation is common enough that it should be addressed by parents, the professional running the group or program, and adolescents from the start as a preventative measure to combat negative social pressure within recovery. Successful recovery for teens is all about support, education, growing, caring, and communication.

The accepted belief in recovery is that teens should be treated within a group of their peers, led by one or two professional (young) adults. This approach has merit if there are group members with a solid background in recovery, because their ability to carefront their peers will be much more effective, even more so than a professional adult. The potential relationship that could develop between someone new to recovery and someone familiar with recovery

can be very valuable for both.

If there are not enough members within a group who can act as role models, or worse, the group is dominated by teens who aren't committed to their recovery, the situation can be disastrous. It could provoke teens to act out, leading to abusive behaviors, the acceleration of addiction, and other very negative consequences.

It can take many months to break down the defenses of an adolescent, as well as those of the family, such as denial. A strong ongoing support system is mandatory for succcssful teen recovery. Teens suffer more intense versions of the same issues that recovering adults do, along with the additional issues of adolescence. Issues can include disinterest in school and poor academics, immature living and social skills, inability to focus, infrequent communication, little self-discipline, low self-esteem, patterns of dishonesty, poor self-image, and self-destructiveness. These issues must be addressed with love and support.

To offer that support, an adolescent's family also needs to be in treatment, working their own program and doing family work. Family members need to make concrete changes as individuals and as a unit. If a large commitment is impossible, at least some involvement of the family is required, no matter how difficult it is due to time or travel constraints. A teen addict and his or her family should be in treatment for at least one year.

Recovering Intelligence

A teen's family needs treatment & to work their own program.

In treatment, along with "Addiction Use," many teens are given an additional (co-occurring) psychiatric diagnoses like Attention Deficient Hyperactivity Disorder (ADHD), Obsessive Compulsive Disorder (OCD), or Opposition Defiance Disorder (ODD). These typically include behavioral problems where teens act out, though some of these behaviors can be a normal part of growing up or are caused by poor diet.

An adolescent treatment program must be structured to include safe and productive activities. Volleyball, rock climbing, and punching bags are examples. Participants need an outlet to vent their excess energy, emotions, impatience, and frustrations.

Teens in recovery need to maintain as much of their normal lifestyle as possible. For instance, an inpatient program may have an arrangement with the local school system to meet the client's educational needs. It's critical to develop healthy ways for teens to experience rituals and rites of passage when it comes to growing up. Examples could be:

- Learning about and using personal strengths
- Spending quality time with parents or a role model
- Challenging experiences such as a rope course or rock climbing with recovering peers
- Goal achievement in an area of personal interest

Diversity

Addicts deserve to be in a treatment program where the staff is sensitive to their personal issues and where they respect the community that the addict comes from. Lack of understanding of a specific person or community can generate negative attitudes and make an addict feel less welcomed into recovery. This increases the potential for dropping out, social isolation, returning to social using, and eventually, a return to additive behaviors.

Sexual Identity and Gender Orientation Issues: The lesbian, gay, bisexual, and transgender (LGBT) community has unique treatment issues. Negative attitudes toward LGBT individuals can still be detrimental to recovery. If you belong to the LGBT community, find a treatment program where the staff is sensitive and knowledgeable about LGBT challenges. Should staff try to deny your reality, or convert you into a mainstream or a religious reality, seek help elsewhere. The staff needs to be comfortable dealing with your unique emotional, family, and medical issues.

Recovering Intelligence

If hidden sexual identity drives your addiction, you must find inner peace.

What if you feel you're not able to openly acknowledge your sexual or gender identity? You must do what it takes to come out, at least to those closest to you, or find peace through healthy diversion, spiritual or therapeutic work, and self-acceptance.

You should be able to locate desirable treatment services in urban areas. Peer run support groups are an option. Keep looking until you find what you need.

Race, Culture, or Nationality: A large part of community

is based on race, culture, and nationality. A few examples of how these communities play a part in recovery include:

- Cultures that use a pub as a social center
- Taboos that disallow leaving a family, gang, or tribe
- The cultural shame of admitting you have a problem for which you need help.

If you can't find the support you need within your family or community, go outside of it. The worst likely outcome would be emotional upset or the need to separate from toxic family and friends. This is hard, so ask for support from someone who's already found outside help. Don't worry about being accepted by others. Most people will naturally accept you once they get to know you personally.

Seniors

Senior drug and alcohol addiction (the silent epidemic) is quite common and often involves prescribed medication, maybe one or more pills that have been abused for many years without a problem. Medication misuse can be abetted by boredom, isolation, lack of connection to other people, or limited options, goals, or the desire to achieve. Mood swings, chronic depression, and thoughts of suicide can coincide with addictions.

Recovering Intelligence

Seniors have a lot to give; reach out and offer to help someone.

If you're a senior addict, instead of obsessing over what you don't have, focus on the time, maturity, and experience you do have. You are a valuable resource. Find a way to help a person or an organization; even tasks as simple as babysitting for a single mom, listening to someone who needs to talk, or answering the telephone for a community group are ways to give and, in turn, receive. Activities that use your strengths are the best ones. Your life isn't over unless you choose to let it be over. Get out and live to the fullest.

Women

Women addicts deal with the same issues as men, yet women experience a double standard with most addictions. They face harsher social stigmas and stereotypes than men do, causing them to suffer more. For instance:

- Women should drink like a lady.
- Women sex addicts are whores; men are just men.
- Women food addicts are fat, while men are hefty.

Women who use sex to support their addictions experience extra shame, self-hatred, and guilt, which may cause them to hide their addictions for years. This is one example of how women have a tendency to feel sensations and emotions more than men do.

Biologically speaking, women and men are different but equal. Women produce less serotonin and endorphins than men, which is one reason why they experience such extreme emotions, and why they are more prone to mood issues like depression. Women also

Recovering Intelligence

Women produce less serotonin, endorphins, & enzymes than men.

don't make enough enzymes to process large amounts of alcohol. This can put women at a higher risk for liver disease.

Men don't stay with addicted women as often as women stay with addicted men. Therefore, women may not have the same emotional support as men, may be limited in their financial resources, and tend to have very realistic concerns, especially about their children. These factors may keep a woman stuck in her addiction and in her dysfunctional (sick) family system longer than she wants. As a result, a codependent spouse may be in denial about their partner's addiction.

Recovering Intelligence

Women need to support women; attend women only meetings!

For women in recovery, at least part of the chosen program structure needs to be female-oriented so that a feeling of safety and understanding is achieved. Women addicts need to involve themselves with positive recovering women to act as role models and who offer support in learning to identify and deal with women's issues.

In recovery activities, women need to refocus on themselves. Generally, women are more motivated towards recovery for the sake of their children than men are. Yet, women still must recover for themselves first. Similarly, recovery is not a time to worry about looking good or taking care of others. It's a time to heal.

Women addicts often have a poor sense of self, defining themselves by the external roles they play, such as by their role as mother, wife, or employee. They need to increase a positive self-identity by focusing on the "Who am I?" aspects of themselves that they value. In addition, they need to work on developing self-assertiveness, self-empowerment, and self-esteem, then putting these new traits into action.

Trauma: Many women addicts have experienced emotional, physical, or sexual abuse. If you are among them, your program must address these issues once you have built some solid recovery. If past trauma is blocking your recovery, then you must contain it until you are stable enough to deal with. (Find Trauma Work in the Index.)

SELF-HELP PROGRAMS

Self-help programs are those ran by members of the recovering community or led by those who have undergone recovery, such as 12-Step programs. Whether you make use of self-help program along with a professional program or as your only program, they can be quite valuable. The community support received from self-help programs is important, though they do have their limitations.

There are low or no-cost self-help resources available seven days a week, offered at various times throughout the day. Many different groups are held in churches, hospitals, sober and community centers, and police stations a round the world. In addition, there are a lot of self-help resources on the Internet. (See APPENDIX 10.)

Working with peers who have similar issues and who will give you support may be more desirable than working with a professional. You learn together, grow together, and hopefully form satisfying and rewarding friendships that last for life. As most self-help programs are ran by recovering community members, there will be variations in style. Try new meetings until you find the ones you like.

Note: Be very careful of advice from rigid, enthusiastic people who are absolutely certain they know what's best for you; they can be quite convincing. Even if their advice has value, it may not be right for you or offer you a complete answer.

12-Step Programs

There are many 12-Step programs all over the world based on the Alcoholics Anonymous (AA) model, which has a long and substantial history. This psycho, social, spiritual program has much to offer. These programs offer support and guidance from others in recovery. They provide a recovery structure which can be adjusted to your schedule and needs. Both the program itself and the social, emotional, and logistical support are important.

Recovering Intelligence

12-Step is a proven model, fits with other models, & it's available.

The only condition for membership into a 12-Step program is a desire to stop your addictive behavior. They have no affiliation with other groups, and their only focus is recovery. Many people will find it desirable or necessary to regularly participate in the program. Anonymity is expected.

There are over 200 different AA-based programs all over the world for people attempting to recover from various addictions and mental health issues. (See APPENDIX 10.) A few of those programs include:

- Al-Anon is a 12-Step based program for the families and friends of alcoholics and other addicts. A similar structure to AA, it is centered on the addictive quality of codependency.
  - » Alateen is Al-Anon's program for younger members.
- Nar-Anon is the same program as Al-Anon but for the families of people addicted to narcotics and other drugs.
- COSLAA and COSA are programs for families of sex addicts.
- Codependents Anonymous (CODA) is a 12-Step program for people who share a common desire to develop healthy boundaries, a positive self-image, and functional and healthy relationships. CODA is influenced by psychology and specific concepts of family systems.

Faith-Based Programs

Faith-based programs are constructed around a spiritual

or religious path to recovery. Christian churches and religious institutions often host 12-Step groups. Some offer their own religious or faith-based addiction recovery programs; these are usually outpatient programs and are run by a member of the church. There also are religious-based (usually Christian) programs not run by specific churches; these are both residential and outpatient.

Celebrate Recovery is a Christian 12-Step program that emphasizes Jesus as the only Higher Power. It sees all hurts, hang-ups, and habits as one issue, and no declaration of being an alcoholic is required.

The Salvation Army is a residential program based on Christian doctrine. They manage charitable businesses to help people in the community.

Secular Programs

Secular programs do not deal with religion or spirituality, nor do they make judgment on faith-based programs. They can be a good match for those whose faith-based program isn't available, those who don't want to explore the spiritual part of life during recovery, and those who don't believe. Well-rounded treatment may include secular and faith-based programs.

Life Ring: The "Three-S Philosophy" of Life Ring is shorthand for their principles of Sobriety, Secularity, and Self-Help. Life Ring:

- Encourages its members to practice abstinence from

drugs and alcohol. Their motto is: "We do not drink or use, no matter what."

- Spiritual beliefs remain private; it supports secular recovery with reliance on human efforts.
- They hold self-help workshops in which members build their recovery plans.

Rational Recovery offers instructional guidance on self-planned recovery from drugs and alcohol through books, videos, and lectures. The program is based on permanent abstinence, self-reliance, and cognitive therapy. Thc foundcr is against meetings, yet meetings based on RR's material and run by individuals may exist.

Secular Organizations for Sobriety (SOS) is a self-help organization for atheists recovering from all addictions. Its philosophy is that recovery is achieved through self-reliance. The program is a simple, rational focus on achieving and maintaining recovery. Religious, spiritual, agnostic, or atheistic beliefs are seen as separate from recovery. Otherwise, it is similar to AA, as the meetings are anonymous, recovering birthdays are celebrated, and recovery is viewed as a one day at a time process. There are also groups for family and friends, similar to Al-Anon.

Sober24 offers free self-help support groups to people who want to abstain from addictive and compulsive behaviors. Cognitive, behavioral, and educational methods are used to change beliefs and attitudes that can lead to negative, addictive behavior. The site has online recovery meetings, a message board, Internet discussion groups, a meeting list, and recommended readings.

SMART Recovery (Self-Management and Recovery Training) is a non-profit, self-help organization that offers tools and strategies to those seeking abstinence from addictive behaviors. This program uses a science-based approach which incorporates motivational, behavioral, and cognitive techniques that foster recovery.

Women For Sobriety is a secular self-help organization that helps members achieve sobriety and sustain ongoing recovery from addictions. Their New Life program is based on personal development including positive thinking, meditation, group meetings, and good nutritional practices. The meetings provide an extremely nurturing environment; most meetings are small, intimate, and supportive.

An extension of Women For Sobriety, Men For Sobriety is a sobriety group for men based on the same format.

The UpSpiralLife Group

12 New Steps for the New Millennium: The UpSpiralLife Group has a specific format to encourage NeuroPositive

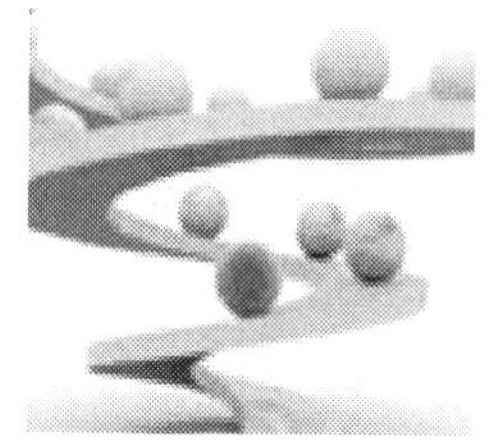

living. The 12 steps outlined within the program cause new positive brain circuits (neuropathways) to grow, forging a strength-based, mental-emotional superhighway that promotes personal growth and well-being. Although designed for normies (non-addicts), the program is very effective for people in recovery when used along with primary treatment or aftercare. This program is based on powerful, cutting-edge knowledge offered by the Applied Neuroscience Institute. Because it is new, meetings are limited, although teleconferencing groups are available. (See APPENDIX 10.)

Online Services

There are many online resources for recovery, and more are constantly in development. No matter where you live, online communities can help you. (See APPENDIX 10.)

DRUG TESTING

Testing is a controversial issue, but it can be used as a deterrent to using, set up by a recovering person who is trying to stay clean and sober. Ask a trusted other to randomly test you through urine screening. Testing services are available, but home testing kits are easier and cheaper. Drug testing provides a way for you to prove to yourself and others that you are succeeding in your recovery.

SUMMARY

Your recovery is too important to "try" to do it. You either do it or you don't; there is no try. You have to make a choice to enter recovery and then stick with it until it's solid – or face the negative consequences that you know will come if you continue your addiction.

In immediate recovery you need to:

- Breathe – a lot
- Stay aware

- Get a medical exam
- Abstain or maintain (with maintenance addictions like food) and stabilize
- Detoxify your body (drugs, sugar, processed foods)
- Use recovery reminders like the Red Dots (or lights)
- Consider amino acid supplements (or compounds), a pro-recovery diet, and a nutritional evaluation
- Choose to trust and accept the help of valued others
- Evaluate your needs and look for solutions
- Choose/commit to a desirable recovery approach
- Build and use your positive support group
- Build and maintain your foundation for recovery
- Start filling your tool box with tools and strategies
- Look at and deal with only necessary issues
- Let go of negative practices that lead to addiction
- Focus on positive people, places, things, situations
- Make sure you are taking care of yourself
- Balance your recovery activities and family needs
- Open up and let down your defenses
- Let go and grieve the loss of your loved addiction; be reminded to practice deep breathing – a lot
- Open up to your Higher Power
- Begin to create and live **Your Recovering Future™**

Stay focused on your desire for recovery. To decrease the potential for relapse, be aware of old patterns and cravings. You must accept the inevitability of change and the reality that little or nothing worthwhile happened while you were under the influence of your addiction, especially in the end.

Know or choose to believe that **Your Recovering Future™** will be a lot better than your past, even better than you thought it could be.

You can do this!
One Step at a Time!

Chapter 3

Early Recovery

Chapter 3: Early Recovery
Table of Contents

EARLY RECOVERY

Early recovery starts after you have created a good support system, have truly given up your addiction, and have started to invest your time and energy into a recovery approach of your choice. Now you are on your way!

Once you start early recovery and set yourself up for success with a quality foundation to deal with urgent issues, it's time to continue building. As you lower your defenses and open up your head and heart, you'll make the mental-emotional shifts that will expand **Your Recovering Future**™. Your life should start to feel easier, more stable, and more hopeful. When you walk your talk, your results will deepen your belief that you can do this.

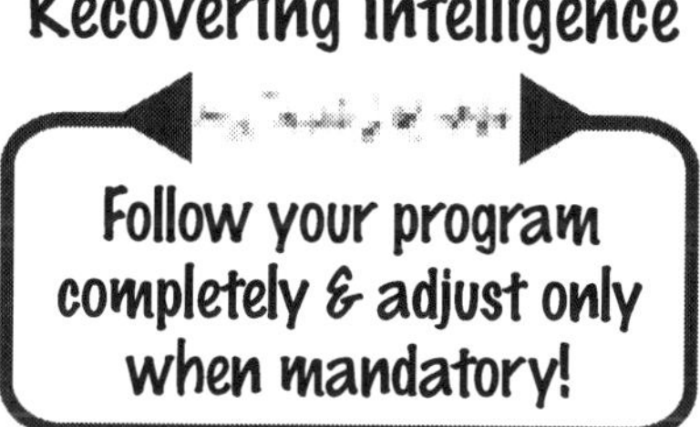

Recovery is a major life transition. You'll need to adjust your negative beliefs, attitudes, perspectives, and assumptions about yourself, recovery, and the world. As a result, your life and your future will change. Transitions are stimulating, yet they can be more positive than negative, depending on how you relate to them. By now, you have had many experiences that show you that you can do what it takes to recover! ***Breathe, Deeply and Slowly!! Relax and Focus on what you can do to get what you need and want!***

Shift & expand your recovering self-image with healthy behaviors!

Your Recovering Future

Recovery is unpredictable, unsettling, challenging, and exciting. It's yours for the asking, to be created as you choose. Many questions will arise during recovery; don't be afraid to ask them. These may include:

- What will life be like without using?
- What will I have to give up?
- How will I deal with everything?
- Can I really do it?
- Am I strong enough?

As in life, recovery can be represented as a glass that is both half empty and half full, meaning there are negative and positive aspects. If you choose to dwell on the half empty glass, you'll be more aware of the negative. If you focus on the half full glass, you'll be more aware of the positive. What you think about most frequently and intensely is what you bring into your life, so focus on the positive while recognizing the trials ahead.

Expect that you will be challenged and that you might become stuck at some point along your journey. If things become difficult and stay that way for months, it is an indication that something needs to change. You'll want to actively explore the possible reasons for the difficulty you're having

Recovering Intelligence

Life offers challenges & opportunities to grow. Accept them!

and deal with them. This doesn't mean that you will get immediate insight and relief. It means that action is your best response for desired results. You may face a problem that you can't do anything about right now. In this case, you will need to grow past it or live with it.

As you embrace your recovery and grow, you'll find your life improving in many ways. Your momentum will increase, and you'll have more opportunities to improve who you are and how you live your life. This can feel scary and stressful, or exciting and desirable. It all depends on you and your approach. Eventually, you will be able to do the things you once only dreamed of, or never dreamed of!

ADDICTION & RECOVERY EDUCATION

At some point, you may want to know about your addictions, how addiction works, its effect on brain chemistry, and how genetics play a part. You may be curious about what drives you to use and how using appears to meet your needs. That knowledge will give you a whole new perspective about your addictions. Yet, in the early stages of recovery, learning how to develop and maintain your recovery is a higher priority than the science behind addiction.

Defining Your Personal Recovery

Defining your personal recovery is necessary so you'll know how to navigate through it. Just like you'd chart travel plans for a personal trip, writing out your recovery plans can increase your motivation and commitment. What's the structure you'll use to create your recovery course? When will you start it?

Developmental Stages of Recovery

There are various theories about the number of stages of recovery and a case could be made for all of them. I've chosen to simplify this for you. Your level of willingness will affect how easily and quickly you proceed through these stages and move into a recovering lifestyle.

Most people's recoveries are not smooth or simple. Yours may be a challenging and complex journey. It may sometimes go sideways and backwards. It can feel like you're in a maze. If you keep going, you will move through all four of the developmental stages of recovery.

They are:

1. Withdrawal and Detox: (drugs, alcohol, and sugar Physical cleansing of your system from toxins; the development of new behaviors.
2. Abstinence & Immediate Issues: Building stability

through the use of this book and other resources without turning back to your addiction to numb out.

3. Foundation Building: Learning new ways to interact with life's problems.
4. Awareness & Lifestyle: A shift in attitude, spiritual practices, and behavior that leads to new way of seeing yourself, others, and the world.

The Healing Environment

A healing environment is a psychological place that nurtures your health, growth, and potential. It is a place you feel safe enough to relax, open up, and do your recovery work – a place to deal with your life as issues come up and challenge you. In a healing environment, you'll have the resources and support to deal with these challenges, if you choose to.

It's vital you feel you are in a healing environment with your self-help and treatment groups and your support team. If you have concerns, talk to trusted others.

Anonymity

Your anonymity, meaning the code that your personal information will not be shared outside your recovery group, is not guaranteed, especially if you're publicly known. Don't share in a public meeting what could result in severe consequences for you or others; instead, discuss it with your mentor, a close friend, or a professional.

Generally, people will keep your personal information confidential, but people are human, sometimes even mature and responsible people make the mistake of breaking a confidentiality.

MENTAL PROCESSING

The mental process you use to evaluate options and make decisions is influenced by your environment and programmed by your beliefs, which thus shape your attitudes, thoughts, and feelings. Keep an open mind throughout recovery, and allow feedback you receive to influence your decisions in a positive way.

Ah Ha Moment

Most people don't have a specific, powerful breakthrough "Ah Ha" moment. Instead, they gradually connect with reality and their real self – the self that got lost in addiction. Remain engaged in recovery until you experience the miracle!

Attitude

Your attitude comes from your beliefs and the way you view and approach life. Your attitude about an experience may affect you more than the experience itself. This is a crucial concept. Changing

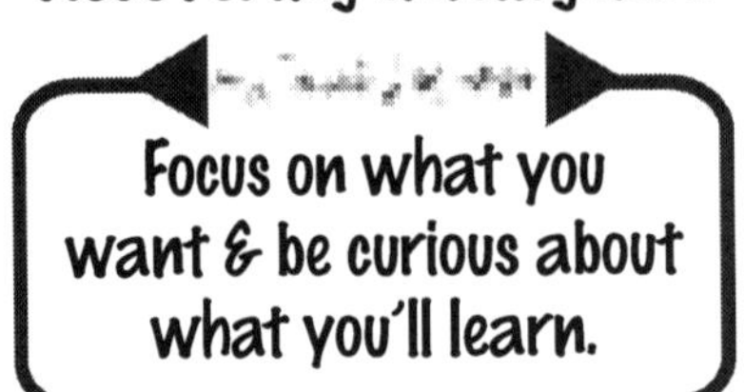

your attitude or your perspective will change your life and the lives of everyone around you.

Don't let negative attitudes define who you are or how you relate to the world. For instance, looking at your life with acceptance and curiosity will offer you a more positive approach than anger, resentment, or denial.

One common negative attitude is saying that you "have to" do something. Normally we do things because ultimately we want the reward at the end. Saying you "have to" do something, is putting a negative pressure on yourself and it's not even true.

Ensure your attitudes work for you, not against you. Most decisions are based on wanting to get something positive out of a situation or avoid something negative. Are your attitudes helping you build a better future?

Attitudes are self-perpetuating. You draw in what you think about most often, most intensely, and most genuinely. Choose attitudes and behaviors that match who you want to be and what you want to achieve – and then stay focused!

Good Enough: You consistently make decisions about how much is "good enough" in any given situation, including recovery. There are negative and positive versions of "good enough." Find a balance. Avoid underachieving by giving in too early and overachieving through false ideas of perfection. As with any decision, it's usually smart to talk with trusted support group members and weigh the risk and the rewards, especially when the risks are high.

Consider: **"In My Experience . . . you don't want to avoid, defend against, or resist desirable recovery options."** (See APPENDIX 7.)

A negative version of "good enough" is when you reach the point in your recovery where the pain of your addiction is lessening, and you choose to believe that you don't need to deal with certain past issues or parts of your personality anymore. You conclude things will be okay or that you can manage (get by, control your addiction, or just hang on) "good enough," even though your recovery isn't complete. This version of "good enough" clearly isn't going to support a healthy and happy recovering lifestyle. Instead, you're settling for limited results, usually because you want to avoid a task or an issue. It is a risky strategy.

A positive version of "good enough" that is highly-acceptable is called satisficing. Satisficing is decision-making strategy, with the standard set at a high level, between good and excellent. Always stay well below the impossible standard of perfection, even if it means you feel your results are only average.

Hope is an attitude based on the belief that you have positive options available to you and that you have the ability and resources to fulfill those options. Hope is what can pull you through many of the challenging periods

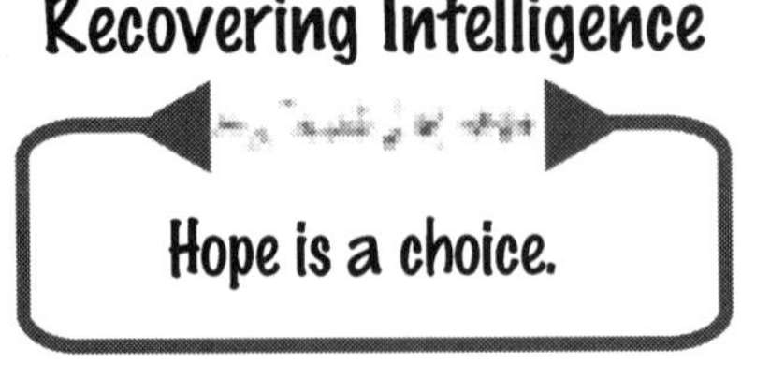

that you may experience. Learn to develop a hopeful attitude early in your recovery. Do this by acknowledging your personal resources and options and by always taking positive action NOW!

Content vs. Hype: A content attitude is comprised of high-quality, positive, and valuable substance, not style. A hype attitude is about presentation, or bling, and is often intense, even angry; it contains limited positive content.

Optimism is a positive attitude or point of view, which you can choose to have, even if it's not your first response. It focuses on the constructive aspects of an issue. You acknowledge negatives and then take on a realistic but optimistic perspective. Gain awareness of an issue by looking at several different points of view, such as the point of view of your spouse, your mentor, or even a person with whom you disagree. Remember, optimists are happier, healthier, and more successful.

Recovering Intelligence

Optimists are healthier!

Belief

Belief is your accepted point of view about something, based on your perception of reality. What evidence do you have that your beliefs are true? Explore the evidence for your beliefs from different

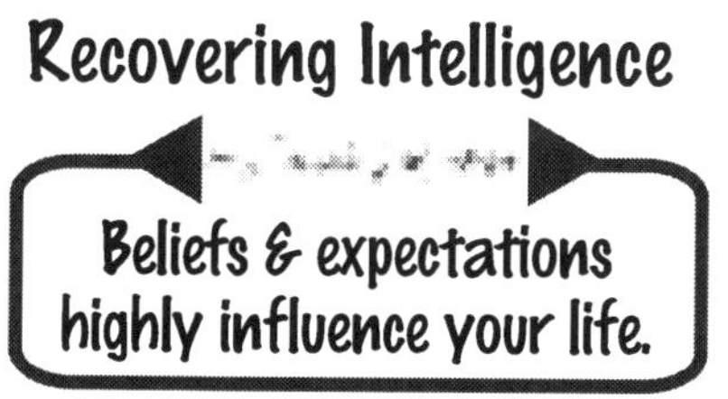

perspectives. Be careful you aren't hanging on to destructive beliefs, which some addicts do so their ego doesn't have to acknowledge their wrong actions.

Your beliefs directly affect your entire life, your perspective of the world, and create your reality. What beliefs would help you create **Your Recovering Future™**?

Commitment

Recovering Intelligence

Your behavior shows the level of commitment to your recovery.

When you can genuinely say to yourself, "I'll do whatever it takes, for as long as it takes," and really mean it, you will already be building a quality recovery. Upon such, you'll be committed to things you've never done or maybe don't do well. This may include listening, reading, talking, watching, and writing – privately or in groups. It'll include exploring the way you think, examining your behaviors, and clarifying your future goals. If you have trouble with any aspect of your commitment to recovery, ask for help.

Expectations are what you think will most likely happen in the future. They'll affect your health, happiness, and recovery. Will your recovery be difficult and painful, or challenging and exciting? Realistic, positive expectations are healthy and desirable, but prepare yourself for disappointments, too. Unfulfilled expectations can feel bad. Look at

the situation, accept, adjust, and move on.

Your belief system is your particular set of beliefs and the way in which those beliefs work together. They are part of your personal map with which you move through the world. In recovery, you need to review and challenge your beliefs. Ask yourself questions like:

- Do I really believe this?
- Does this perspective match those held by others whom I trust and respect?
- Does this belief work for me?
- Would I benefit from changing a specific belief?

Endurance

Recovery is a focused, life-long journey. Even with a quality program structure, it will take endurance. Not every day will be great, and you must endure disappointments. If you look at the big picture, you'll find that your worst day of recovery is still better than your best day of addiction.

Mental Recovery Resource States

You have mental and emotional states that will help you through recovery if you consciously connect with them. For example, visualize a time in the past when you had courage to get you through a difficult situation. Remember what it felt like and then bring those emotions into the now. The situation in which you felt courage could be minor, but reconnecting with that courage is vital. Some examples of mental and emotional states to reconnect with are:

- Commitment: Your decision to do whatever it takes

to get an outcome that you want.

- Courage: Being brave enough to move through any fear, even in a very difficult situation.
- Curiosity: Being interested in something; your desire to find information or a solution. Curiosity is a valuable mental state if used carefully.
- Enthusiasm: Feeling interested in something and being excited about having it or experiencing it.
- Learning: Choosing to know more about something.
- Optimism: Choosing to believe that a situation will turn out well and that you can succeed, or that you'll learn and grow, even from a negative outcome.
- Resourcefulness: Believing in your personal knowledge and skills and your ability to find the outer resources (people, money, situations, etc.) that you need to be successful.

Motivation

At the most basic level, your motivation comes from your desire to avoid pain and gain pleasure. The way in which you have mentally wired your recovery will influence your recovery as being either painful or pleasurable, hard or easy, etc. Your motivation will come from your eagerness to:

Recovering Intelligence

Open-up & connect with who you are & what you want & you'll find your motivation!

1. Avoid all the negatives of using you have endured
2. Gain all the positives of quality recovery

It's likely you'll mostly be motivated by avoiding the negatives, later more by gaining the positives. You must take the time to repeatedly develop a pleasurable association with recovery and a negative association with using. This can be developed through real-life involvement with other recovering individuals who are in a program and through personal development using recovery tools and strategies.

Just prior to recovery, when you have "hit bottom," you will have a strong connection with the negatives of your addiction and an equally strong desire to avoid them. This is called being "sick and tired of being sick and tired." If you are willing to open up to the reality of your addiction, you'll raise your "rock bottom", experience less pain and negative consequences, as well as cause less negative consequence to others.

Note: Connection with your motivation can be quite emotional, so seek support throughout the process.

Early in recovery, it's important to build momentum. The best time to do this is during primary recovery, while you are still in contact with the negative aspects of your addiction. After you have built a stable foundation to recovery, you can ease off from your intensity, just as a pilot will go full-throttle to get the plane off the ground, but once in the air, the pilot pulls back on the throttle.

Over time, the negative consequences of your addiction will become less intense or fade from your awareness, so it's essential to have ways of staying motivated. It is usually more desirable and effective to focus on positive motivators. These include healthy family and friendships, increased self-esteem, and purposeful goals.

Programming

Programming is the training of your computer-like unconscious mind with information and experiences. What you put into your mind will highly influence how you think, what you believe, and how you feel about yourself and the world. It's important to work with your unconscious mind by programing it with accurate information. From the computer programming world comes the joke GI = GO (Garbage In = Garbage Out). This means if you program the computer incorrectly, don't blame the computer for the results. Be responsible for how you are programming yourself.

Reprogramming: If you continue to think and act the same way you have been, you'll continue to get the same results. To build a better future, old behavioral patterns need to change. Learn to pay attention to what you say, think, and do. Be as clear, specific, accurate, and positive as you can be about **Your Recovering Future™**. (See APPENDIX 9.)

Consider: **"In My Experience... you don't want to think inaccurately."**
(See APPENDIX 7.)

The Iceberg Principle: Icebergs rest 10% above the water and 90% below the water. This idea is similar to the human mind. 10% of our self-knowledge is conscious and 90% of it is unconscious. To connect with the real you, you need to connect with your unconscious mind. You can do this using tools such as journaling, meditating, or repeatedly asking yourself important questions. Connecting with your unconscious grants you knowledge and resources.

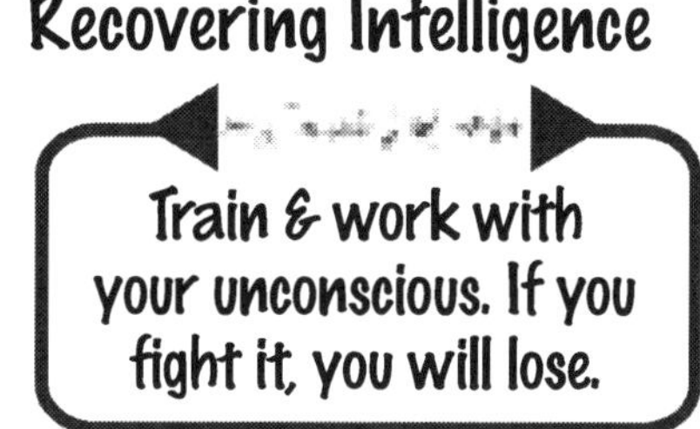

Don't fight your unconscious mind. You may win some battles, but you will lose the war. Learn to stay aware of and work with your unconscious mind by teaching it what results you want. Your Addict Self has evolved and thrived because, early in your addiction, using worked. Now you must develop a strong Recovering Self. Over time, you will see that recovery works much better that using.

Success Response

You want to build your internal success response. That will encourage you to set yourself up for success. This is your response to always do what is best for your recovery; what you know will move you forward in your recovery. As you begin to build a strong success response, you will focus more on solutions. Examples include:

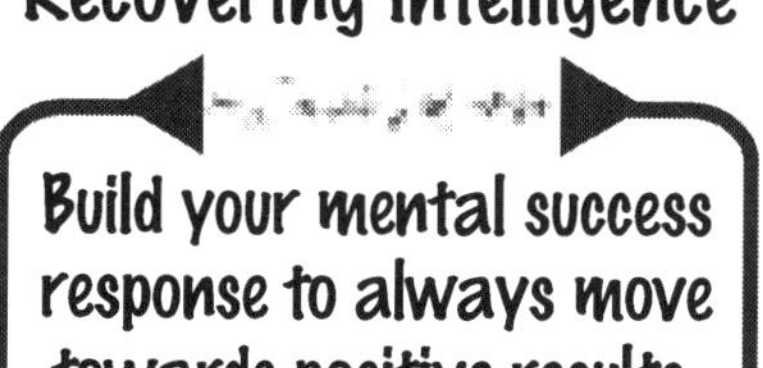

- Always going to your core meeting(s).
- Regularly using reminders such as alarms, chips, and

red lights.

- Having your heart-felt reason for recovery, strongly "wired-in," ready, and available.

Willpower

Willpower can be thought of as your mental-emotional structure which causes you to act on what you want and prevents you from acting on what you don't want. Having willpower is necessary in recovery. Fortunately, you do have some willpower; otherwise, every time you encountered a trigger, you'd use. Through willpower, instead of using, you'll rely on your inner strength to choose a desirable response, such as reviewing your options card, calling your support people, or asking (praying) for spiritual help. You can strengthen your willpower by practicing accurate and positive behavior.

Recovering Intelligence

Develop & use willpower until you can get to your support.

Using willpower alone or as the main strategy in a recovery approach is unlikely to succeed because recovery is complex, requiring structure, support, and other tools to navigate through the highs and lows. Negative results of using willpower alone may include:

- You probably won't grow, leading to a more rigid and controlling personality, and less happiness.
- Your focus will mostly be on what you need to avoid, rather than what you want to become.

- Your desire and focus around recovery decreases.
- You miss out on the positives of recovery, like a more adaptable, flexible, open style – one centered on personal abundance, happiness, and health.

If your addiction must be maintained, as with food addictions, willpower is essential, but willpower is a resource, not the answer. Willpower can be developed by repeating patterns of inner strength until it becomes habit. Habits are in your long-term memory, so you'll remember them. Develop your willpower but never test it needlessly, especially in a high-risk situation.

BUILDING YOUR RECOVERY

Decide what the structure of your program will be and build from that. The following are some suggestions.

A Foundation For Your Recovery

Your recovery is founded on your acknowledgment that you have an addiction. Look at the major life problems your addiction has caused and would continue to cause if you returned to it. Don't allow ego, finances, or social status to compel you to reject the chaos and powerlessness you experienced as an addict. You have cravings and behaviors you struggle to control.

See Your Recovering Future™ & build it up: One decision, action, & outcome at a time.

Your Recovering Future

Accept this lack of control and learn from it.

Recovering Intelligence

If you have control over your using & it's manageable, why stop?

Healthy people wouldn't tolerate losses or chaos the same way an addict would. As an addict, your life has become unmanageable, disrupted and out of control due to your using. To what degree was your life unmanageable, disrupted, or out of control?

Powerlessness is your inability to predict with certainty your ability to control your use. Acceptance of your powerlessness is vital. If you aren't at all powerless, then you must believe that you are in control of your behavior and aren't an addict. Choose to focus on what you can control, and create positive results in your life from it.

Powerless vs. Helpless: Powerless and helpless are similar but different terms. Used here, powerlessness is a positive and proactive term – taking control of your life by letting go of what isn't working. It doesn't mean that you're helpless in general. Believing that you're helpless is harmful, and it blocks your desire to grow and thrive.

Recovering Intelligence

Let go of your addiction & gain control over your powerlessness & your life.

Surrendering: Think of surrendering as letting go and yielding to reality. Surrender the illusion that your addiction had any healthy value for you. Surrender to the truth that recovery has more value than your addiction. Surrender to the fact that using isn't valuable enough to you to continue wasting your time, money, health, and happiness on it.

Like most mental shifts, surrendering is often unconscious, occurs over a period of time, and concludes when you become aware of it. Usually, there is no big surrendering event, no burning bush. As your unconscious and conscious defenses break down and change, you have the opportunity to genuinely open up to the truth about your addiction, and maybe for the first time, you are able to walk down the path of recovery.

Upon surrendering, you may have an experience of calmness and relief, like a heavy load is being lifted from your shoulders. There is no longer any desire to defend or embrace your addiction. You know that you don't have to continue your addiction, and you can recover.

Recovering Intelligence

Surrender & believe that your Higher Power will guide your recovery.

In the 12-Step model, surrendering means you give up your own will and submit to the will of your Higher Power or the God of your understanding, who will guide your recovery. This belief assumes that there is a spiritual consciousness with a bigger plan for you, that you have agreements with The Source to fulfill a general or a specific life purpose. It can feel hard or impossible to trust an unknown Source and turn your life over to that Source. Yet, it's an experience and a process that so many before you have chosen with great results, especially when a more ego-centered approach hasn't worked.

Addiction Completion

To achieve addiction completion, you must abstain from your addiction or, for maintenance addictions, cease excessive behaviors. This psychological shift regarding the relationship you have with your addiction needs to be felt at a deep level. Certain activities can assist you as you move along in your recovery towards addiction completion. Examples include:

- Ending relationships with other users
- Changing your phone number and eliminating all using persons' phone numbers
- Eliminate trappings: credit cards, pipes, deep fryers
- Eliminating all hot and secondary triggers:
  - » Removing all items connected to your addiction
  - » Changing your lifestyle so you reduce contact with triggers
- Having a funeral (burial/fire) for your ex-addiction

As you move through these activities, stay focused on your recovery. Think of what you want in your future and why your future will be better as a result of your recovery.

Balance

Staying balanced in every aspect

of your life is important, especially in early recovery. You will gradually develop your sense of balance over time, but there are immediate actions you can take that will help you find some stability: breathe, slow down, pay attention, relax, and limit extremes.

- Behavior: Observe; feel your body sensations
- Emotional: Identify and connect with your feelings
- Mental: Focus and think accurately
- Nutritional: Eat so your brain functions at its best
- Social: Maintain healthy supportive relationships
- Spiritual: Connect with yourself and the Source

Behavior

Your behavior is how you act, including what you say and do. It reveals who you are and what you want. Words genuinely felt, and often easily spoken, can be hard to carry out. Strive to have your actions match your healthy desires and values. Are you walking your talk?

If repeated over time, even negative behavior will become familiar and accepted, to the point it no longer seems unusual or unfavorable. This makes it more likely to continue. The remedy is awareness and a willingness to stay connected to your desire to change and be healthy.

Positive behaviors: Become fully aware of, experience, and appreciate all of your positive recovery qualities, patterns, and behaviors. Attempt to repeat them as often as possible while keeping them in balance. Remember the 3 positive to 1 negative ratio for happiness.

Negative behaviors: Become clear about what your

negative behaviors are and connect with your desire to change them. Stop, breathe, and look at your situation. With feedback from your support group and other resources, start letting go of and changing these behaviors. New actions create new feelings.

Challenging Life

Just as life is challenging, recovery can also be challenging. If you accept and embrace recovery, you'll be working towards a more desirable life. If you don't fully accept recovery or healthy living, or if you continue your addictive behaviors, you'll have a tough life. Recovery is your opportunity to practice accepting challenges that allow for personal development and lead to success.

Recovering Intelligence

Accept the challenge to live fully engaged, aware & excited!

Change

Change is inevitable. How you respond to change makes the difference. If you relax and work with it, even embrace it, your life will be easier. Develop your ability to be adaptive, curious, flexible, and self-accepting, and strive to grow and improve.

Change will happen as you clear out inaccurate information and emotional blocks from your unconscious mind through the use of healthy resources. Make small but consistent changes by a) increasing the amount or intensity of the positive and b) reducing the amount or intensity of the negative. Your outer world will change as you transform your inner world.

If you resist the positive changes that come with recovery, the process can be unnecessarily difficult. Recovery will be easier if you address and work through each issue and turn your focus towards **Your Recovering Future™**. Not letting go of negative behaviors is similar to being pulled apart by The Rack, an ancient torture device that is very painful.

Changing can feel like you are losing a part of yourself, but you aren't. Who you are is much deeper than your ego, your programing, or your behaviors. Who you will become is up to you. Your willingness to go deeper into yourself may feel scary but will have big benefits. Take a deep breath and ask yourself, "Who am I?" and "Who do I want to become?" Breathe, be still, and listen for your answers.

Recovery takes courage. Courage is not the absence of fear but rather the ability to move through your fear, doing what you need to do in spite of it. Tap into the courage you used to get through past situations. Visualize what you want. Then clarify what it will take to achieve it and take action, even when you are afraid. Focus on goals over which you have direct control or you can develop control over, such as your beliefs, attitudes, feelings, thoughts, and behaviors. What will cause you to change? Have you built that into your recovery?

The experience of being in a close, quality friendship is a vehicle for change. It starts with learning about yourself, then connecting with others. The feeling of connection can be intense and desirable. The feedback you get will be invaluable. It's easy to react when a friend's feedback appears to be negative; breathe, let go of self-judgments, and listen.

Evaluation

Consistently evaluate your life, yourself (see Self-Evaluation), and your goals, relationships, and environments. Learn to scan, paying attention to potential triggers and possible relapse symptoms, especially as you move through slippery situations. Ask yourself, "What's really going on, and is this a good place for me to be?" If the answer is yes, great! If it's no, change the situation or leave. What desirable situations do you want to be involved in?

Following Suggestions

Follow suggestions from valued others whenever possible, but be careful. Rigidly following suggestions that conflict with other essential priorities can backfire on you; for example, attending so many meetings that you feel guilty about not taking care of family priorities. When

you are given suggestions that don't work for you, ask other trusted resources, and attempt to find another, better option.

Friendship

There are four levels of personal friendship, each with their own benefits and responsibilities, depending on the closeness of the relationship. Each level of friendship builds on the prior one. The deeper the level is, the more rewarding and the more demanding it will be, as the emotional connection can be extremely powerful.

1. <u>Acquaintanceship</u> is defined by the social setting. Time spent together is based on mutual interests. You're friendly and exchange public information.
2. <u>Casual friendship</u> is based on common interests, activities, and concerns. There's interest in each other's personal goals, hopes, and opinions. Strengths and weaknesses are known, and some trust develops.
3. <u>Close friendship</u> (fellowship) promotes a sense of oneness. Both of you share some life goals and help each other achieve those goals. There is moderate caring, support, trust, etc.
4. <u>Intimate friendship</u> is based on loyalty and a commitment to generously invest in each other's lives to help one another grow, mature, and achieve your dreams. This level of intimacy requires honesty, lowered defenses, trust, and at times forgiveness. In an intimate relationship, it's likely you'll agree to offer and accept feedback about personal issues.

- Professional friendship can be intimate and fulfilling, but it's limited by boundaries.

Keeping a Friendship: A long-term quality friendship needs to be based on maturity, nurturing, and respect. A friendship that is not based on these attributes should be questioned or ended. You want to match each other's depth of emotional connection, whatever it may be.

Letting Go of Using Friends: At the beginning of recovery, even true friends whose behavior or presence triggers you can't be in your life. Find a way to tell them about your recovery in a way that's respectful and acknowledges your friendship. This can be painful, so be ready, especially if they react negatively.

Recovering Intelligence

Review, understand, & let go of your past. You will heal & find peace.

Gratitude

Feeling grateful for what you do have and for the opportunity of recovery can go a long way towards making your life work. Research has found that it's more difficult to experience a negative emotion when focusing on a positive emotion. Focus on what you appreciate and what you are grateful for. Make a list and read it daily.

Gratitude is the positive emotion that connects us to others. Acknowledge others for the blessing they are in your life. If you choose to feel good about them, it may improve your relationships. Share your appreciation for someone in your life who has been especially helpful and kind. Write them a letter of gratitude describing why you're grateful to them. State what they did and how it affected your life. It's even better if you can read your letter aloud to them and then give them a special copy. This is a powerful, positive experience that will not soon be forgotten.

History

You must acknowledge your using history by completing three tasks. First is your "Abuse-A-Log" (similar to AA's Step Four "Moral Inventory"). Make a complete list of your using history and note the problems it caused. Describe the impact using had on you, your life, and others. This will give you a clear and powerful picture of your past abuse and the resulting consequences. As you work on your log, practice slow, deep breaths and relax. Upon completion, take a step back and absorb the full impact.

The second task is to write out your life story. Include all significant life events and a review of your using and treatment history. Again, breathe and take in the full impact of the experience.

The third task is to write about the significant life issues that are prominent in your history. Be honest and thorough! The following are examples of issues you can include, if they apply:

- Abandonment

- Abuse or trauma
- Anger
- Character defects: blame, dishonesty, selfishness
- Disturbing feelings: bitterness, envy, jealousy, rage
- Disturbing thoughts: self-harm, suicide, revenge
- Dysfunctional behaviors
- Fears
- Guilt, regret
- Harm to others
- Resentment
- Misconduct: criminal, sexual
- Values: personal, family, social, spiritual
- Unthinkable thoughts (that are thought of often)

Share your history with someone who cares about you, is non-judgmental, emotionally uninvolved, and empathic. This will increase the positive impact of the exercise and help you process and release your heavy feelings. As you hear the listener's accepting response, you will connect with your humanity and the human reality that everyone makes mistakes. In addition, sharing your history with your Higher Power will connect you with your spirituality.

Moving On

Moving on from one step to the next can be positive or negative in terms of your recovery. If you're considering changing your recovery focus, approach, or activities, carefully explore the reason behind the change.

If you have completed your current goals, or you realize that you must change your approach to meet those goals, great! Completing goals will inspire you to set further ones and meet more milestones. Changing focus because you want something different is also good; set a new goal, take positive action, and make it happen.

However, moving on because something is hard, you're blocked, or you're trying to avoid an issue may work temporarily, but the issue will still be with you until you address it.

Always start your next goal before you have completed your last one. This will give you a smooth transition between goals and will reduce the likelihood that you are running away from an issue. It will also motivate you to keep moving forward.

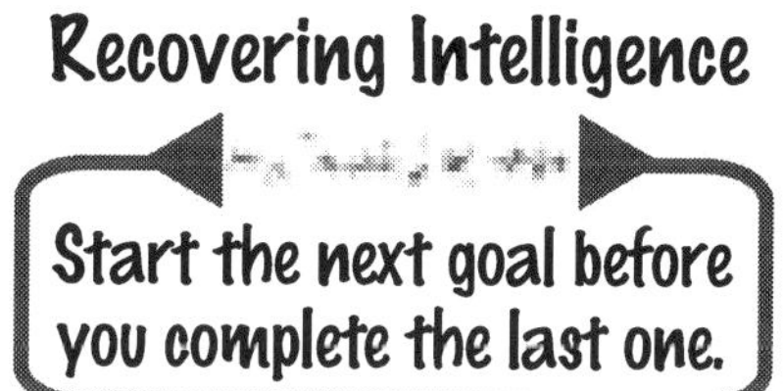

Opening Up

Opening up to your authentic self is a choice to be more genuine, sensitive, curious, flexible, and expansive. It involves connecting to your unconscious mind, exploring new things, studying and observing, shifting your reality, and letting go of your fears. To open up, you need to be honest about your past, who you are, and who you want to become.

Opening up will serve you in many ways, such as strengthening your knowledge and resources. In recovery, you will learn to accept life on life's terms while being fully aware, fully alive, and fully involved. It can be overwhelming at first, but it's necessary to the recovery process. Pace yourself!

Embracing reality: Your attitude towards recovery will shape your approach. If you embrace new and different beliefs about your addiction, desirable paths for recovery may open up to you. This is because your mental filtering system allows desirable alternatives to be recognized by your conscious mind once they are made known. For example, you buy a new car, and suddenly you begin to see identical-looking cars that were always there, you just didn't notice them before because your mind was not open to it.

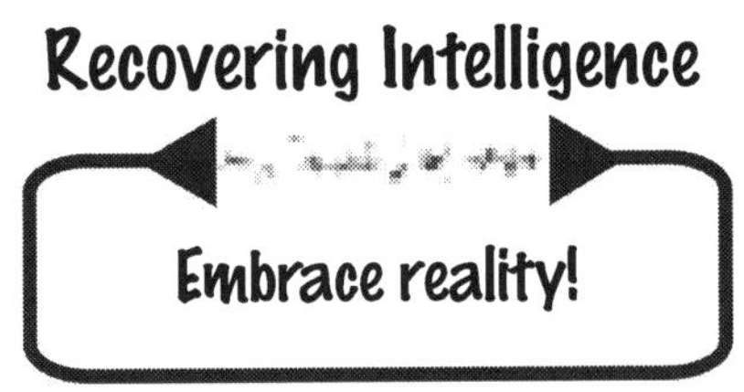

Changing how you see reality isn't easy, even when you want to. Listen to or read about how respected others see reality. (Find *Reality Testing* and *Seeing Reality* in the Index.)

Connecting with yourself: Embrace all of your experiences – the negative, painful ones, as well as the positive, pleasurable ones. In the beginning, you will most likely be processing a backlog of suppressed emotions that could go back years, causing you to focus on negative experiences. This is much like unplugging a drainpipe. You must clear the blockage and push out the sludge before you will have clean, pleasant, and healthy water. With recovery, your blockages will become smaller and less frequent; clean,

Recovering Intelligence

A healthy relationship with yourself is required for a healthy life.

clear energy will flow more effortlessly through you.

Opening up to your feelings results in a healthier mental-emotional state. Through the process of opening up, you will grow and the fullness of your life will expand, offering you in-depth knowledge about yourself. It will also allow you to interact with yourself and your environment more effectively and with greater personal rewards.

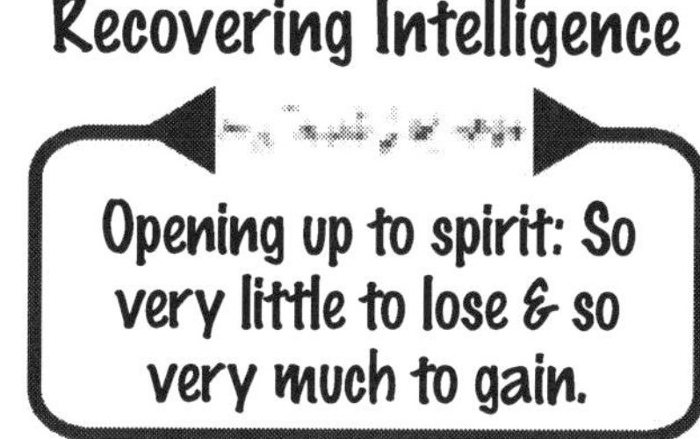

As you move through your recovery, you will deepen your connection with yourself. You will become more aware of your personal value. Understand that by unearthing your authentic self, you are improving the use of your natural ability, creativity, and strengths. You don't have to become a sports hero, scientist, or explorer to discover a new frontier. Setting up a recovery structure, clarifying your personal needs, writing your goals, developing your recovery plan, and carrying it out is an equally exciting and creative discovery process.

Connecting with others: To have an emotional or intimate connection with someone, you both must be willing to open up to your needs and your feelings toward each other. This may be difficult, threatening, and scary. Yet, if you don't, you will never develop an emotionally connected and caring relationship. Furthermore, insensitivity to others is a negative aspect of an active addiction and does not fit with any version of recovery.

Increase your sensitivity to life's subtle pleasures: Savor

the joy of a small moment so that you fully connect with and enjoy all the experiences life has to offer. Such activities include a child's laugh, time with a friend, or the scent of a rose. Over time, your ability to enjoy simple pleasures will increase and offer you a fuller and deeper connection to life.

Embracing spirituality: You made your addiction your Higher Power, tuning into it in celebration, boredom, happiness, etc. Opening up to a different Higher Power should be a low risk, high reward option. Many who choose to open up are amazed at the knowledge, peace, and overall value that they gain.

At some point, you may want to follow a specific spiritual path. Many people will tell you that their brand of spirituality, usually an organized religion, is the right way or the only way to true spirituality. The important thing is that you make your own decisions and that you feel a strong connection with The Source. Start slow and be sure you fully understand what is being presented to you.

On your spiritual journey, you need to let go of your fear and doubt, and open up to your desire to explore and connect with the universe. Minimal or detached participation, such as consciously willing yourself to be spiritual or only attending a one-hour weekly church service, won't work. Let go and focus on the idea that the universe will listen and respond. As you open up to your spiritual nature, strive for a partnership with your Higher Power.

Seeing Reality

It takes time to develop the desire and the ability to

see and embrace our truths. Welcome the idea of looking

at and accepting reality, without being defensive. Start with small observations and continue until you comprehend the deepest truths about yourself and your life. Be careful not to focus on too much too quickly. Small steps make perceiving reality easier, but be consistent.

Denial is an unwillingness to accept truth, even in the face of objective reality. It is a defense, one that could continue the rest of your life unless you pull your head out of the sand.

Recognize your self-deceiving mental styles, illusions, and other defenses you've been using to block reality, and change them. Start by admitting that seeing reality accurately is vital to recovery and that it's something you may need to improve on by paying attention to your thoughts, feelings, and behaviors. Commit to always look for the truth in a situation, including the part you play.

Serenity

Serenity is a clear, calm, and comfortable state of mind that's part of a quality recovering life. Serenity and happiness come as you surrender to your new life, achieve milestones, and live a healthy recovering lifestyle. You will increase your serenity by using tools such as meditation. (Find *Serenity Prayer* in the Index.)

Create **Your Recovering Future™** with structure, especially your personal recovery plan and vision. Set yourself up for success by living within this structure and working your program to the best of your ability. Visualize your new identity as a happy, healthy,

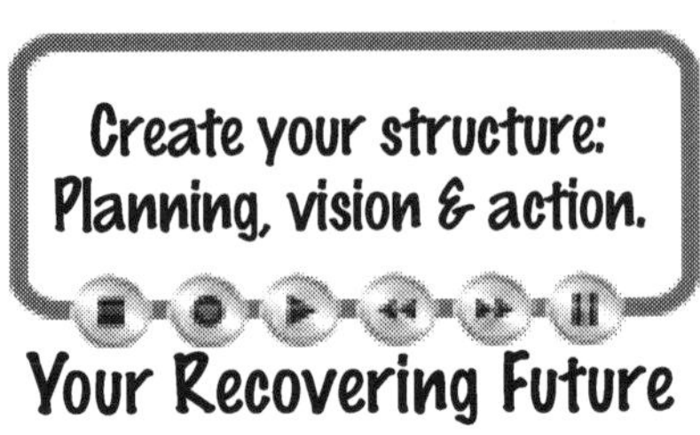

and successful person pursuing a quality recovering lifestyle and replacing your old addict self-image with the new, much more desirable you. The vision will take time to become a reality, yet without the vision, the reality is less likely to become real. See (APPENDIX 8.)

SELF-RECOVERY

Even with many outside resources, you must have the inner resources to pick up the phone, go to a meeting, or turn to your partner and ask for help. A quality recovery program must have at its core a personal approach, a "self" recovery program. A self-recovery approach takes you through an internal process of personal growth and change. You must take full responsibility for your past, present, and future, your recovery, and for changing yourself from the inside out. This gives you the ability to face yourself and tap into the inner resources you will need to deal with your addiction and create **Your Recovering Future™**.

Self-Trust

Overtime, you'll learn to develop self-trust, but until you do, you must choose to trust your support group. If you are uncomfortable relying on others, make the agreement you share very clear and specific. If things don't work out, you can then look over your agreement to clarify and work on any issues. The trust you build with others will demonstrate that people are reliable.

Learn to begin trusting yourself by completing small tasks; you'll build from there. Fully experience your successes. Once you are comfortable trusting yourself, trusting others will come ever easier. (Find *Trust* in the Index.)

Self-Awareness

Self-awareness is your most important self-resource. If you don't have awareness, you don't have much. Knowing what you believe and what you want are part of self-awareness. This knowledge allows you to take control over the direction your life is headed.

Start by observing yourself. Increase your awareness of what you're saying, thinking, seeing, and doing. Listen to your self-talk, notice your thought patterns, and observe your programmed behaviors.

Recovering Intelligence

Awareness increases your chances to control your life & your future.

This naturally leads to self-reflection, which can lead to a desire to change, and so you likely will. (Find *Observing Self* in the Index.) Pay attention to:

- The Red Light reminders
- What am I saying, thinking, seeing, and doing?
- What am I feeling about myself and my recovery?
- The ways that my behaviors support what I want?
- Am I living in my values and moving towards my goals?
- What do I need to pay more attention to?

Self-Discipline

Discipline is the practice of controlled and orderly behavior. It will facilitate you in completing goals and other commitments, no matter what. That is called self-efficacy, but commonly known as "walking your talk."

Discipline has a negative feel for many, as it may be hard at first, but with good self-discipline, you will be able to build your recovery foundation and life will eventually get easier. After deciding what successful recovery is for you, train yourself regularly by engaging in activities that are positive and proactive. Start small and gradually build up to where you want to be. For example:

- Read about addiction recovery
- Attend self-help group meetings
- Participate in a recovery program
- Work with a coach who will push and support you
- Commit to personal and lifestyle changes

Breathe, relax, and focus on your desire for the discipline that you'll need to achieve your recovery and life goals. Practice behaviors that move you towards your goals.

Self-Knowledge

You likely lost yourself during your addiction, and now you have an opportunity to learn or relearn who you are. If you practice self-honesty, you can get to know yourself pretty well. You will learn what you like and don't like, what you want and don't want, and what you value and don't value in any given situation. This is self-knowledge.

Don't buy into the illusion that you're going to totally find yourself; just commit to gradually learning more about yourself. Self-focusing activities like journaling, meditating, and praying will offer you a lot of insight.

Self-Evaluation

After awareness, your most valuable self-resource is honest self-evaluation, the process of continually examining your inner self to ensure you're on track with your recovery goals. Acknowledge your true attitudes, feelings, thoughts, and behaviors. This is who you are despite ego or outside factors. Are you functioning the way you want?

The intention of self-evaluation is positive change. Explore how you want to be different. Keep in mind your personal and spiritual beliefs, values, and goals. Make this a part of your recovery plan. Opinions from valued others will help in your evaluation. Seek them out and listen to them. Review your recovery goals daily, weekly, monthly, and yearly.

Self-Acceptance

Self-acceptance is your ability to accept yourself for who

you are, as a whole person with all of your strengths and weaknesses. It will allow you to lower your defenses and admit and accept the reality of your life, which will fortify your foundation so you can build your recovery. What have you been unable to accept about yourself, and what would it take to be willing to start dealing with it?

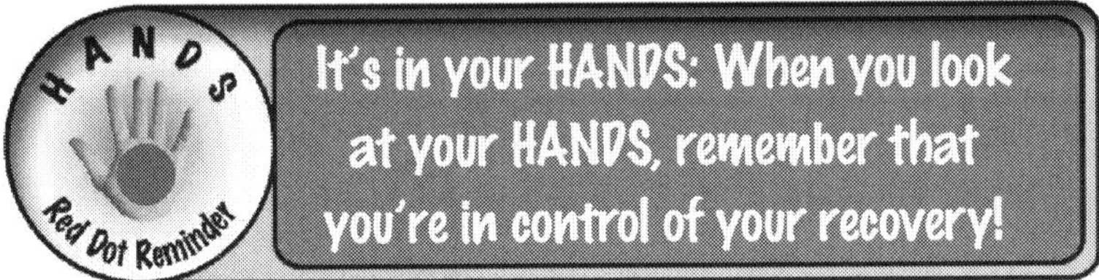

Self-Development

Start your self-development by doing the *VIA Strengths Assessment* and then a detailed review of your using history ("fearless personal inventory"). You will thrive by evolving both your personal strengths and your character defects. For support and feedback, you will want an experienced guide to help you through self-development.

Self-Esteem

Your self-esteem is how you regard yourself. Many people suffer from low self-esteem, and addiction impairs it even further. Life's experiences may have negatively programmed

your self-esteem. Believing that *you* are your negative past behaviors or current circumstances will pull down your self-esteem lower than is justified.

One personal reward of recovery is a higher self-esteem. As you follow through and build on your achievements, you'll learn to trust yourself, and your self-esteem should improve. If it doesn't, you may want to take a look at why. Don't hold your self-esteem hostage. Allow it to grow as you succeed and build your life. You'll know your self-esteem has improved when you feel okay about responding to a compliment with "thank you" or a question with "I don't know, but I'll find out."

Recovering Intelligence

Improve your self-esteem by self-acceptance & by working a good program.

Having solid self-esteem is very desirable. However, you can achieve recovery without it. Stay engaged in your program, and you'll build the quality life that recovery offers. Let yourself feel good about that.

Self-Forgiveness

Everyone makes mistakes. Your ability to forgive yourself for your mistakes requires patience and kindness. Self-forgiveness isn't a one-time task; it's a process you may need to do regularly over time. You'll need to examine the wrongs you did and humbly accept that you did the best you could at the time. Let go of your guilt and remorse, and move on.

Recovering Intelligence

Forgive yourself & focus on growing past it.

Self-Healing

Healing is an emotional experience. Self-healing is a choice. To heal, you must relive and let go of the feelings you are stuck on, especially the painful ones. Healing can sooth and perhaps eliminate the pain caused by your past.

Apologizing and accepting apologies, forgiving yourself and others, saying goodbye to enabling people or negative love objects, grieving your losses, nurturing yourself and accepting the nurturing of valued others, and letting yourself laugh and feel happy are all things that can be healing. If the issue doesn't heal on its own, get the support you need and deserve. This may include professional help.

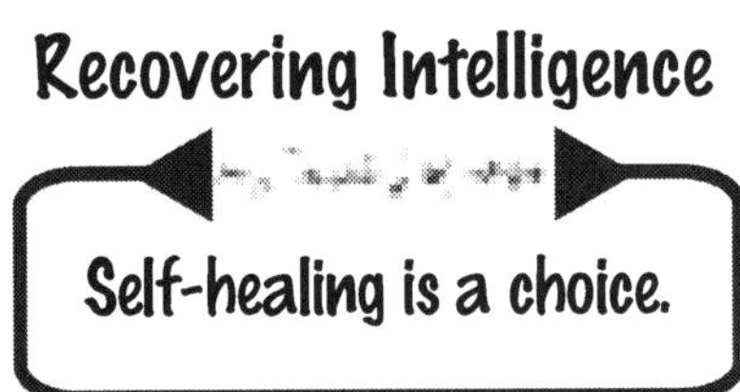

Healing Your Past: Accept your history, face the issues it created, and rebuild your life. You need to forgive yourself and respectfully apologize to and make amends with those who you have hurt. Similarly, forgive those who have hurt you. If sharing certain experiences of others, ask for their permission, and reveal only what will help them heal without re-injuring them.

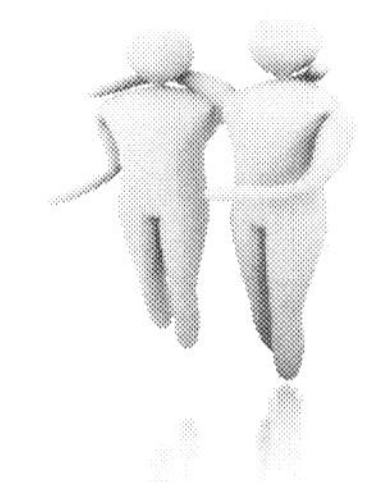

Start by viewing your past from a positive point of view, or if this is too difficult, from a neutral one. Believe that you are not your flaws, weaknesses, or traumas. Your past behavior may cause you healthy guilt or remorse, but it shouldn't incite toxic shame. After looking at, and processing your past, complete your healing by living a desirable life in the present.

Self-Honesty

Self-honesty is mandatory to develop self-trust and self-confidence, quality relationships and family life, and a solid foundation for recovery. Are you totally honest with yourself? (Find *Self-Evaluation* in the Index.)

Self-Image

Your self-image is the person you see yourself to be in your mind's eye. It's usually part of your ego, not the deeper, spiritual you. Therefore, it is a more superficial self-concept, one that can waiver depending on your circumstances. It's important to try to maintain a healthy self-image where you see your full value and potential. This may be a stretch and uncomfortable at first, but well worth the effort.

You must let go of your addict self & picture your recovering self.

Your Recovering Future

Quality recovery will cause your self-image to change. Expect your inner addict self to resist this change. Your addict self will attempt to maintain addict beliefs and behaviors and pull you back into your addiction. Practice over and over seeing yourself in **Your Recovering Future™** and your self-image will shift for the better.

Do you have a negative, addict self-image or a positive, healthy self-image?

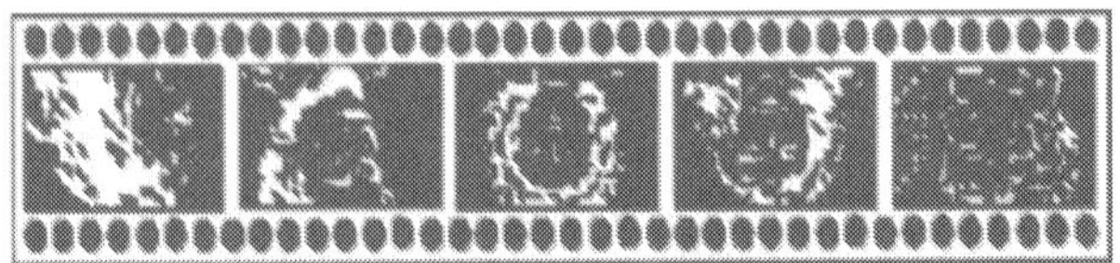

The best way to change your self-image is to change your inner vision of who you are and want to be. Expand and grow your new self-image.

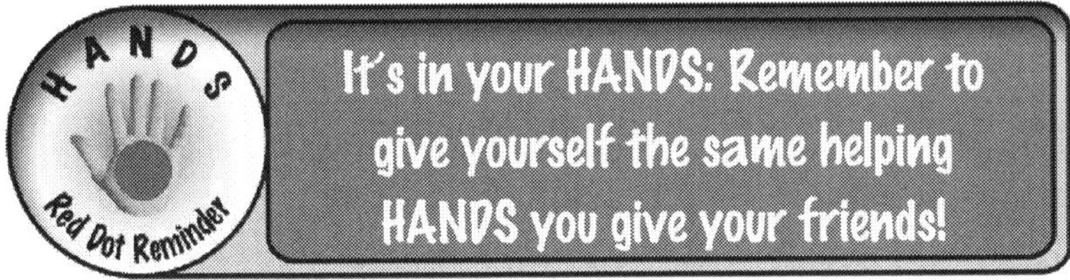

Self-Love

Self-love is very important. In self-love, you explore self-valuing, and you find and live a life that reflects who you are and what you want to be. Start to show your self-love now by committing to **Your Recovering Future™**. Self-love fills up emptiness, moves you through your fears, and eliminates your loneliness. You'll learn to care about yourself first-and-foremost and start living the type of life you have been wishing for.

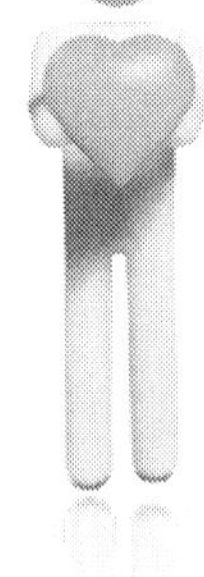

Self-Nurturing

Early recovery is a particularly difficult experience; it's

a good time to practice self-nurturing. Part of self-nurturing is doing healthy things for yourself as a reward (self-validation) and for the pure delight of it. Some simple ways to self-nurture are deep breathing and letting yourself feel a genuine sense of joy. Meditation, prayer, and mindfulness activities are other ways to self-nurture.

As time goes on, you'll find yourself healing from the wounds of your addiction. It'll be important to continue to nurture yourself. You deserve it, and it's a healthier pattern than only nurturing yourself when you're hurting. It's also very important to nurture your inner child – the little voice from your childhood that's buried deep inside of you and may feel battered and bruised by life. Today, he or she deserves to be nurtured. Take him or her out for some healthy playtime.

Remember to Breathe Deeply & Slowly!

SUMMARY

Your commitment to overcome your addiction increases in quality and longevity if you apply structure into your recovery approach from the start. You may have bad days and tough periods, and barriers may present themselves, but the structure of your approach is set up so you stay on your path of recovery.

By following a structure in early recovery, life will continue to improve. When positive thoughts about using come into your mind (and they will!), you deal with them more easily and more quickly than ever before. You take immediate action and get back on your recovery path. You focus on the solution rather than the problem, and you, with the help of your resources, usually find answers quickly.

Your knowledge about yourself, recovery, and life continues to develop. You have a sense of balance and stability that feels good, yet may be unfamiliar. You're finding a new, lighter, and happier style that works for you. Your healthier lifestyle brings you more energy. You commit yourself to doing what it takes!

You receive positive feedback from the world around you that verifies you are improving. People and opportunities from your past come back into your life, and new ones present themselves. This is because they now like who you are becoming. You're starting to experience more and better things coming into your life.

Your addict self recognizes you're trying to starve it, so it will attempt to regain control. Stay aware by using your inner and outer resources to keep your healthy self in control. Acknowledge that recovery feels better and is a much more rewarding lifestyle than an addicted lifestyle.

Change is constant, yet you might resist it, especially if you hold onto your old patterns. So accept and embrace change, and let go of old ideas and images that don't fit with your new ones. Build change into your recovery.

Tap your inner resources, like curiosity. Accept the many outer resources available to you. Move past your fears and embrace what you can already see as the beginnings of **Your**

Recovering Future™.

In early recovery:

- Accept and embrace change
- Breathe slowly and deeply and use your reminders
- Consistency and hope become easier
- Develop self-caring practices
- Encourage your positive emotions
- Family life increases and smooths out
- Goal setting and evaluation become comfortable
- New, healthier patterns develop
- Nutritional supplements may no longer be needed
- Nutritional needs are met with a high-quality diet
- Open up personally and emotionally with valued others
- People open up and trust you
- Practice engaging in purposeful activities
- Self-care, self-esteem, and self-image improve
- Start to give back to others regularly
- Urgency and crises give way to stability and growth
- You walk your talk and keep your commitments
- Your recovery foundation keeps growing
- Your tool box is filled with personalized strategies

Chapter 4

Continuing Recovery: Strategies & Tools

Chapter 4: Continuing Recovery – Strategies & Tools Table of Contents

TOOLS & STRATEGIES

In early recovery, it's critical to have strategies for how to abstain from an addiction, and tools that will assist you in doing so. A strategy is a plan or goal. A tool is a device for carrying out the strategy. Together, tools and strategies are the means to work through a recovery plan.

For example, as part of your recovery plan, you may set a goal to stay sober for 24 hours. This is a strategy. As part of the strategy, clarify the tools you'll need to achieve the goal, such as talking with your mentor, going to a meeting, fishing, reading, exercising, personal quiet time, church, etc.

You will keep using tools and strategies into continuing recovery, the next stage of addiction treatment. Continuing recovery starts when:

- You have a solid recovery foundation and you're living a consistent recovery program.
- You've made the needed mental-emotional shifts into recovery, with openness and hope, or even faith.
- You have embraced and are living a healthy and growth-oriented lifestyle.

Throughout recovery, you must consistently grow, or you'll stagnate and slide back towards addiction. Your strategies and tools can help. Use them to go over, under, around, or through the blocks you'll bump into as you grow. Be aware of the most effective strategies and tools. As your life changes, so will your

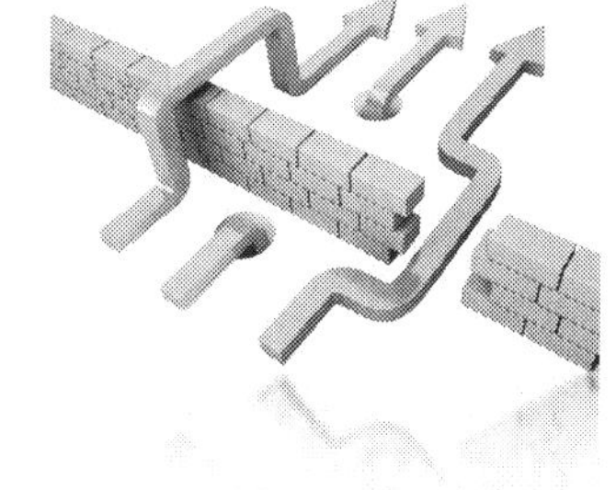

recovery approach. If you want quality recovery, you'll need to evolve your strategies and adapt them to different situations.

As you are developing strategies for recovery, ask detailed and accurate questions about what you want to solve, create, or achieve. The most important questions are those that provide you with a different mental perspective on an issue and give you new options to consider. Examples are: "If I knew the best answer, what would it be?" or "If I were able to build quality recovery, what would it be like and how would I do it?" Find someone who appears to have quality recovery and talk to them. What do they think quality recovery is? What does it feel like to them? What's their mental image of their recovery?

Recovering Intelligence

Mental strategies will change your outcomes & rewire your brain.

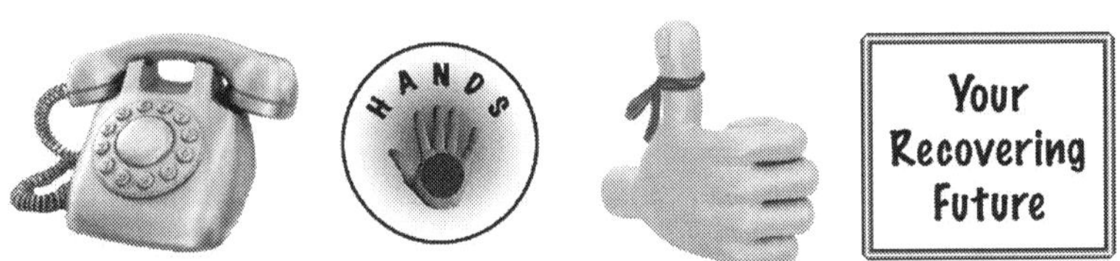

Tools: There are countless tools to aid you in your recovery. Some tools are physical, like a telephone and written reminders. Others are mental, like affirmations and imagery. And some are relational, like family, support groups, and your Higher Power. The most effective tools will change your feelings, thoughts, attitudes, and beliefs for the better. Like a mechanic who works with many different gizmos, you'll want a tool box full of useful tools for creating **Your Recovering Future™**. The more you use them, the more familiar they will feel and the stronger your recovery muscle will grow. Practice using your tools often, before you need them!

Approach

Both abstinence and maintenance approaches require commitment. Remain aware of yourself and your thoughts and feelings about using or not using. Use your structure to set yourself up for success by making it easier to succeed than to fail. Your approach needs to include:

Recovering Intelligence

With your best approach, success will be easier than failure.

- Healthy people for support and guidance
- New ways of having fun through engaging and purposeful activities

By the continuing recovery stage, your recovery needs to have grown in its strength, stability, and depth. There may be more demands on your time and attention, especially from your family. Your recovery should have a balanced team approach with many vital teammates: family, support groups, professionals, faith community members, co-workers, etc. All the players on your team need to be helpful and healing people; thank them and at times reward them.

As you move through your recovery, your needs and issues will change; therefore, your approach will need to be adjusted. Issues such as use of free time, physical health, and family need to be re-evaluated. Update your recovery plan at least every three months. Keep a consistent program, yet remain flexible so you can adapt when situations change (and they will!).

Accurate Questions: Ask questions that will lead you toward the results you want. Inquisitiveness helps you learn and grow, but being overly cynical when you ask questions won't. Your inner critic only judges; it doesn't have an open mind. Ask questions with positive intent and curosity, and you're likely to find answers that move you toward **Your Recovering Future™**. Such a question could be, "What isn't working well enough, and how I can improve it?"

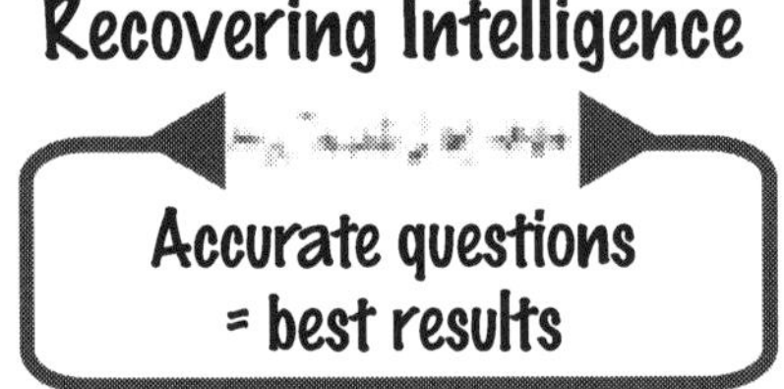

From Self-Defeating Critic To Helpful Learner

"Why am I such a loser?" **To** "What change will help me?"

"Why do I always relapse?" **To** "What can I learn?"

"Why are they such jerks?" **To** "Why do I let myself react?"

Art Work

If you are willing to let your artistic energy flow, art therapy can help you express and process your issues and feelings. Join an art class and let yourself go. Don't analyze your project until it's finished. There are many artistic formats, such as building, dancing, drawing, music, painting, photography, pottery, singing, sculpting, and writing. Experiment with those that interest you. When you find a good match, you will find artistic expression to be incredibly therapeutic.

Change Strategies

There are preset strategies available that focus on what you want to change. One is A.C.T.S.

- Awareness & Openness: What do you like and don't like about the situation? What do you want or don't want?
- Connection: Pay attention to your thoughts, goals, and emotions, especially your desires. Be aware of any pitfalls and challenges to your recovery. Ask trusted others for feedback and support.
- Timing: Connect to your readiness to act now.
- Structure: Use a solid approach with effective strategies and tools to set yourself up for success.

Choice

Life is a long series of big and small choices. You choose to act on feelings and instincts, or to make thought-out decisions. You choose to move towards or away from what you desire. You choose to behave functionally or dysfunctionally. One day, you'll wake up and ask yourself, "Where did the time go?" or "How did I get here?" You'll think back and realize that you made critical choices during meaningful moments that sent your life towards or away from what you really wanted.

You want your "wake-up" experience to be a positive

one; you want to be pleased as you look back on those decisions that you now know will lead you into **Your Recovering Future™**. You'll be happier with your life review if you set yourself up for success by living the Three Cs. You need to be:

- Conscious of your beliefs, thoughts, feelings, behaviors, and situations.
- Connected to what you really need and want, especially when you're making important decisions.
- Clear about your short-term and long-term goals.
  - » Decide how you're going to achieve your goals, and then let them take their natural course.
  - » Review them regularly.
  - » Train yourself daily.

(Find *Goal Achievement* or *Self-Awareness* in the Index.)

Connecting Inside

Recovering Intelligence

Connect inside: Breathe, self check-in, mindfulness, & meditation.

Most people don't know what they're feeling. Exploring their emotions can feel scary or out of control, so they don't. To develop your emotional awareness, start with slow, deep breathing techniques, and pay attention to your thoughts and feelings.

Feelings are both:

- Negative: Loss, sadness, failure, and bodily pain
- Positive: Fun, happiness, and success

Connect to your feelings by:

Crying: Crying is the natural, desirable, and healthy response to an intense emotional experience. It's an indicator that you are connected to your emotions. Allow yourself to cry in private or, better yet, with trusted others.

Deep Breathing: Slow, deep breathing has many health benefits. Besides relaxing and energizing you, it puts more oxygen in your blood, which is valuable for your brain. Breathing during an emotional situation can make the difference in how well you deal with the situation.

Most people don't understand how to breathe correctly or the value of a proper technique. Practice breathing for its calming effect, for developing mindfulness, and as training for deep meditation. To the degree you are physically capable of doing so, breathe deeply and slowly by inhaling and exhaling for 6 seconds or longer for up to 20 minutes, once or twice a day, ideally at the same time of day. You can start at 3 minutes and build up. Practice deep breathing before and during stressful situations.

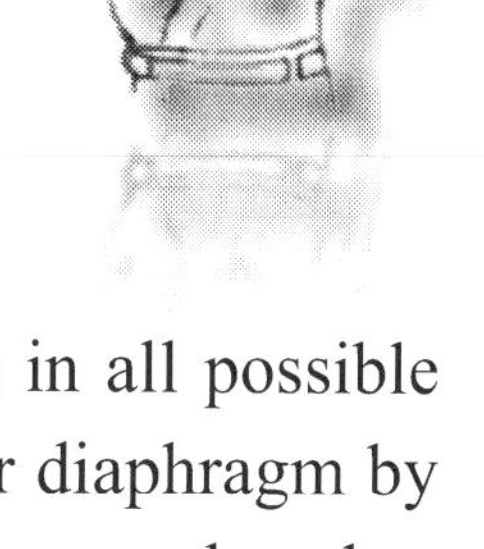

Correct breathing, commonly called belly breathing, utilizes your diaphragm muscles. When you breathe in, expand your diaphragm, pushing your belly out. This pulls out the bottom of your lungs, which inflates them fully and allows them to take in all possible oxygen. When you breathe out, tighten your diaphragm by pulling in your belly, which pulls in your lungs and pushes out all of the carbon dioxide.

Internal Check-In: The goal of an internal check-in

process is to raise your awareness of what's going on inside you mentally, emotionally, and physically. The check-in can be brief. Take a deep breath and ask yourself:

- How am I doing?
- What am I feeling?
- What am I thinking?
- What am I saying to myself?
- What's my attitude?
- How am I behaving?
- How am I breathing and holding my body?

Meditation: Meditation is a term for a group of mental practices where people teach themselves to rest their mind and sink into a natural state of relaxation. Usually, meditation is guided by a visual or audio focal point. By softly focusing inwardly, you can passively explore or actively process information. Meditation offers many benefits including reduced stress, clearer thinking, more energy, less sleep required, and increased recall of unconscious information.

Recovering Intelligence

Meditation is a valuable & pleasant experience.

There are many versions of mainstream meditation techniques, such as biofeedback, mind clearing, self-hypnosis, Silva Mind Control, and Transcendental Meditation. There are also many versions of spiritual or religious oriented meditation, which are quite useful.

Neutral: Being neutral is being present, calm, centered, and connected to a place inside of yourself (heart or center of head) to a point where you feel okay in the moment. It is the ideal state of mind for letting go of conflicts, pressures, and toxins, and for physical healing and mental clarity.

Personal Resources: Throughout life, you naturally utilize your personal resources. These could be your ability to hustle, develop friendships, or to relax. Explore how you can use more of your personal resources in healthy ways.

Progressive Relaxation: This is the experience of relaxing your large muscle groups, one at a time, as you draw in slow, deep breaths. Tense each large muscle group throughout your body as you breathe in for about 3 to 6 seconds, until you feel your muscles are stretched. Then starting with your feet, progressively relax each muscle group as you breathe out. Repeat this process twice. Be sure to breathe deeply from your diaphragm. (Find *Deep Breathing* in the Index.)

The ability to consciously relax all your muscles at once is called the relaxation response. It offers you the opportunity to choose to relax at any time.

Connecting With Others

Friendship is very important for your recovery, but only about 75% of Americans have connected friendships with supportive people.

Some of the people in your recovery fellowship will only be acquaintances, of which a handful will grow to become friends. There are four types of relationships in recovery fellowships:

Recovering Intelligence

Develop & nurture close, intimate friendships.

- Acquaintanceship: Superficial social interactions
- Casual friendship: Shared social experiences
- Close friendship: Shared personal experiences
- Intimate friendship: Bonded emotional connection

The emotional intimacy that comes from sharing may bring up feelings of fear from core childhood and family of origin issues. It can be beneficial to process your feelings beforehand with a recovery friend, a psychotherapist, or with your mentor.

(Find *Friendship* in the Index.)

As you begin your recovery, it's a good time to develop new, healthy friendships or reconnect with old, healthy relationships, which often need nurturing or repair.

Consider: **"In My Experience... you don't want a poor connection to your inner and outer resources."** (See APPENDIX 8.)

Professional Ally: A professional ally is an experienced confidant, someone you trust and respect, who's knowledgeable and skilled at helping you deal with life's ups and downs, and who is solid support. In addition, they are someone who's not emotionally involved with your challenges. Personal coaches, counselors, and psychotherapists have different training and skill levels, but they all offer you an opportunity to discuss concerns, talk through difficult issues, and explore solutions. What issues do you need to explore?

Healthy Boundaries: Develop and keep healthy physical and emotional boundaries with others by paying attention to your words and actions, and being clear and assertive. Learn how to say NO without guilt. (Find *Boundaries* in the Index.)

Decision Making

Making decisions may feel uncomfortable if you don't trust yourself. Learn to make small decisions and build up to making big decisions. When new to recovery, make decisions based on the objective, or factual, feedback you receive from your recovery support group. Your addict brain will tell you that you are an independent adult and should be able to make decisions without checking in with anyone. DON'T BELIEVE YOUR ADDICT BRAIN!

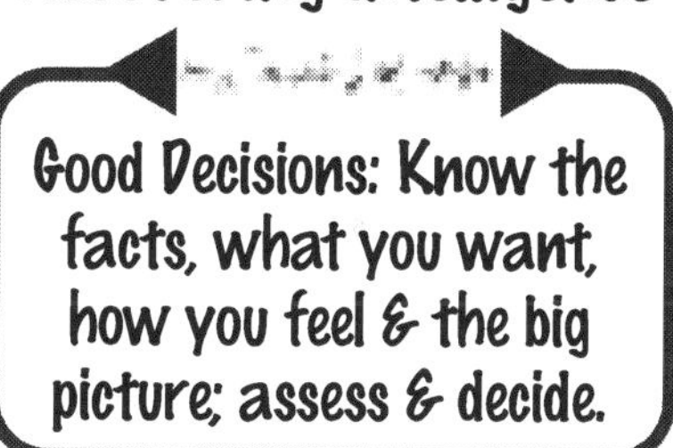

When learning to make decisions in sobriety, the process below may help you:

1. Clarify and define the issue or problem.
2. What are your options? List them.
3. Have you solved this issue in the past? How?
4. Weigh your options –
    - Which options seem the most practical and desirable?
    - Feelings: What do your feelings tell you? It's always important to consider your feelings when making a decision, yet it's equally well advised to overrule them in favor of rationality. Get feedback from someone in recovery that you

trust.

- Intuition: What do you sense you should do?
  - » Check your values. How does the solution fit with your value system?
  - » Which option will satisfy your overall needs and not cause problems or regrets?
  - » Consider other potential negative and positive consequences:
    - ◊ What will be the immediate results?
    - ◊ Future View: Will the option you select be beneficial in the long run?
- Prioritize: Best options first.
- Perspectives: What do valued others think?

5. Make your decision and own it.
   - List the steps, tasks, and actions it will take to implement your decision.
   - Take action. (Find *Goal Achievement* in the Index.)
6. Short-term evaluation:
   - How is your decision working? Scale from 1 to 10. If it's working well, continue. If not, adjust or change it.
   - Are your results good enough?
   - Review your decisions every 1 to 4 months.
7. Long-term or completion evaluation:
   - Same process as short-term review.
8. Acknowledge your success, even partial success.

Assessing Scale: Accurately assessing your results is essential. At times, you'll need to evaluate if a solution to an issue is working, even though there is no visible evidence or concrete facts to prove one way or another. Your assessment will be subjective; you must determine what is happening in a situation based on how it feels or what appears to be going on.

Either of these scales will be helpful in your assessments:

Least 0 – 1 – 2 – 3 – 4 – 5 – 6 – 7 – 8 – 9 – 10 Most

Least -10– -8– -6– -4– -2– 0– +2– +4– +6– +8– +10 Most

Financial Organization

Putting your finances in order should be part of your recovery structure as it is a positive step forward. Furthermore, it's important for your mental wellbeing that you have a healthy relationship with money. Clarify your current financial situation and rethink future plans. Set up and follow a realistic budget. Get your spending under control and pay off your bills (credit cards) ASAP! Define your financial goals, whether it's paying the rent or investing. Consider seeking help from a consumer group or a consultant to guide you to financial health. More than anything else, you must spend less than you make!

If your addiction is about money, like spending and gambling, take action. Cut up your credit cards and sell whatever you can. And get the additional support you need.

Goal Achievement

Setting and achieving goals provides those little stepping stones that, as a whole, create a strong recovery approach. You can achieve large goals, such as long-term recovery, one small goal at a time. Your goals should be significant enough to push you forward, but not so demanding that they're unlikely to be met. Start by taking a step of any size, even a baby one, in the direction of your target.

Identify the final outcome you're aiming for after accomplishing certain tasks, goals, and milestones. Regularly evaluate your approach, adjust, and set new goals, if needed. Adjusting your approach later is better than taking no action at all.

Goals act as guiding marks. If you don't set specific goals, your unconscious mind will hit and miss, having to guess if it's helping you succeed in your recovery. When you set a clear goal, your unconscious has a target on which to focus. Examples are:

- Not Specific: I will improve my physical condition.
- Specific: I will walk for 20 minutes, a minimum distance of one mile, three times a week for the next three months. Then I will evaluate and reset my goal.

Your personal style of goal setting needs to match you.

Some people want their goals to be very specific and detailed, and others are more ambiguous. Pay attention to the results you get and adjust your style as desired. Consider:

SOBER goals need to be:

- Specific: Clarify the who, what, when, where, how, and why; therefore, it's measurable and you'll know what you have achieved or not achieved.
- Obtainable: With the correct structure or approach, and with the right plan and motivation, your goals should be obtainable.
- Believable: Your goals make sense, and you believe that you can achieve them.
- Realistic: Your goals are valuable enough to be worth pursuing, yet realistically achievable.

As your recovery progresses, optimize your recovery plan by determining a time line for your goals.

- Immediate Goals:
  - 1 Day to 1 Month: These goals should be very clear and include a one-hour daily recovery activity. Make any changes before you go to bed so you are ready for the next day.
- Short-Term Goals:
  - 1 to 12 Months: These goals need to be clear. Know they may change before they're complete and that's okay.
- Intermediate Goals:
  - 1 to 3 Years: On New Year's Day, review last year's goals and write next year's.
- Long-Term Goals:

» 3 to 5 Years: Long-range goals will multiply the likelihood of your long-term success.

Have ongoing goals. Plan the next one as the current one is near completion. That way, you have something to look forward to and work towards, which can help prevent depression or a relapse event. Achieve your goals by taking action NOW! Part of that action is to let go of control and allow your goals to take a natural path.

Humor

Humor is a powerful and desirable resource; it can even be a life saver. Humor can lighten up the emotional heaviness of issues like depression, fear, or grief. Develop and use a good sense of humor that allows you to laugh at yourself and at situations in which you find yourself in. It's unwise to laugh at other people or their circumstances. People often laugh at cutting, put-down, or sarcastic humor, but healthy people don't like it. Sarcastic is Latin for "to cut."

Recovering Intelligence

Humor is a fun, powerful & healthy tool, unless it's misused!

The structure of most humor is a punch line that's unexpected. This causes a release of natural tension. Develop healthy humor and use it often.

Information Gathering

Closely observing and processing your experiences in

recovery is required for accurate information gathering, used to make good decisions and to achieve your goals and milestones. This happens when you open up and pay attention to the feedback you are receiving from both outer and inner sources.

Recovering Intelligence

To receive information, you must be open to it & pay attention.

Inner or internal information can come from your unconscious mind, yet it usually doesn't offer you answers unless you ask for it. You may attain this internal information by using the easy technique of sentence completion. Repeat a specific question to yourself, over and over, until an answer comes to you that fits and is useful. (Find *Sentence Completion* in the Index.)

Outer or external information is gained by paying attention to the circumstances that surround you and asking others for more information.

Learning

A good way to learn is to ask someone who has achieved quality recovery what they are thinking. Watch their style, speech, and movements, and practice or mimic them. Make their recovery approach your own by developing a version that feels natural to you.

Learn from others: observe, picture & practice the behavior!

Your Recovering Future

Your mind has what are called Mirror Neurons. Their job is to help you learn new skills by imitation. If you mimic what you see people doing in recovery, and practice those behaviors over and over, they eventually become familiar. Keep practicing and the new, clean, and sober behaviors will become automatic.

Lifestyle

You will want to rearrange, upgrade, or change your past using lifestyle to a present-time recovering lifestyle. There are many lifestyle changes to consider. These may involve:

- Activities: fun, purposeful, spiritual, value driven
- Free time: activities, fun, happiness, humor, emotional and mental health, personal development, physical health, relaxation, social needs
- Goals: personal, family, spiritual, work
- Home: environment, involvement, trigger-free
- Relationships: family, friends, primary partner, and acquaintances; communication, quality of time, and interaction; toxic-free
- Self-care: emotional and physical; hygiene, presentation, nutrition
- Work: environment, performance

Be honest about your lifestyle choices; nothing should be untouchable or beyond evaluation.

"Living in the Grays"

Many people see reality in black and white, which allows them to label and compartmentalize life. It's a clear, simple, and easy approach. Unfortunately, reality is mostly a range of grays. You may choose to interpret a situation as good

Recovering Intelligence

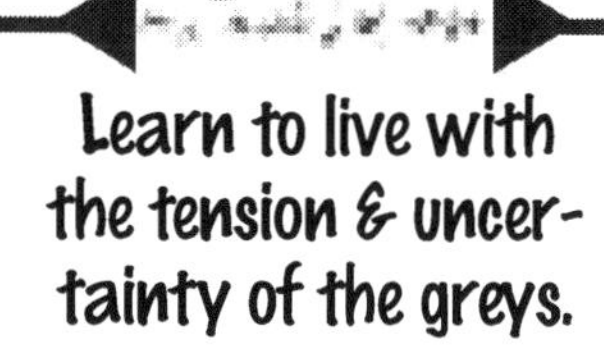

or bad, but if you examine life more closely, you will learn that reality is a pattern of grays, much like an old TV screen where the picture was formed by a series of black and white dots. If you looked too closely, the dots were all you'd see. If you pulled back, you'd be able to see that the dots formed a picture. Your ability to pull back and to try to understand the whole picture will assist you in tolerating the gray areas of life. Life is not black and white.

You are multidimensional. It's important to expand your view of the world to include the gray areas of uncertainty, like not being able to forecast the future, and admitting that you might not have all the facts of any given situation.

Mental Imagery

The mind can store information in mental images, which determine how you experience and move forward in your recovery. Your mind's eye visualizes what you think and feel, who you are, what you have, what you have done in the past, and how you view your recovery.

Mental imagery is a powerful self-help tool.

Your Recovering Future

There is clear evidence that whatever your mind's eye can see, hear, and feel, your unconscious mind will accept as a real experience.

You want to create a picture of your successful future. What does your picture of **Your Recovery Future™** look like, feel like, sound like, smell like, and taste like? How often do you picture yourself living in your desirable future? (See APPENDIX 4.)

Note: After mentally examining any negative images from your past, disconnect from them. Breathe and know that those past experiences are not a part of your life today!

Mental-Emotional Shifts

Many of your perspectives, beliefs, and attitudes will need shifting throughout recovery. Shifting is the mental and emotional process of letting go of old points of view and embracing new ones. This will cause new, positive behaviors in **Your Recovering Future™**. In real time, verbally affirm, visualize, and practice daily these mental-emotional shifts. Such a shift is: "That's just who I've always been," to "This is the person I choose to be now."

You'll make a shift because you choose to open up to your desire for recovery. As you do, you'll begin to accept and embrace a new way of life.

Recovering Intelligence

The symbol for crisis & opportunity are the same in the Chinese language.

Examples of shift changes:

- <u>Crisis changes into Opportunity</u>: In the Chinese language, the symbol for crisis is also the symbol for opportunity. You will likely enter recovery in crisis. Recovery offers you an opportunity to learn to live free of chaos and the stress of getting your next fix. It also grants you the chance to develop the ability to deal with life in a responsible and effective way.

- Darkness changes into Light: Darkness symbolizes the negative – a lack of awareness, illness, or evil. Light symbolizes the positive – awareness, health, and spirituality. Darkness cannot exist in the light.
- Defensiveness changes into Openness: Choose to relax rigid thinking and be more accepting. Open up to your support group, especially your closest friends, family, and a carefully chosen therapist, coach, mentor, and/or sponsor.
- Hope changes into Faith: Hope is a belief that good outcomes in life are possible. Faith is complete trust that what is desired will happen. In recovery, choose to have faith that you will be a living testimony for the "Promises of the Program."
- "Life is Unfair" changes into "I Empower My Life": Cast aside the concept that life is unfair and accept life for what it is. Realize that life is what you choose to make it. You are in control of how you respond to life experiences.
- Negative changes into Positive: Change your negative view of a situation into a positive one. Learn from every circumstance by seeing the value of what is happening.

- Not Understanding changes into Embracing Spirit: Choose to let go of not knowing and open up mentally and emotionally to the possibility of a powerful intelligence that can help you. Truly consider engaging with and embracing this spiritual source by opening your heart up wide. Ask for help.
- Stressed Out changes into Relaxed: Monitoring your stress levels provides the opportunity to control your reaction to tense situations. Accept your stress symptoms as feedback that you need to regularly practice how to relax instead of allowing stress to take over as a response mechanism.

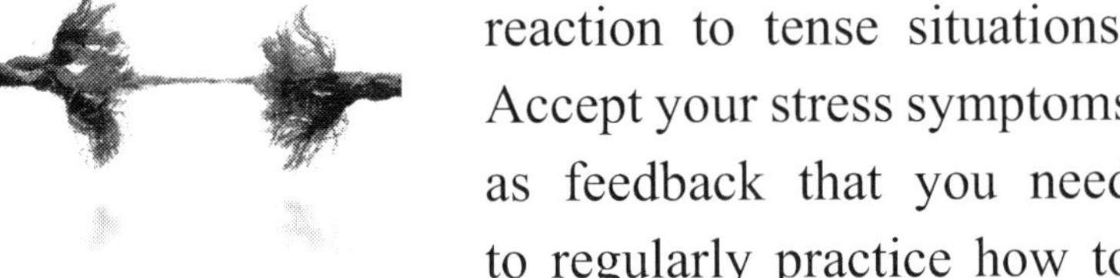

- "Try" changes into "Until I'm Successful": With commitment, "I'll try to make an effort," changes into, "I'll make my best effort," then into, "I will complete the... task." Eventually, this final statement evolves into, "Until I'm successful," meaning you won't stop until you achieve your recovery goals. The "until" promise becomes the only option.
- Worthless changes into Value and Power: "I am worthless," changes into, "I have value," then into "I'm worthy," and finally into, "I am valuable and powerful." You have the ability, strength, and value that you need to live fully.

Modeling

In early recovery, it is essential that you lean on the

wisdom of those who have gone before you. Check out who might be a good role model – maybe your minister for spiritual guidance or your therapist for personal growth? Did a speaker at a meeting touch your soul? Who has spoken wisely about recovery?

When you look for role models for your recovery, you need to seek out those who are living their lives as you would like to live yours. Select your role models carefully, for they are the ones who have endured recovery challenges successfully. They will be your guides through many situations that present themselves to you, through both early and continuing recovery. Ask them what path they took to set their lives straight.

Options Card

A 3 x 5 options card is a vital go-to resource that will physically remind you what to do when you are triggered, craving, depressed, upset, or hurting. It will remind you of who to call and what to focus on. It has two parts:

- Support group's phone numbers.
- Powerful reminders: Ones that will always put you back on track.

Carry it with you always; keep it in your wallet or purse. Review it regularly, daily at first, so you remember to use it when you need it. (Find *Options Card* in the Index.)

Perception

Your perception is how you see or experience something by having observed it and attributed meaning to it. When you change the way you look at something, you change the way you experience it. If you're looking at recovery as not worth the effort, open up and let in new information. Change your perception.

Recovering Intelligence

Your first impression could be right or wrong - clarify & reassess!

Here is a simple example of an incorrect perception: As you enter a local support group, you smell a foul scent and think, "These people stink." Then you see a table with a variety of cheeses – that's what you were smelling. New information (the cheese) has changed your perception, and therefore your experience as well.

Personal Free Time

When new to recovery, having fun may seem unlikely. Your "fun" was your addiction; therefore, you must avoid returning to what was "fun" before you began recovery. Instead, participate in healthy fun during your free time, like the type you had before you started using. Make healthy fun a regular part of your life. Plan and schedule your free time with new activities. Learn

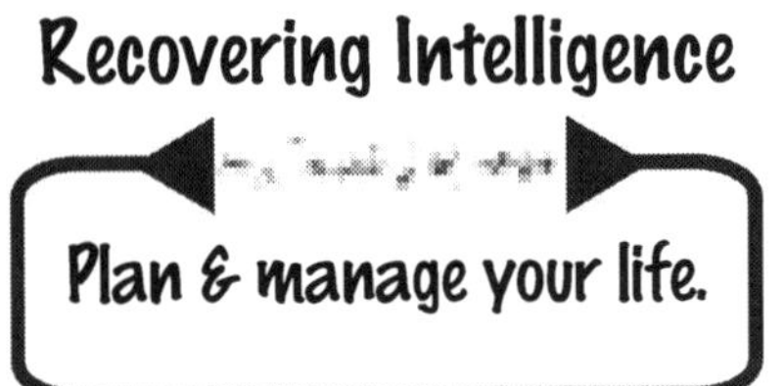

to socialize with recovering friends, develop hobbies, or work on a favorite project. If you are having difficulty thinking of things to do, ask your recovering pals what they do for fun.

Play: What you consider playful is personal. Whatever it is, make playing a daily part of your life. Think of your younger days. What did you relish doing? Remember. Then DO IT.

Note: For the first year or two of recovery, fill your free time with positive activities. Idle time can lead to relapse.

Personal Healing Time

Taking care of yourself is very important. Relaxation and rejuvenation will allow you to experience a better quality of life. Personal healing time can come from a variety of activities and from both time alone or time interacting with others. Examples of such activities are taking a bath, meditating, reading, talking with friends, playing sports, listening to music or a speaker, or writing.

Personal Organization

Lack of personal organization makes it harder to function well and can be self-defeating. It may reflect how you're feeling inside. Clutter, forgetfulness, and lateness are examples of poor personal organization. Old, dysfunctional habits like procrastination need to be

Recovering Intelligence

Start with one approach that you are committed to using & use it.

changed into healthy habits. Organize yourself; start with just a little at a time and build on that.

Personal organization will help your life to be easier and simpler. You will be more effective and efficient in everything you do. Structure and consistency will add to your productivity. Utensils such as Post-its, lists, a calendar, personal organizer, and smart phone can help. Clean up your personal space. Develop and use your personal structure for successful recovery and follow through. It will pay off!

Time Management: Use your time wisely and do not waste it. This is time management. In continuing recovery, time must be divided between personal priorities (relaxation and play can be priorities) and tasks you are working on.

Recovering Intelligence

Time management is about task management.

Time is precious – use it wisely, yet share it willingly. Value others' time by being punctual and focused when you're sharing, and by being clear about what you want from them. Communicate your expectations in a respectful manner.

Positive Psychology

Recovering Intelligence

It takes 62 muscles to frown & only 26 to smile. Smiling is easier!

Positive psychology incites well-being, but it is not happyology. It is based on sound research and includes traditional psychology to help many people who are experiencing emotional pain to find relief. It also assists healthy people to become even happier, healthier, and more successful.

By the time you have established a solid recovering foundation, start learning about positive psychology, because recovery must be happier than addiction. The sense of joy and peace that stems from positive psychology will help you to develop and expand your recovery. It works well with the philosophy of 12-Step and other self-help programs, some of which incorporate positive psychology into their structure.

Positive psychology focuses on building your happiness in the following ways:

- Using your personal strengths. (Find *Strengths* in the Index.)
- Raising your level of happiness by fully experiencing positive emotions.
    - » Raw pleasures: Example: Eating ice cream
    - » Complex pleasures: Example: Watching opera
    - » Positive Emotion: Example: Connecting with feelings such as curiosity, excitement, gratitude, hope, joy, love, peace, and trust.
- Experiencing Flow ("zone") activities: Happiness comes from being engaged and focused on the "dance of life."
- Participating in purposeful activities: Engaging in something bigger than you. Example: Being active with your family, church, or a social cause.
- Building and maintaining a meaningful life.
- Fulfilling your emotional needs.
- Paying attention to negative self talk and

implementing ways to eradicate it.

- Building on positive emotions with a 3:1 ratio – for every negative, find three positives in your life.

Recovering Intelligence

Happiness grows with three positive experiences to every one negative experience.

You'll be a lot happier and healthier. Set yourself up for happiness by creating this ratio regularly.

- Increase your happiness with:
  - » Daily activities from which you derive pleasure. Take the *VIA: Signature Strengths Questionnaire* and use the results to plan activities. (See APPENDIX 10.)
  - » Acting as if... smile, and you'll feel happier.
  - » Close relationships and shared intimacy.
  - » Focusing on your personal control. Choose to focus on the things that you can control instead of focusing on the things that you cannot control.
  - » Choosing to have faith; believe that things will be okay or as they are supposed to be.

Prayer and Meditation

Prayer and meditation are two separate tools in recovery. They are similar in their ability to calm the soul, but they each have a different approach. Prayer is an action. It is a way of communicating with your Higher Power. There are many ways to pray, most of which involve talking directly to the Source. After talking, spend at least the same amount of time listening. One prayer that has helped many is called the Serenity Prayer (short version):

"God grant me the Serenity to accept
the things I cannot change, courage to
change the things I can,
and the Wisdom to know the difference."
Reinhold Neibuhr, 1926

With meditation, you focus on quietness, your inner self, and your Higher Power. There is no talking. Only the inner voice, which is so often ignored, is heard. Research shows that meditation helps heal damage done to your brain in your active addiction. (Find Meditation in the Index.)

Present (Being)

The present is the only moment in time over which you have any control. Everything that ever happens only happens in the present. That's why it's called the present; it's a gift. There are three aspects to being present:

1. Physical awareness of time, your physical body, and the outside physical world
2. Mental awareness and your specific focus
3. Heart-centered awareness

Be present by being aware of yourself, your thoughts and emotions, and what's going on around you now. Focus on the here and now and not the past or the future.

Problem Solving Strategies

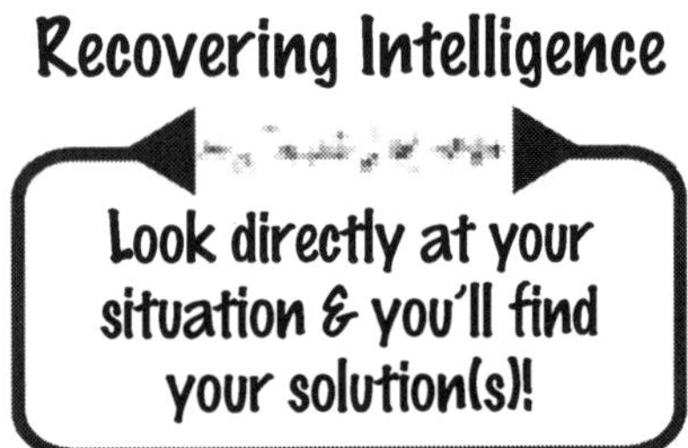

Problem solving strategies help you develop options that will lead to adequate solutions. Examining the cause of an issue can assist in problem solving. Search for how your behavior, attitude, or beliefs have helped create the problem. Ask yourself what is it that you need to change. Get objective feedback from someone you trust.

Example Problem: I'm invited to a wedding. I usually relapse at such events.

Example Solutions:

1. Pre-agreement with a friend to talk (live/by phone)
2. Step outside with a friend
3. Arrive late and leave early (call and/or meet a friend)

Products

Learn about nutritional, herbal, health care, and personal growth products for recovery. Educational products include books, audio/video resources, and computer software. (See APPENDIX 10.)

Purpose

Most people want a reason to live. They want to be

engaged in something bigger than themselves that gives their life additional value and meaning. Early in your recovery, your purpose will be to stay clean, deal with life and family issues, and to build a recovery foundation. Opening up and growing in continuing recovery should allow your life purpose to become clearer. Find purpose in more than one thing. For instance, by helping other newly recovering people start their journey, you may discover a reason for remaining committed to your own recovery.

Recovering Intelligence

Be a part of something that is desirable & bigger than yourself.

Recovery Shifts

As you begin your recovery, you may feel fairly negative. If you accept that these feelings will change with time, you will be able to work on shifting those negative attitudes to positive ones. Many have reported making the following shifts:

Recovering Intelligence

Key shifts are vital!

- Thoughts shift from "I can't recover" to "I wish I could," to "I want to" to "I can," and finally to "I will recover."
- "Thoughts shift from "Maybe," and "Could be," to "I choose to believe!"
- Thoughts shift from "Recovery is hard," to "Recover is challenging," and "Recovery is work," to "Recovery is desirable," and "Recovery is valuable,"

and finally to "Recovery is a blessing!"

- Thoughts shift from "I am a using addict," to "I am an abstinent addict," to "I am a recovering addict," and finally "I am a healthy recovering addict!"

Recovery Strategies

Recovery strategies exist for expected and unexpected situations. In addition you can develop your personal ones. Practice them and be ready for the triggers that will appear at some point in your recovery, often when you least expect them.

Act As If (Fake It 'Til You Make It): Avoid getting stuck in a negative self-fulfilling prophecy. Pretend that things are the way you want them to be. Practice this by acting as if you are happy. Research shows people who seek activities that stimulate laughter, like watching a comedy or flexing your smile muscles, are happier. So smile!

H.A.L.T. (Hungry, Angry, Lonely, Tired): These feelings mimic the craving to use and could trigger a relapse. In recovery, it's crucial to avoid them. Eat three meals a day. When you are angry, talk to a healthy recovering person about your issues so that you have some assistance in how to proceed. Your addiction kept you company when you felt lonely. Plan what to do when you are alone. Get enough sleep so you won't think you need to use to stay awake. Practice balance. Take care of yourself by eating, relaxing, accepting, and connecting.

Honest Carefrontation: *Carefrontation* means to confront someone with kindness, caring, and concern. There are times when you will need to confront a person(s) who is endangering your recovery. Be clear about what the issue is. (Find *Carefrontation* in the Index.)

K.I.S.S. (Keep It Simple Somehow): When new in recovery, everything can appear to be complicated. Recovery basics can be simple, but they're not always easy. Do simple things like deep breathing.

Reach Out: The emotional and social support of your core group is necessary and an imperative and powerful resource. Call someone if in need; don't be alone.

Recovery Attitude: Stay aware of your attitude towards recovery. What are the most important reasons you want to recover? This list may include the positive future you desire or the negatives past you're sick and tired of. What will always turn your focus back onto your recovery? Your children? Your spirituality? Not wanting to go to jail (again)? Write these motivational factors on your options card. (Find *Options Card* in the Index.)

So What: (Also known as a cure for a case of the "F___ its" and "Screw its.") When you feel like recovery is a waste of time, and you just don't want to participate in it anymore, you have a case of the "Screw its." To pull yourself out of this hole, say to yourself, "So what?" or "So? I'll do recovery anyway!"

Reframing

Recovering Intelligence

Reframe - look at things from a more desirable point of view!

Reframing requires you to look at an issue and develop a different perspective to your initial understanding of a related event or experience. It's a powerful tool for decreasing resentments, guilt, self-loathing, and self-blame. You can reframe anything by filtering your perspective through a more useful point of view. In recovery, you must reframe the shame you felt as a result of your use to compassion for yourself.

Resiliency

The ability to overcome the challenges that life presents us with is the backbone of resiliency. It is a term that describes one's ability to cope and bounce back from daily struggles, normal hardships, and the tragedies of life. Some people are born with more resilience than others. But you can develop resiliency by changing how you think about adversity. If you consider adversity to be drama or trauma, chances are you will be less resilient. Consider adversity to be a learning opportunity, and you will increase your resiliency.

Recovering Intelligence

Resiliency is the ability to bounce back from adversity.

Developing your ability to be resilient is extremely

valuable. Staying optimistic is a strength that will help move you through life's challenges.

Review

Consistent review of your recovery program will give you important feedback as to the success and depth of your recovery. A review of how you acted on the day will assist you in taking an inventory of your behavior and personal interactions. Reviewing longer periods of time (6 months to 5 years) will clarify the bigger picture of your recovery and your life in general.

> **Recovering Intelligence**
>
> **Regularly review your program - daily, monthly, & yearly.**

Review:

- Your immediate recovery goals regularly.
- Your long-term goals occasionally.
- Your progress with overcoming character defects.

Remember that every aspect of your recovery program will benefit from evaluation. Set yourself up for success by taking action now. Ask trusted others to help you, listen to their feedback, and then take action!

Rewards

Creating a reward system for achieving goals can be very motivational. If you set a goal to attend 90 meetings in 90 days, your reward for

this type of daily recovery activity could be having coffee with recovery pals after each meeting. A positive reward system works better than making negative consequences for yourself, unless you know that you are motivated by fear of failure. For many people negative consequences can feel punitive and lead to lack of interest.

Rewards can be concrete, like money; personal, like a hug; or educational, like enrollment in a seminar. What type of reward would give you the most drive to obtain your goals? While working on each task, set yourself up for success by enjoying the experience and the rewards.

Self-Talk

Many of us talk to ourselves in ways we would never address another human being. How you talk to yourself affects how you feel, your attitude, and your behavior. As you learn to pay attention to your internal self-talk, you will have the opportunity to change it. Negative self-talk will not build quality recovery. Substitute negative self-talk for that which is positive, or at least accurate. This takes time because, for years, you may have practiced beating yourselves up with guilt, blame, and put-down statements. In recovery, you need to replace your well-rehearsed negative self-talk with positive affirmations.

Your self-talk will help you develop Your Recovering Future™.

Your Recovering Future

Examples: Replace:

- "I can't" with "I can" or "I will"

- "I'll try" with "I will" or "I'll do my best"
- "I have to" with "I want to"

Focus your self-talk on your desired future rather than your negative past or current problems. Affirming and picturing a positive future will move you more easily towards that future. (See APPENDIX 7.)

Affirmations: Affirmations are statements that something is true or will soon become true. They are short, positive thoughts about what you want or whom you want to be. Personal affirmations will help you focus on desirable changes and establish an image of **Your Recovering Future**™.

Affirmations will help you develop the vision of your desired recovery.

Your Recovering Future

Select one affirmation at a time. Say it to yourself until it becomes familiar and comfortable. Soon enough, you will begin to believe it. Place your affirmation in visible places. Review it many times a day so its message will sink into your long-term memory. Once you believe your affirmation is somewhat true, select another one. Keep adding to your repertoire. Before you know it, you'll have many positive beliefs about yourself. Consider making an affirmation CD. Play it often. (See APPENDIX 10.)

Social-Emotional Intelligence

Emotional intelligence is the ability to identify, assess, and control your emotions. Social intelligence, also known as street smarts or people skills, is your ability to know what others are feeling or care enough to ask. It includes

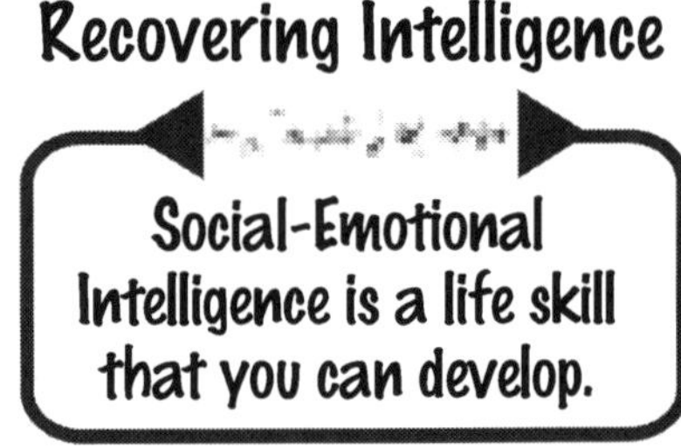

the empathy that helps you get along well with other people and refers to one's capacity to negotiate and navigate through complex social interactions. The socially intelligent person usually has emotional intelligence as well. In recovery, you can improve your social-emotional intelligence by attending meetings and learning the skills you may have missed or which have become rusty because you were preoccupied with your addiction. (See APPENDIX 5.)

Strengths

Your character strengths are your virtues, your personal assets. Are you able to identify your character strengths? The following list might help you. Character strengths include: appreciation of excellence, bravery, citizenship, creativity, curiosity, discipline, fairness, forgiveness, gratitude, hope, humility, integrity, kindness, leadership, love, love of learning, open-mindedness, persistence, perspective, prudence, self-regulation, social intelligence, emotional intelligence, spirituality, and vitality. Using and developing your strengths is an effective life strategy. You'll be happier and more successful if you base your life and your career on your strengths.

Recovering Intelligence

Using personal strengths will make you happier & more successful.

Start promoting one or two of your strengths immediately and then slowly add more. Learn what your personal strengths are by taking these strength assessment questionnaires:

(See APPENDIX 10.)

- VIA Survey of Character Strengths
- StrengthsFinder 2.0 (career focused)

Stress Reduction

Stress can become so familiar that it feels normal. If you have become accustomed to stress, you may find yourself seeking tense situations. (Find *Stimulation* in the Index.)

Reducing stress is vital for your health. There are many tools to reduce stress such as creative activities, biofeedback, deep breathing, relaxation, meditation, physical activities, and self-soothing. Find a way that works for you and use it until you can reduce your stress response.

If you're finding it difficult to reduce stress, your body may be producing too much cortisol. You can learn to mentally control this, and there are nutritional supplements that can help. (Find *Stress* in the Index.)

Structure For Change

How are you going to change? What is your plan to stay abstinent from your addiction and to stop engaging in your using rituals? What is your plan to leave behind all those "fun" using activities? It takes dedication to change your thought patterns, character, and concept of what fun is. Without a plan and a structure, recovery doesn't happen. Find someone with

Recovering Intelligence

Live in your recovery & life structure. Let it carry you the distance.

long-term recovery. Ask them what structure they put in place and how it helped keep them away from their addictive practices.

Time

You're accustomed to spending your time planning to use, using, and recovering from use. In continuing recovery, you may find yourself with an abundance of time that you don't know how to fill. You must plan what to do with that free time so that you're not tempted to use. Consider creating a daily time line, an overview of how you'll spend your day. The structure of a time line will increase the chances of fulfilling your recovery goals.

Include a daily recovery activity into your time line. For many, this will be attending a meeting. Schedule around the activity. A time line might start with getting up at 8:00 am, at 8:15 am showering and attending to personal hygiene, eating breakfast at 10:00 am, going to an 11:00 am meeting, and so on. You will find scheduling your day to be a very helpful tool. Make it a daily practice. If you don't, you won't likely be as productive in your recovery as you could be, and you might find yourself drifting back to old using behaviors.

Writing

Writing can be an effective recovery tool, particularly journaling, which offers you the chance to process your feelings, emotions, and

Recovering Intelligence

Writing is an excellent tool for processing & reviewing later.

experiences in print. Many in recovery have discovered there is something magical about journaling. It provides a method for purging resentments, negative emotions, and upsets. A journal also gives you a resource to review your history, see patterns, and make sense of past situations. You can use a journal to focus on specific issues like your recovery, intense events, feelings, relationships, or personal growth experiences.

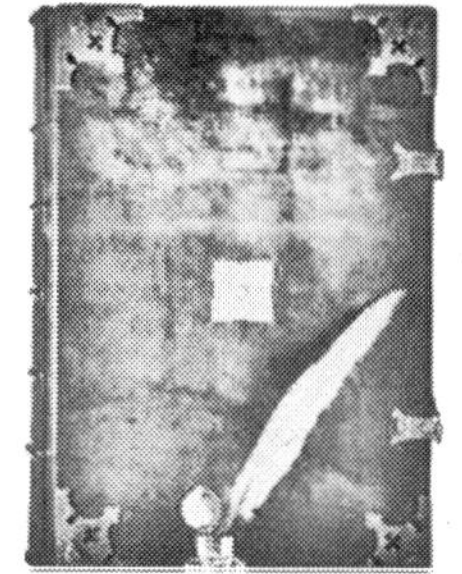

An activities journal is what is commonly thought of as a diary. On a daily basis, write about your experiences, including the underlying circumstances, the outcome, and your response to the experience. This type of diary is valuable for charting your recovery.

A feelings journal is a systematic way to explore, clarify, and vent your feelings. It can be valuable for recovering people who need to work on being aware of, identifying, and processing emotions.

Letter journals provide a way to say things to others that you have stored in your resentment "basket." Writing a hate letter to your sibling about all the terrible things he or she did to you as a child can be a way of letting go of pent up emotions. Writing to a deceased parent about how much they are missed can help release stored grief. Writing is cathartic.

Most often, the letters written are not mailed. They are either burned or shredded. The point of letter writing is to act as a recovery tool to assist you in letting go of people, places, situations, and things over which you are powerless.

All wounds of the past are forced out of your system so you can focus on becoming the person you have always wanted to be.

Letter writing is also a tool for making amends. When circumstances prevent a face-to-face apology, a letter can be written. Remember, just because you took the time to write a letter doesn't guarantee that someone you've wounded will forgive you. Letters don't allow for expectations about how the recipient will react.

Letters have many other functions. Many write letters of gratitude. Some write letters to their Higher Power. Others write about how someone else's behavior affected them.

Consider journaling as little as 5 minutes a day. Don't worry about how good it is, whether it will help, or what others would think if they read it. Just give it a try!

SUMMARY

For those who have the courage to embark on the path of recovery, there are many strategies and tools available to help you work through the challenges that may arise. Select the tools that feel right, those that motivate you to become who you want to be, even if they require more time, energy, and effort. These are the tools that will assist you in the development of **Your Recovering Future™**.

Take a Tool Inventory. Write down those tools you have become skilled at using, and then write down those you need to adopt in order to transform a negative, using lifestyle into a positive, healthy lifestyle. When the tools you have practiced become second nature, look for different ones to put into your tool box.

Give unfamiliar tools the time and effort they deserve so they can become valuable resources for you. Humor, prayer, and meditation are often overlooked. Tools like an options card, acknowledging and honoring your character strengths, and reframing may be unfamiliar to you, so they will take patience and enthusiasm to master.

The day will come when you have tried most of the tools and strategies suggested here. Your tool box will be filled with options that are comfortable because you have practiced them, over and over.

- Try new tools & strategies, even if you think you have enough.
- Fill your tool box with enthusiasm.
- Utilize the Red Dot Reminder System and complete your options card.
- Practice using your tools and strategies.
- Take a personal inventory, and identify your character strengths.

Chapter 5

Continuing Recovery: Personal Issues

Chapter 5: Continuing Recovery – Personal Issues
Table of Contents

ISSUES

Everyone has issues. What are issues? They are problems or matters of contention. They are those little prickly topics that you wanted to avoid dealing with – so much so that you used or you became involved in addictive behaviors, hoping that if you ignored them long enough, they'd go away. In the first months of recovery, when you are no longer able to avoid your issues, you may feel like you are carrying the weight of the world on your back.

AVOIDANCE

For many of us, avoidance goes hand in hand with other addictive behaviors. Avoidance causes negative consequences such as, financial challenges, interpersonal problems and general frustration. Examples of avoidance: telling your partner you'll mow the lawn but you watch sports all day instead; putting off making a bank deposit because you have to go shopping on the opening day of a store sale.

In recovery, overcoming avoidance can be one of the toughest challenges you face. It requires becoming a person of your word and living up to your responsibilities. How do you overcome avoidance? Take one issue at a time and solve it. If you don't know how, find a recovery person who does. Model their thinking, emotions, and behaviors until it becomes your own.

Addiction Interaction Disorder

Compelling research indicates few addicts (about 17%) have only one addiction. Having a mix of addictions and compulsions is known as Addiction Interaction Disorder (AID). Simply put, if you are addicted to one thing, chances are you are addicted to other things.

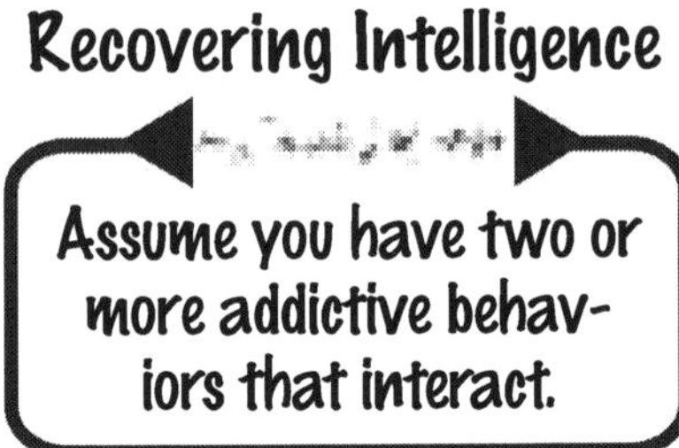

AID addresses your propensity to have addictions that coexist with others. For example, if you are an alcoholic and are also addicted to Internet gaming, these two will interact, fuse together, and reinforce each other. They become part of the package that is Addiction Interaction Disorder. For those in recovery, it's crucial to identify other dependencies and discuss them with one or more support friends.

Most recovering people aren't aware of all their secondary addictions, or the complex interplay between them. Untreated secondary addictions are often part of a using ritual, making them a gateway back into your primary addiction(s). If not identified, treated, and brought into your recovery, your secondary addictions will lead you into relapse.

Recovering Intelligence

Deal with your secondary addictions or they'll trigger you.

Some examples of Addiction Interaction Disorder:

- Returning to one addiction lowers the resolve not to participate in other addictions.

- One addiction leads into another because there is a connection between them.
- Two or more addictions increase at the same time.
- One addiction is replaced with another addiction.
- Doing two or more addictive behaviors together to achieve a greater effect.
- Ending a secondary behavior brings stability.

Switching Addictions and Cross Addiction are aspects of Addiction Interaction Disorder. Switching is when you transfer your desire for one addiction to another addiction. The new addiction may be seen as better than the original one. Usually, each successive addiction creates a more intense high. Total abstinence from all mood-altering substances and addictive behaviors is always the best approach to recovery, when possible. (See APPENDIX 2.)

Cross Addiction is when you are addicted to two or more substances simultaneously. For addicts, it is easy to be cross addicted because the pleasure pathways in the brain have become acclimated to mind-altering substances.

How do you deal with AID? You treat multiple addictions very much in the same way you deal with a single addiction – with an effective recovery plan. Pay attention to the interactions between all of your addictions and addictive behaviors so that you can approach your recovery appropriately.

Consider: **"In My Experience... you don't want to cling to other secondary addictions or addictive behaviors."** (See APPENDIX 7.)

Altered States

An altered state is any state of mind differing from the normal state of consciousness. A negative altered state can be caused by drugs or other addictions, or a mental disorder. Positive altered states come from listening to music, meditation, or reading. Research shows that altering one's state of mind in a healthy way can be healing and restful for the brain. It breaks our practiced ways of obsession, stress, worry, and anxiety. Meditation is an easy, relaxing, and helpful tool to encourage a healthy altered state of mind. It can help you deal with cravings, obsessions, and negative emotions.

Compulsions and Obsessions

An obsession is the domination of thoughts or emotions by a persistent idea, feeling, or desire. Compulsion is a strong urge to take action on one's ideas, feelings, or desires. A component of the disease of addiction is obsessive thinking and compulsive behavior. Obsessive thoughts precede compulsions. Therefore, if you intervene on an obsessive thought, you will diminish the urge to take action on it. How? There are many ways. One of the most popular ones is to wear a rubber band around your wrist, and whenever thoughts about using come up, snap the rubber band and remind yourself, "This is NOT an option."

Habits

Habits are behavioral patterns that have been practiced enough that they have become involuntary. When you repeat a thought or a behavior often enough, it becomes mentally wired. The more you repeat it, the bigger the circuit gets and the stronger the habit becomes. When you build positive habits, life becomes easier and better. When a negative habit starts causing you problems, change it by replacing it with a new, desirable habit. Stay aware of your thoughts and actions so you catch negative habits early on, and commit to changing them!

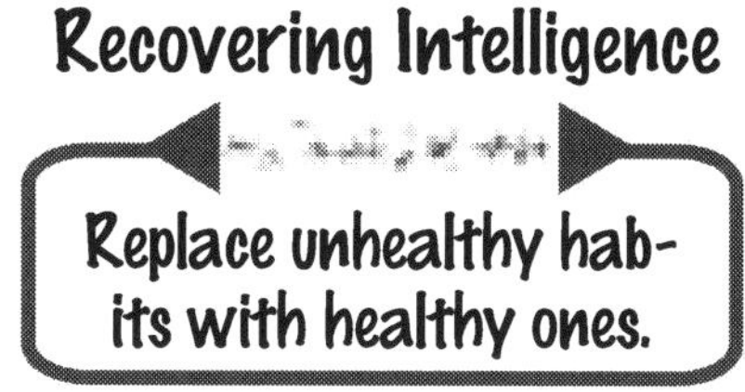

Consider: **"In My Experience... you don't want to do anything to strengthen current negative habits or start any new ones."** (See APPENDIX 7.)

Rituals

Similar to habits, practiced behaviors known as rituals may activate a return to your addiction. Some examples are:

- Happy hour after work
- Weekends at a casino resort
- Living for shopping sales

For sustained recovery, rituals that have been part of your past using lifestyle will need to be left behind and replaced with new ones that support a healthy lifestyle. These might look like:

- Spending time after work at a sober social center
- Weekend activities with family or friends
- A new approach, like exercising, meditating, team sports, or volunteering with a purpose

Stimulation

Stimulation refers to excitement, invigoration, and sometimes irritation. People with addiction issues may seek out or create exciting, risky, and often thrilling and dramatic situations that induce a rush of hormones, like adrenaline. Stress produces adrenaline, DHEA (a feel good hormone), and cortisol (the stress hormone). These hormones are supposed to diminish after a short period of time. If not, they will hurt your body.

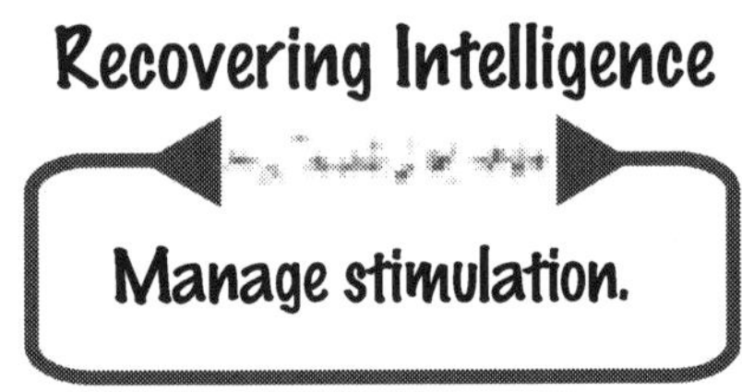

During your addiction, it is likely that you experienced an intense level of emotional, physical, and neurotransmitter stimulation. In recovery, you will need to learn a new "normal." You will still require spiritual, mental, physical, and emotional stimulation. Without it, boredom, a powerful instigator for relapse, might derail your recovery. But you must create positive, healthy ways to enjoy the excitement life has to offer.

Note: Don't create an addiction to your adrenaline!

Healthy stimulation:

- Physical: Learn to rock climb.
- Spiritual: try learning meditation or finding a church service that touches your heart.
- Mental: do crossword puzzles or a new video game.
- Emotional: learn new ways of communicating with significant others or watch tear-jerker movies.

It's important to mention that some types of stimulation can feel irritating at first, such as trying to practice a new communication skill and having the attempt turn out to be a dismal failure, or trying to practice meditation and finding yourself thinking about what to buy at the grocery store for twenty minutes. If at first you don't succeed, try, try again! You might even learn to feel pleasure from smelling a rose, listening to music, or watching a child play.

Even if you are involved in a positive activity, it's possible to become over-stimulated. Getting used to or habituated to a high level of stimulation can cause problems, such as exhaustion or burnout.

Risk-taking behavior: To continue the brain stimulation they experienced throughout addiction, some people engage in risky, highly-stimulating behaviors during recovery. Instead, chose healthier options like exercise, creative hobbies, meditation, or just relaxing. Nutritional supplements like amino acids, GABA (relaxation), or L-tyrosine (stimulation) may also be helpful in curbing risk-taking behavior. Check with your physician.

Stress

Stress is similar to stimulation, yet more intense. If your stress response continues after the actual stimulation or trigger ends, it can hurt your recovery performance and harm your body. How you respond to positive (eustress) and negative (distress) stressors will help or hurt you. If you deal with stressors well, it can improve

your performance, and vice versa. Everyone has many small stressors which can build and cause pressure. Examples of positive and negative stressors include:

- Positive stressors: a big vacation, graduation, moving to a nicer home, a new job, a wedding, or other positive events
- Negative stressors: the death of a loved one, divorce, illness, loss of a job or other financial problems, or other bad news

Stress ignites a chemical reaction which causes a relapse response. In turn, this can lead to an intense emotional obsession in your brain that causes a craving so strong, it overrules your ability to consider other options. Once this chemical response exists, it can happen again at any time. This is why it's very important to stay calm and self-aware all of the time.

Because of the hormones stress produces, you can become addicted to stress. The attempt to do it all may cause you to feel alive. In reality, you're hurting your body, emotionally and physically.

Nutritional stress: This is a biological response to poor nutrition or to foods which cause an allergic reaction. Allergic reactions, such as to gluten (wheat protein), can cause relapse in alcoholics. Nutritional stress taxes the body and brain and reduces your ability to function correctly. (See APPENDIX 3.)

(Find *Stress Reduction* in the Index.)

MENTAL HEALTH ISSUES

Many people with chemical or behavioral addictions also have a mental health diagnosis. This is referred to as *dual diagnosis*. Information on mental illness and diagnoses can be found in the Diagnostic & Statistical Manual of Mental Disorders or on the internet.

Many mental illnesses are biological conditions affecting the brain and its function. In the brain, a group of chemicals categorized as neurotransmitters serve to keep us seeing, hearing, feeling, and thinking within the same reality as the majority of the population. How this is accomplished is too complicated to address in this book, but simply put that if there is too little of some neurotransmitters, we get depressed, lack energy, or feel pain. If there is too much of certain other neurotransmitters, we can see and hear things that aren't there or don't feel good.

Drug abuse can induce symptoms that resemble mental illness in both the intoxicated state and during withdrawal. In some cases, symptoms like anxiety, depression, or psychosis (a disconnection from reality) can persist for months after the initial period of detoxification.

An intense lifestyle, such as drug use, can increase the likelihood of activating a genetically predisposed mental illness. Those who have an addiction problem are more likely than non-addicted people to have a mental illness. Without a period of abstinence, it is extremely difficult to tell apart a mental illness from substance induced symptoms that mimic a mental illness. An addiction is always treated first so clinicians can identify what was caused by a drug versus what was caused by neurotransmitter production.

If you have symptoms of a mental illness, consult a skilled professional immediately. Be honest about your addiction issues. If you don't, your therapist will not be able to give you an accurate diagnosis.

If mental symptoms do not respond to treatment after a period of three to six months without substance abuse, get another evaluation. Talk to your therapist or physician about arranging one. If available, SPECT (preferred), MRI, or PET scan technologies can offer help for understanding what's going on in your brain. Such tests can aid in determining what areas of your brain are over-active or under-active.

PERSONAL ISSUES

An issue is a belief, feeling, thought, attitude, or behavior that causes a concern, small or big. Each person has their own set of personal issues. Each issue may need a different approach and a different set of skills to deal with it. To resolve an issue, you may need to:

- Define what the issue is.
- Determine if you should address it now or later in your recovery.
- Take an inventory of yourself.
- Radically change your own behavior.

- Explore your history, even your childhood.
- Go to personal or family therapy.
- Meditate or pray, or both.

Whatever your issues, if you don't actively and effectively deal with them, usually they'll undermine your recovery.

Recovering Intelligence

Deal with your mental-emotional issues or face the consequences.

Make a list of what bothers you, what responsibilities you are avoiding, and what you'd like to change about YOU. Address one thing at a time. Go slowly. Look for progress, not perfection. Do this work with someone in recovery or with a recovery coach or therapist, whatever is desirable.

Abuse – Physical, Emotional, Spiritual

Abuse is a systematic pattern of behaviors in a relationship used to gain and maintain power and control over another, usually with the intent to manipulate. Abuse leads to feelings of shame, anger, lack of trust, and the inability to make an emotional connection with others.

Types of Abuse:

- Emotional: Characterized by behaviors that are hurtful, undermine, or control. It can lead to fear, guilt, humiliation, anxiety, depression, and trauma.
  - » Absence: Whether through being physically distant, emotionally unavailable, or due to

neglect or avoidance, absence can be a form of emotional abuse.

- Physical: Behaviors that cause physical injury; also verbal threats of violence.
- Sexual: Forced and unwanted sexual behavior of any kind – pressure as well as molestation and rape.
- Verbal: Using words to put-down, humiliate, or disgrace with the intent to control or manipulate.

Childhood: Childhood abuse is a common issue for people in recovery. Many addicts' parents were addicts themselves and were abusive while under the influence. Victims of childhood abuse may suffer from a mental illness. Severe abuse can cause PTSD (Post Traumatic Stress Disorder), emotional disconnection (dissociation), and even Dissociative Identity Disorder (multi-personality disorder). Early recovery may be too soon to explore childhood abuse. If these issues are not undermining your recovery, wait to address such issues in a later stage of recovery. If you don't wait, you can easily trigger a relapse due to intense emotions resurfacing. If they are causing you to relapse, then they must be dealt with sooner. This can be a successful approach.

Every type of abuse is a boundary violation and can be traumatizing. Abuse can happen at any age. If you have a history of trauma, seek help from a trauma specialist.

Adult Child of an Alcoholic Issues

An ACA (Adult Child of an Alcoholic) is an individual who was raised in a dysfunctional household in which one or both parents were addicted or emotionally ill. In such a family, destructive behaviors control the household. One or both parents are caught up in their using, and the other is focused on taking care of his or her spouse. Kids come in second, at best.

At a young age, ACA's learn to be responsible, flexible, calm, and enabling. They often select partners that help them replicate their families of origin because the style feels "normal." ACA's in recovery need to re-parent themselves so that the "don't talk, don't trust, don't feel" rules, and the chaotic family controls, are diminished.

To assist you in overcoming your ACA issues, find a process style therapy group or get involved in individual psychotherapy. Trust is essential if you are to open up to the process work necessary to heal yourself. It's important to believe you have the right to feel and talk about your childhood experiences. The goal of ACA work is to process, let go of, and move beyond the wounds, violations, neglect, or abuse that you experienced in childhood. With support, learn to embrace the needy parts of yourself.

The Answer

Some people are convinced there's "One Solution" or "The Answer" that will fix all issues and allow them to live a "normal" life, one that includes controlled using. "The Answer" is usually dependent on another person or on an external event such as their job, their spouse, or money. "If only my partner was more supportive, I wouldn't use so much." When you catch yourself saying, "If only," realize that you are looking for an external excuse to participate in an addictive behavior.

Research indicates that once a reward system has become permanently changed by addiction, controlled use is only temporary. It doesn't last; eventually, you return to using and behaving addictively. Let go of trying to find "The Answer." Focus on your recovery first. Put, "If only," in the closet for another day. Be in the present!

Assuming

Assuming is guessing the cause or outcome of a situation without evidence. There's an old saying, "If you ASSUME, you make an ASS out of U and ME!" Take a vacation from your assumptions. They are false judgments. Examples of potentially risky assumptions that can derail your recovery are:

- It'll be okay... I'll go next time.
- It'll get better... I'll try harder.
- I basically get it... I'll learn more later if I need to.

Don't set yourself up for failure by making overly optimistic assumptions. Telling yourself that "it's no big deal" when you are about to enter a high-risk situation can and will hinder your recovery. Don't assume you can get through:

- A using family gathering

- Visiting a place where you used in your addiction
- Any situation that has often caused you to experience significant negative emotions

Attitude

Your attitude or personal view about something is based on your beliefs and perceptions about a person, place, or situation and can have a dramatic impact on your life.

The new science of epigenetics has shown that your genes are NOT 100% in control of your destiny. This is known as *epigenetic control*. According to epigenetics, your genes are only a blueprint and can be changed! If you have a genetic predisposition for addiction, you don't have to act on it. Protein (made up of amino acids) in every cell can be altered by outside influences, including your beliefs, attitudes, thoughts, and feelings. This protein influences DNA, and therefore your destiny. This means you can change yourself at a cellular level, immediately! So pay attention! There are two ways your attitude plays a part in changing your blueprint, including how it affects your recovery:

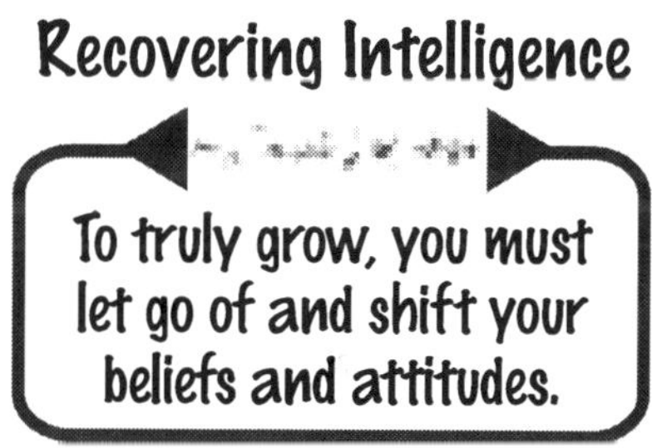

1. A positive belief can heal you (placebo effect).
2. A negative belief can cause illness (nocebo effect).

Boundaries

Boundaries are your physical, emotional, psychological, and spiritual property lines. They define who you are, what's yours, what your roles are, etc. Boundaries also define what belongs to others, what their roles are, and who they are.

Clear boundaries are important for building and maintaining healthy relationships. They clarify what's allowable, comfortable, reasonable, and safe, and what's not. It's important you know your boundaries, and at the same time, acknowledge and respect the boundaries of others.

Learning what your boundaries are, and honoring them, can feel very difficult. Needy loved ones can often try to make you feel guilty about having boundaries that affect them. For example, in recovery from alcoholism, you must honor your boundary about not drinking. How many times do you hear someone say, "Just taste this; it is SO good!" or "One sip won't hurt." If this happens to you, recognize you are with someone who is violating your boundaries. What will you do then? Have a plan! If you waiver on your no using boundary, you are teaching the person you are with that you are not committed to your recovery. You will be violating your own boundary, and much more.

Types of boundary issues include:

- Abuse: I will not allow you to hurt me. If you attempt to do so, our relationship will be over.
- Addiction: I'm in recovery; please don't tempt me.
- Distance: I prefer talking at arm's length.
- Gifts: We agreed on a $10 gift limit, and yours cost $100. I can't accept it.

- Language: I don't like off-color language.
- Sex: I don't want to have sex, and I don't have to.
- Space: Don't bump into me with the grocery cart.
- Touch: I don't like being touched, so please don't.
- Time: Every time we meet, you are at least 30 minutes late. In the future, I will only wait 10 minutes.

There are many more types of boundary issues. For those of us who are codependents or addicts, we often don't know what our boundaries are, or we are afraid to say no to someone lest we make them angry. Allowing boundary violations to occur is a trigger and an excuse to return to addictive behavior. Doing boundary work, while initially scary, will assist us in protecting our recovery.

How do you set a boundary? First, you must become aware of what type of situations cause discomfort for you, and then you must outline to others what those situations are. In the grocery cart example, turning around and graciously saying, "I'd appreciate it if you would stop bumping me with your grocery cart," is a clear and polite statement. With the person trying to tempt you to participate in your addiction, saying, "Thanks for the offer, but I don't use, so in the future, please don't offer me any," is another clear and polite statement.

Let go of the outcome. There is no need for further explanation. Step back, and see if your boundary is respected. If it is, hooray! If it's not, decide if you want to be around someone who won't honor your personal boundary requests.

(Find *Personal Growth* and *Boundaries* in the Index.)

Committee

A committee is a collection of past and present voices that internally comment on your behavior, thoughts, and decisions. They are usually the voices of people you've dealt with in your past or past versions of yourself. Your committee tries to provide "rules," "rationalizations," and "formulas" for ways to solve problems, leading to patterns and habits that ultimately take on a life of their own. Each committee member quietly whispers to you through your thoughts. If all these voices conflict, as they do at times, your options for the road ahead may become confusing.

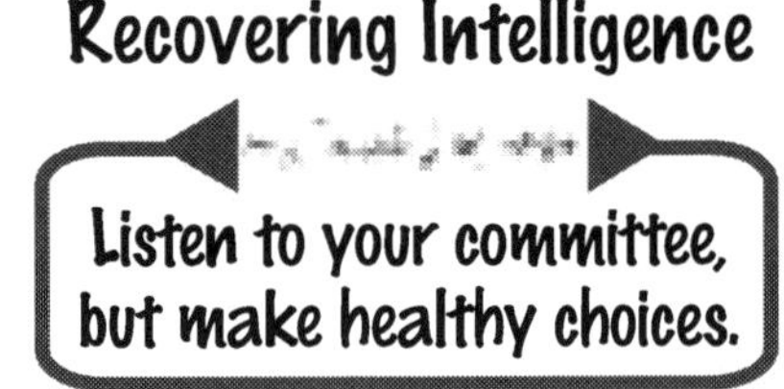

Identify each committee member. Have they become functionally obsolete? For example, has the voice of Uncle Henry, who tells you that you are a lazy loser, worn out its welcome? After all, Uncle Henry died 20 years ago when you were unemployed. But now you've had the same job for 10 years. Bid him goodbye, and when his voice arises again, say, "Oh, there you are, Uncle Henry! I'm good. Bye."

Write down and review what each voice tells you. Then burn it, bury it, or put it in your circular file or your God Box. Let it go and move on!

The following are some examples of common "parts" or "self or selves" of people's committee:

- Addict Committee Member: Remembers the positives of using. It wants you to repeat your past and to satisfy your addiction needs.

- Adult Committee Member: Out of your rational intellect comes a logical, factual self able to negotiate between the other selves and your environment.
- Child Committee Member: From childhood experiences emerges:
    - » Positive: Good, carefree, needy, open, playful, and rebellious selves
    - » Negative: Abused and abusive, fearful, acting out, and damaged selves
- Healthy Committee Member: It knows what's healthy and best. You want this part in control.
- Parent or Relative Committee Member: From experiences with your parents and other authority figures comes a nurturing, or strict and judgmental, self.
- Survivor Committee Member: It knows you can and will survive. It knows how to accomplish survival.
- Other Committee Members: People, places, and situations have offered positive and negative learnings and have become the voices of your committee.

Compensating

Like most addicts, you probably feel bad about yourself. You want to make up for all the negative behaviors that resulted from using. Your desire to make reparations may continue well into your recovery, but you must grow out of your low self-esteem, poor self-image, or feelings of regret

and shame about who you used to be. These feelings will hurt your recovery if you don't. Are you trying to make up for who you used to be? Working a quality program will provide a structure for making amends to those you have harmed, allowing you to let go of the need to compensate.

Completion

It's essential for you to deal with and let go of the negative memories from your past. Unfinished business is an energy drain. It blocks your ability to grow, heal, let go, and move on. This means that at some time in your recovery, you must turn and face difficult issues. It's important to rank past events that were wounding in order of severity. Start with the issues that were less hurtful and work your way to those that have inflicted the most pain. Facing life's wounds can be scary. Do it with a therapist, mentor, or sponsor. If trauma is in your history, get a therapist who specializes in trauma. A completion list might look like this:

1. I'm angry that my aunt didn't remember my birthday.
2. I'm hurt that when I was eight, my mother slapped me.
3. I'm furious that when I was eighteen, I was raped.

In early recovery, items 1 and 2 can be dealt with. Item 3 may needs to wait until you have solid recovery, unless the issue cause you to relapse. Progressing through a completion list by letting go of resentments can be very freeing.

Not only do you need to work through wounds from the past until they come to completion, but you also must let go of using rituals and addictive behaviors. The comfort of familiar patterns that occurred while you were using can be alluring, but cannot be continued, including those that involve other people. Family and friends who used with you or who played some role in your addictive lifestyle must be addressed. You will need to let go of, or limit any of those people who trigger you, or aren't 100% behind you.

Grief work is a part of recovery. You will feel many losses as you enter recovery. Grief about not being able to engage in your addiction and about lost time, money, or opportunities can feel like a tidal wave hitting the shore. Likewise, many people experience intense feelings of loss in regards to coveted activities, employment, friendships, primary rclationships, and social situations that they no longer participate in. A completion ceremony involving writing, burning, breaking, or burying items can help you to work through your grief so you can move on.

The hardest losses are the absolute ones, like the death of a loved one, or the loss of any important relationship or love object. In these situations, it's necessary to go into your heart and accept, release, and forgive yourself and others. Ask your Higher Power for forgiveness and guidance. The support of your recovery community will also be very helpful.

Find healthy ways to express your feelings through talking, writing, or other healing activities. Until you release your emotions, you may experience anxiety, depression, confusion, and doubt. Pay attention to the physical sensations and symptoms of pent-up grief such as aches, illness, pain, tension, or tightness.

When processing your grief, take breaks to renew yourself, especially if you are overwhelmed by emotional flooding. If overwhelmed, secure the issue in a symbolic mental container and leave it there temporarily while you go to a safe place in your mind. Grieving is about:

- Accepting the loss
- Coming to terms with your feelings of loss about being abandoned and left alone
- Possible survivor guilt

There are five stages of grief that you must move through. They are:

1. Denial: "No, not me."
2. Rage and anger: "Why me?"
3. Bargaining: "Yes me, but..."
4. Depression: "Yes, me."
5. Acceptance: "It is what it is."

Trauma work is often needed in recovery as natural and human perpetrated traumas, especially towards women, are all too common. Traumas can be emotional, physical, sexual, and verbal. Victims usually need treatment, and perpetrators always do. Trauma is a big issue that must be addressed. Find a competent psychotherapist who is trained in effective, modern tools to treating trauma, such as Eye Movement Desensitization & Reprocessing or Cognitive Processing Therapy.

Compliance

Compliance is the willingness to go along with a prescribed course of treatment. In recovery, following a structure might feel foreign. Remember, the healthy part of you wants recovery, but your addict self is still alive and well. It will point out all the ways you are different and don't need to follow your recovery plan. It will try to explain why you were okay in your addiction. Keep participating in your recovery structure until your beliefs make the necessary shift to keep you on course.

Consistency

The human mind tends to ignore what is the same and focus on what is different. You will be more consistent in your approach if you set yourself up in a structure that reminds you to pay attention to recovery thinking and behavior. You will be served by:

- Increasing the consistency of your positive thoughts and recovery behaviors.
- Decreasing addict thinking and using behaviors and staying away from your using rituals.

The occasional indulgence of your primary or secondary addiction (an affair, a bet, a box of candy) psychologically strengthens that behavior, increasing the likelihood of repeating it and triggering a full relapse. The more frequently you indulge, the stronger your response.

Defenses

Everyone has and uses psychological defenses for self-protection. They provide you with a social mask to keep others from knowing who you really are or how you are feeling! Psychological defenses can help you cope with difficult situations, but they can also deny or distort reality.

You develop strong defenses during addiction to keep outside influences from discovering the truth about what you are actually doing. They can become so much a part of you that you don't notice you're putting up blocks. In recovery, defenses prevent openness, change, and growth. You can be calm, pleasant, and attentive and still be defensive. (Find *Defended into Openness* in the Index.)

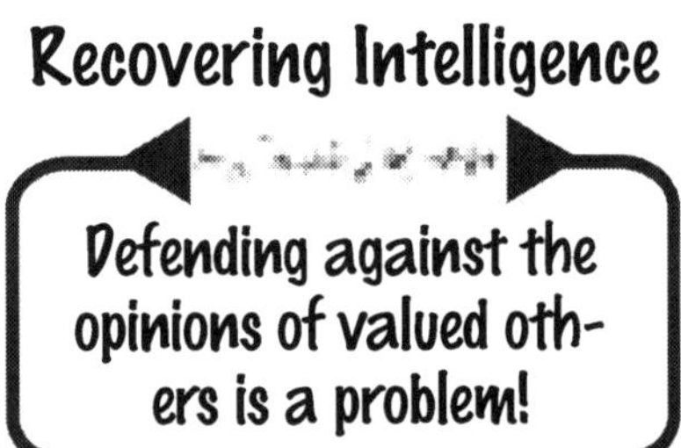

Common psychological defenses are:

- Avoidance: You avoid a feeling or situation.
- Denial: You refuse to accept the truth, even when given feedback from people you trust.
- Disassociation: You mentally and emotionally disconnect from the present.
- Intellectualizing: You think and communicate your mental experience, but not your emotions.
- Minimization: You see a behavior or a situation as less important than it actually is.

- Projection: You place your feelings or experience onto another and believe it's theirs.
- Rationalization: You make up an excuse to justify a behavior or relieve a disappointment.
- Repression: You unconsciously block out experiences that are too painful.
- Sublimation: You redirect unacceptable impulses.
- Suppression: You dismiss unpleasant thoughts, feelings, or memories from your consciousness.
- Other: Many behaviors are used as defenses such as anger, being right, humor, and the need to look good or present yourself well.

Of these defenses, denial and minimizing are the most commonly used by addicted people. You will continue to use these and other coping strategies during your recovery. It's very important for you to stay aware of your defenses. Ask trusted others to tell you when you are defending.

Disabilities

Everyone has physical defects, real or imagined, but some are more obvious than others. The loss of sight or a limb and obesity are more visible than being hearing impaired. It's vital that you discover, acknowledge, and accept your personal disabilities. Most programs are wheelchair accessible, but few have staff who can work with major disabilities like being deaf or blind or having a severe brain injury. When considering a program, clarify their resources.

Recovering Intelligence

You can recover any way.

Chronic Pain: The abuse of psychoactive medications is common among chronic pain patients. Managing ongoing pain can be very difficult, yet there are solutions. In addition to seeing a medical doctor, consider consulting a nutritionist, pain clinic, or a trained pain specialist.

There are personal activities that will help you manage pain without using medication. Develop self-awareness, self-control, and a relaxation response through journaling, meditation, prayer, self-hypnosis, yoga, and martial arts like QiGong and Tai-Chi. Other non-medical approaches to pain control are acupuncture, amino acids (DLPA, DPA), biopuncture, chiropractic therapy, electronic stimulators (ECS), processing audio CDs, and cold wave lasers.

Recovering Intelligence

Try amino acids & non-addictive pain medication first.

Pain medication can be the best option to managing pain, if you can accept the dangers of addiction. Discuss this with your physician. (See APPENDIX 10.)

Emptiness: A Big, Deep Hole

Some people have a big, deep empty hole in their psyche that feels like it's a bottomless pit. If you feel this way, be careful you don't continue to fill it with addictive behaviors, meaningless activities, or other temporary fixes. Instead, fill it with positive recovering people, healing activities, and desirable situations. When you are ready, the permanent fix will come from deep personal work, bonded relationships that are fulfilling, and growth producing adventures.

Expectations

Develop positive expectations, yet know that things may turn out differently – for better or worse. Learn to accept outcomes and see the good in them. Be curious, optimistic, and gain perspective. Have options, like a plan B, in place.

Guilt

Guilt is an emotion that occurs when a person determines, accurately or not, that they have violated a moral standard that they believe in. You can stop guilt by accepting what you've done in the past and by changing your behavior to match your present beliefs and values.

Some people use guilt to manipulate other people. Learn how to recognize when you are being manipulated or when you are trying to manipulate someone else through guilt. Connect to how you want to be.

Idealizing

Idealizing means to think about yourself, others or situations as better than they actually are, or even as being perfect. This will inevitably lead to disappointment. Take yourself and everyone else off of the pedestal and see people for who and what they really are.

Identification (or lack of)

For those in recovery, it's essential to identify and socialize with other recovering addicts who have a similar history. Such identification enables you to accept and embrace recovery. It assists you in shedding the mask that has abetted you in keeping your addiction a secret. Lack of identifying with those in recovery or as a person in recovery may come from one of two issues:

1. You believe your level of using wasn't as bad as the "real addicts." (Maybe denial?)
2. You want to see yourself as different or better than other addicts. Therefore, you avoid them and their clean and sober ways of socializing.

These issues are bad excuses and can lead to the rejection of your recovery community or even recovery itself, which may cause you to slide into an unhappy, dry lifestyle or back into using.

Lack of identification with a recovery community or as a recovering person is mostly an unconscious defense mechanism and a major block to being healthy. Get past the "addict" and "non-addict" labels. Focus on how your thoughts, feelings, attitudes, and actions are similar to other recovering people.

One of the ways in which you can manifest positive identification is the *them and us* attitude. *Them* are the people who can control their using, also called normies. *Us* is the recovering community who couldn't control our addictions. This attitude serves as a cohesive force for the *us*. If you aren't comfortable identifying with *us*, maybe you are a loner, have judgments about addicts, or are still emotionally committed to your addiction. Work on shifting

Recovering Intelligence

You are likelier to get involved with people you can identify with.

your identity to a more positive one.

Identity

Your identity or self-concept is who you believe you are in relation to the world. The degree in which you have created an identity and chosen to present yourself as that person becomes who you think you are. But the identity you have created might not be who you actually are or who you really want to be. Sometimes two or more identities can be in conflict with each other.

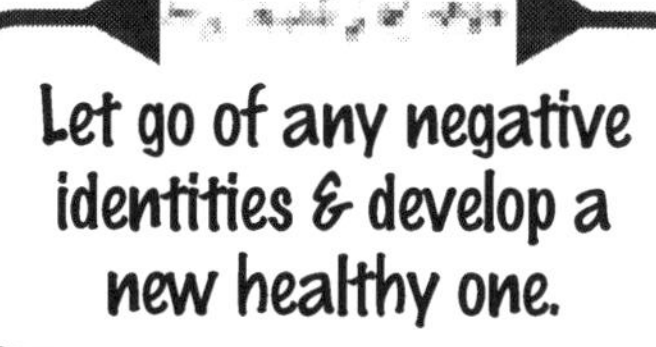

You may have created a tough guy, user identity for the world to see, but inside you long to be open, soft, and engaging with others. Your identity may be a nice person who is always helpful, when a strong part of you sometimes wants to take care of only herself and say no to others. What is your identity? Who do you want to be?

Illusion

An illusion is something appearing to be or interpreted to be true, but isn't. Illusions distort reality. Often they are harmless, but illusions about your addictions can be very harmful, even deadly. Here are some examples of the illusions that addicts tell themselves and distort their reality:

- "Since 'X' wasn't my addiction of choice, it'll be

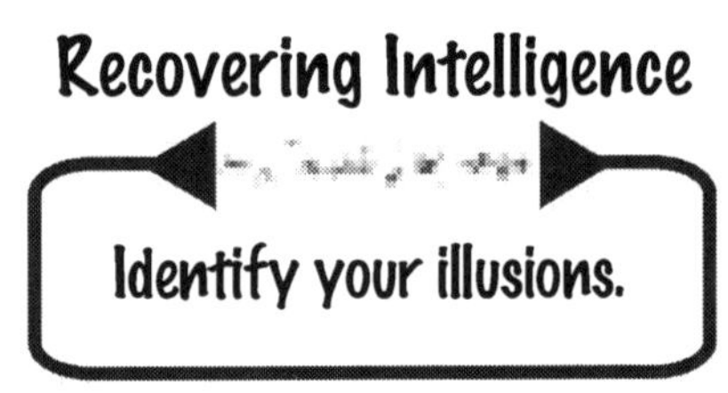

okay to indulge in it while I'm getting through early recovery from my addiction of choice."

- "My family knows me, and they're the best people to help me through this." Even worse if they know nothing about recovery and have been the "co."
- "Starting a new romantic relationship helps by giving me support and a positive focus while I'm dealing with early recovery stuff."

Illusions involve magical thinking, the belief that there's a connection between what you think is true and what is actually true. Counter the seductiveness of magical thinking by doing things in real, concrete ways – thoughtfully focus on information received in recovery, call the phone numbers you get at meetings, and really get to know people before and after meetings.

Recovery is reality based. An illusion can be a relapse trigger or symptom and set you up to use. What are your illusions?

Immediate Reward

Learning to delay pleasure is a huge challenge after practicing immediate gratification for so long. Practice delaying rewards. Start small and build up. Use the tools and strategies you have in your tool box. Then, when the urge comes to return to your old addictive substance or behavior, you'll be much more prepared.

Inner Critic

Your inner critic is the voice in your head that can insult you, guilt you, or shame you by directing you to focus on your faults, shortcomings, and past mistakes. This causes you pain, weakens your good efforts, and blocks you from getting what you want. Your inner critic is an accumulation of negative feedback about your past actions and how you have wounded others. It is the nag that never shuts up about all the wrongs you have committed in your entire life.

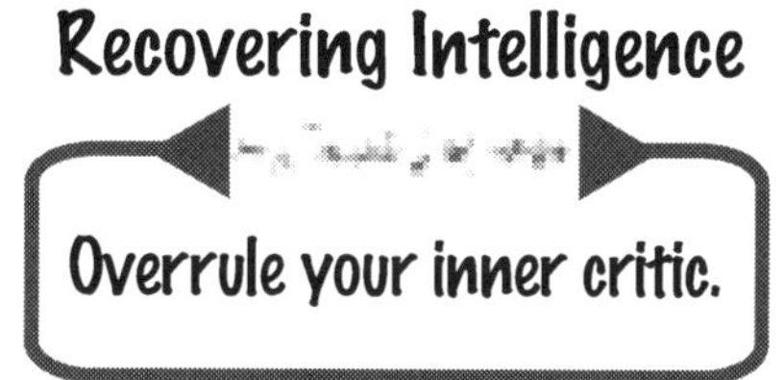

Listen but don't believe what your inner critic is telling you, or it will derail you from your recovery! Manage it by setting yourself up with a quality recovery program. Stay aware that your thoughts, feelings, and actions positively affirm who you want to be and how you want to live your life. Remember, don't believe everything you think!

Insecurity

Insecurity is about doubt, uncertainty, and inadequacy. Psychologically, it arises from your acceptance of negative programming and your refusal to acknowledge your strengths and talents. Spiritually, it's a disconnection with who you really are.

As you grow in your recovery, you can leave your old,

insecure addict self behind. Through positive feedback from valued others, you'll learn to believe you have value. Confidence will naturally build, one step at a time. Gradually, you'll accomplish your tasks, goals, milestones, and dreams. Still, at times you may have to consciously overrule your inner critic and affirm your self-worth!

Isolation

Isolation is lack of social contact to avoid dealing with your problems and issues. This is common in addiction and leads to being stuck in mental-emotional relapse or using. In recovery, you must move past your discomfort, fear, or insecurities and reach out to connect with positive and supportive others. Spend some time alone doing positive activities, but never isolate!

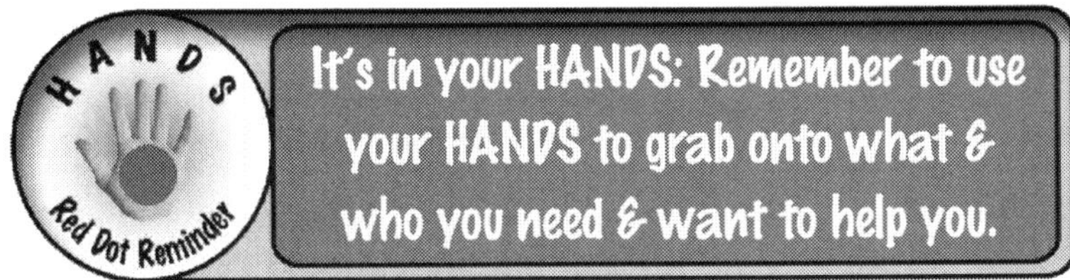

Legal Issues

If you have legal issues as a result of using, satisfy your legal obligations and clean up the wreckage of your past. For some people, court-mandated requirements can be a useful but imposing form of motivation. It's what gets some people to take a look at reality and stop their addiction.

Loneliness

Loneliness is a state of mind. It comes from a disconnection from yourself, others, the world, and the Source. If you were connected, you would not feel lonely or alone. No matter what, you always have yourself, so get to know the inner you. Start by listening to your inner thoughts, and exploring and applying what you learn to your life. Then connect to others by showing an interest in them. Even if you have no friends or family, you can have new recovering friends. Choose connection – not loneliness.

Lying

Lying is common in addiction, especially those that are illegal. Lying hurts your self-esteem, self-image, your recovery, and your relationships. Practice rigorous honesty, unless it would bring unnecessary harm to others. Live your life so you have no reason to lie.

Manipulation

Some addicts have become skillful masters at manipulating others for their own advantage. Hopefully in recovery, that will be unacceptable to you. Pay attention and respect your and others' boundaries, feelings,

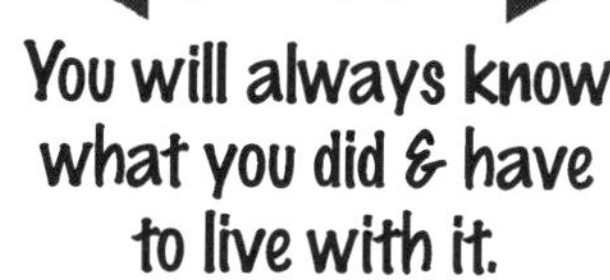

desires, and needs. Also, pay attention to your addict self attempting to manipulate you to use.

Maybe Now

After a period of time in recovery, it's easy to forget that your addiction caused you many problems. With this forgetfulness often comes the thought, "I am not really an addict!" or "I've had enough recovery that, maybe now, I can use." Resist "maybe now" thinking and the temptation that comes along with it to experiment for the sake of seeing if you really are an addict. "Maybe now" thinking comes and goes. Stay committed to your recovery, and remember the reality about your addiction.

More & Better

More and better is the need for external things in a much larger amount and higher quality than they already are. Called *other-esteem*, you may desire more and better to help you feel better about yourself. It's a facade, an artificial and deceptive front which helps you present yourself to the world in a manner that hides who you really are. More and better can momentarily appear to fill up the deep, empty hole in your psyche and raise your self-esteem, but this is short-lived because it's based on the external and not the internal. More and better even has a motto: "It's not about who you are, it's about what you have and how you look."

Accept that just because you can have more and better things, looks, and experiences in your life, it doesn't mean you should or that your life will be improved. If you connect with yourself, your life, and your Higher Power from the inside out, you will realize that an internal focus can lead to a greater satisfaction and happiness than focusing on the external could ever provide.

Recovery is an inside job. Focus on being satisfied with who and where you are, and be open to the gifts of recovery that are "more" and "better" than expected!

My Way In My Time

Many of us want to create our own recovery program. We don't want to follow the tried and true paths of recovery because they are "too strict," "make me give up all my using friends," and "require meeting attendance." Hanging onto illusions such as, "Willpower can keep me abstinent," can also encourage us to live our own program.

Your fears, your ego, your control issues, and your desire to continue to use provide rationales for "doing it my way." It's a very wise person who follows recovery suggestions. It was your own thinking that got you to where you ended up in your addiction, so relying on the wisdom of your recovery resources might be a much more prudent way to replace *stinkin' thinkin'*.

"Others" Focus

There is a certain self-centeredness that coexists with addiction. In active addiction, the world is all about you. "When can *I* engage in my addiction?" "My addiction is causing problems in our relationship? Well, *I* can't stop!" The emphasis you have put on yourself in addiction must be refocused onto other people. If you struggle with this idea, look at it as the new way that you want to relate to others.

Focus on:

- Being in the present and focused on listening to whomever you are speaking with.
- Doing recovery service for other addicts, like providing a ride to a meeting, supporting a newcomer, or making the coffee at your recovery group.
- Volunteering in your community at a soup kitchen, an animal shelter, or by walking a neighbor's dog.

Don't focus on:

- Feedback given by people who have no knowledge about addiction or recovery.
- The opinions of your using friends about recovery or your life issues.
- Your judgments about another person's addictions or their recovery program.

Oversensitivity

When you are being oversensitive, you excessively respond to or are aware of your emotions. Oversensitivity usually manifests when you are feeling fearful, suffering from low self-esteem, or are experiencing depression. Often, you feel like you have no control over your emotions and are unable to manage them. Therefore, the goal in overcoming oversensitivity is to regulate your emotions.

When you have extended periods of being oversensitive, serious problems can arise. Monitor to see if you're:

- Too emotionally open and vulnerable.
- Experiencing a lot of negative emotions.
- Unable to adjust your emotions.

Personality

Starting in childhood, your personality is influenced by genetics, life experiences, and the choices you make, including years of practiced adaptive and maladaptive behaviors, inner thoughts and emotions, interpersonal relating, control of (or lack thereof) impulses, and natural temperament. In addiction, many of us have personality traits that deviate markedly from those accepted by our culture. This can cause significant distress.

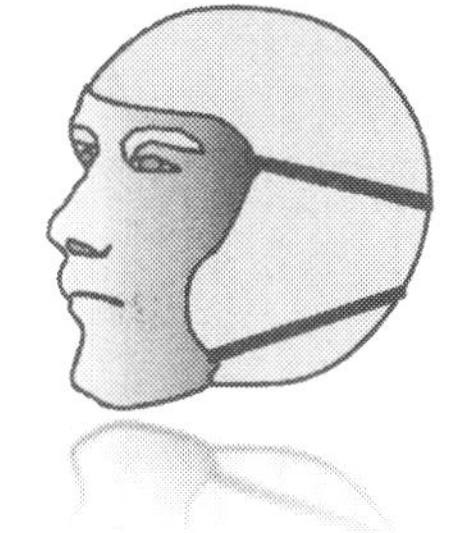

If parts of your personality feel uncomfortable or false, chances are you have adopted non-authentic personality traits to help you mask your inner self. Maybe you developed them to take on a presentation of how you think others want you to be. Maybe you adapted yourself to fit in with your environment. These non-authentic personality traits are not permanent. In recovery, your personality may return to its original state.

Returning your personality traits to their original state will take some time and effort. You will benefit greatly from observing yourself and others and trying new behaviors. To be successful at changing addict characteristics, you have to make a commitment that is similar to your recovery commitment. You have to commit to be open and not defensive, to be curious, self-observing, and willing to change those personality components that aren't serving you well.

The goal of recovery from the negative personality traits we develop from long-term addiction is to have our inner self and outer self match. Therefore, you will need to change the way you interact with your day, the people around you, and the situations you face. Observe yourself objectively to grasp how others perceive you. You will benefit by writing down what you see and where you think you need to change. What will you need to alter in order to feel good about your behavior?

Many in recovery say they have an addictive personality. Research does not support this belief. There are much more specific aspects that play a part in addiction. An inherited predisposition or tendency toward addiction can be the result of genetics. The reward system, the way pleasure is processed in the brain, can be permanently changed from exposure to addiction; this is especially true of drugs and alcohol. Addictions can become habit from years of practice and reinforcement. All of these can influence why someone becomes addicted. Managing key aspects, like how you reward yourself, can facilitate healthy personality changes.

Personality components:

Childhood: The more intense your childhood was, the more it influenced your personality and way of being in the world. Those with traumatic childhoods will likely have personality traits that are protective, avoidant, dependent, and needy. If you are like many addicts, you will feel enthusiastic about working through your childhood issues and want to start immediately. A word of caution! WAIT until you have a firm recovery foundation.

Recovering Intelligence

You need your ego to run your life, but you need to keep your ego in check for your life to run well.

Ego: Your ego is the sense of self which is distant from other people and the world in general. It enables you to be a thinking, feeling, conscious being who is distinguishable from others. It lets you know that there is a YOU within. Egos can often be inflated so that people become prideful and self-important, like the "control freak." Egos can also be small and diminished so that people become passive and non-assertive. In recovery, figure out the state of your ego and whether or not it needs adjustment.

Temperament: Your temperament is an aspect of your personality. It can be scientifically explored by measuring your irritability, activity, frequency of smiling, and by determining if you have an approachable or avoidant nature when you find yourself in unfamiliar situations. Temperament is also defined by traits such as introversion or extroversion. If parts of your temperament have led you to your addiction, examine what you would like to modify and make a plan for how you want to change it.

Child State: A child state refers to adults behaving, feeling, and thinking in a manner that is similar to how they did in childhood. Sometimes, a child state which has never been satisfied is called King or Queen Baby because, in an attempt to have their needs met, adults act in an infantile or childlike manner.

Most addicts carry with them inner wounds from childhood. The Wounded Child manifests in adult life through feelings of being unsafe, unvalued, and unloved. In recovery, become aware of your behavior and determine if it's mimicking how you navigated through challenges in your childhood. These wounds require healing with therapy.

Personality traits that may need changing in recovery:

Grandiosity: Many addicts display an unrealistic sense of superiority. They appear to deem themselves better than others and view others with disdain or as inferior. In truth, grandiosity most often stems from overcompensating for low self-esteem or an underdeveloped sense of self. This can result in a demand for immediate gratification through extreme feelings of power and self-importance.

Immaturity: When addiction begins at an early age, emotional development doesn't mature because addiction and addictive behaviors block emotional growth and breed immaturity. If you began using marijuana to a large degree at age 12, for example, you greet the world with 12-year-old emotions and thinking – even at 50! You can develop maturity by watching and discussing with mature others how they would handle various situations. Then practice what you learn. Eventually, you may bring up your emotional age to match your chronological age.

Paranoia: Paranoia is a thought process based on anxiety and fear. It often leads to irrationality and delusions. Paranoid thinking typically includes beliefs of being persecuted or conspiracy concerning a perceived threat towards yourself.

In addiction, out of fear of being discovered, it is easy to believe you are constantly being watched, which can lead to becoming irrational. In recovery, when there is nothing to hide, paranoid thinking often declines or ends.

Rebelliousness: Rebelliousness against not only authority but everyone and everything else, even yourself, can be expressed in self-destructive ways, like using. This can be an outgrowth of unmet childhood needs.

Self-consumed thinking: Being so self-focused that there is a lack of concern for others is self-consumed thinking. This type of thinking is rampant in addiction. Practice self-awareness, and when you notice you are self-consumed, choose to stop, step back, and refocus on how you can be of service to others.

Physical Care

Pay attention to the physical care of your body. Your physical appearance indicates outwardly how you feel about yourself mentally and emotionally. When you are cleaned up and looking your best, you feel better inside, making you more able to take on issues while living your life fully. In addition, others will relate to you in a more positive way.

More importantly, taking care of your brain, bones, muscles, and other parts of your mind and body will accelerate your recovery.

Learn about your:

- Brain and body: (See APPENDIX 3.)
- Mouth: See a dentist or physician.
- Stomach and intestines (GI tract): Gather

information about how good bacteria can help your GI tract, and contact your physician to ask about probiotic supplements or eating foods that contain probiotics.

Preoccupation & Obsession

Preoccupation refers to excessive concern and constant thoughts about one thing. Obsession is uncontrolled and compulsive preoccupation. A tendency to be preoccupied or obsessed is less of a negative when used constructively. Choose to focus on the positives in your life – finding solutions to your issues, achieving goals, helping others, etc. – as you work towards **Your Recovering Future™**.

In the extreme, preoccupation and obsession (Obsessive Compulsive Disorder) can be a big problem. It can lead you to resist your recovery and fixate on why you need to participate in your addiction. Psychotherapy is usually helpful. Often, brain chemistry needs to be adjusted either through nutritional remedies or medication. Consult a mental health professional and possibly a nutritionist for evaluation.

Pride

Having genuine pride in your real accomplishments and self-respect for who you are is great, but pride is too often based on lies or illusions to boost up your ego, known as false pride. Be proud of yourself for being in recovery, living a good and full life, and walking your talk. Let go of false pride. People can see right through it, and the lies and illusions you tell yourself will sabotage your recovery. If achieving personal success does not help you develop genuine pride and self-esteem, there is likely an underlying issue you need to work on.

Psychological Problems

In many cases, the mental, emotional, psychological, or psychiatric symptoms people have in early recovery are due to their past addictive behaviors, especially with alcohol and drugs. With sustained abstinence, these symptoms will often fade. In some cases, they will go away sooner with short-term use of medication. However, sometimes they don't go away, or they get worse without medication.

In early recovery, it's difficult to diagnose psychological

HANDS Red Dot Reminder

It's in your HANDS: Handle All Negative & Disabling Symptoms, use effective tools and strategies!

problems because so many of them are induced by substance use. To assist you in determining whether or not a psychological symptom is due to your addiction or to brain chemistry, you have to buy yourself some time. Implement techniques such as deep breathing, self-awareness, exercise, journaling, meditation, and prayer to get you through the abstinence period necessary to separate addiction-induced symptoms that are lingering from true psychological problems. Nutritional supplements may also be helpful.

The combination of addiction and psychological issues is called *dual diagnosis*. If you have been drug free for at least six weeks and are still experiencing psychological challenges, get professional help. If you had a preexisting psychological issue before you started using, especially drugs or alcohol, let your physician know.

Our culture is firmly embedded on the assumption that a pill is the best way to treat any and all physical and psychological problems. While there are many positives to this medical model, there are also some alternative options – ones that don't involve prescribed medication and its potentially negative side effects. A combination of psychotherapy with nutritional and self-help approaches, such as breathing, meditation, 12-Step programs, and movement work, can be very helpful. Psychotherapy can be effective for most problems without side effects, yet there are some exceptions, especially severe mental illness, where pharmaceuticals are the best or only answer.

Recovering Intelligence

Many people have psych issues. What are you doing about yours?

Common mental health challenges in recovery include:

- Anger about not being a "normie;" about having to give up your addiction, your friends, and the life that you have known; anger regarding family and friends.
- Anxiety is very common. There are many different

types of anxiety including panic and phobias. Be mindful that withdrawals, cravings, hunger, lack of sleep, and loneliness can all feel like anxiety.

- Bipolar Disorders (previously called Manic-Depression) come with emotional highs and lows. Symptoms can be mild or extreme and sometimes include psychosis, a disconnection from reality. The highs and lows of behavioral and substance addictions can initially present themselves as a bipolar disorder.
- Compulsiveness is a strong desire or urgent need to DO something. It's the behavioral aspect of obsessiveness, the carrying out of the obsessive thought.
- Obsessiveness is a powerful need to think about something a lot. It's usually paired with compulsion, as in Obsessive Compulsive Disorder.
- Depression is the condition of feeling sad, despondent, and often vegetative. At one time or another, many people experience depression, usually due to a temporary situation. For those in early recovery, it's common to feel sad about having to give up one's addiction. A depressive disorder is diagnosed when you feel depressed for a couple of months for no reason. It can be mild to unbearable and is often caused by a neurotransmitter imbalance.
- Impulsiveness is the need to act now, without thought or regard for possible consequences.
- Mind racing is fast thinking that is out of control.

- Personality disorders are extreme behavorial styles that impair social or occupational functioning. Such behaviors can result in poor coping skills, which may lead to personal and life problems, inducing extreme anxiety, distress, or depression. There are many types of personality disorders. (Find *Personality* in the Index.)
- Psychosis is loss of contact with reality. Sometimes, psychosis can be caused by consuming a substance. If so, the person will come back to reality once the substance leaves their system. Otherwise, psychosis should be treated with medication.
- Self-harm (self-mutilation, self-inflicted violence) is moderate to severe injury like cutting, burning, or hitting that someone inflicts on his or herself. It may appear that the person is trying to commit suicide, but in actuality, in most cases it's a way to relieve frustration and anxiety. They experience temporary relief from emotional pain through distraction and through brain produced endorphins, due to the injury.

Reacting

Your gut reaction or overreaction to stimulus is often due to a past event or person. At times, you must react to an immediate, here-and-now situation, such as a matter that requires fight or flight. When you respond to something, it's with thought after weighing the options, but when you react, it's without thought.

Regret

Regret is the feeling of shame, depression, or guilt after acting in a manner you later wish you had not. With regret, there is usually an element of self-anger. Regret is about the past, which can't be changed. Grieve your losses, and refocus on the present and your future. Make decisions based on love and joy, not fear or regret. If you are in a 12-Step program, you will learn how to let go of regret.

Remorse

Remorse is closely linked with guilt and self-directed resentment. It's the pain of accepting responsibility for your past actions. While those of us in recovery must acknowledge the harm to others that came from our addictive behaviors, it's unhealthy to live in remorse. You cannot reverse the past. You must forgive yourself and focus on the present. Your life may depend on it!

Resentments

Resentment involves the memory of real or imagined wrongdoing. It is often sparked by expressions of injustice or humiliation. Thinking about resentments can elicit negative emotions including anger and hatred.

Discuss your resentments with a recovery mentor who has shown wisdom in such matters. Make a plan outlining how to get rid of each resentment. Look at your part in each situation.

This can be very difficult due to our natural inclination to be right! Forgive, apologize, let go, and move on from your resentments so that you have more energy for the more important things in life.

Rigidity

Rigidity, being firmly fixed or unyielding, presents an obstacle to problem solving. There is an over-dependence on prior experiences. If we make our future reliant on the beliefs and practices of the past, we will never be open to change. Rigidity blocks being sensitive, open, aware, flexible, and adaptive, all of which are traits that help in happy, healthy, and successful living.

Recovering Intelligence

Rigidness limits your options, flexibility, & adaptability.

There is one positive to being rigid in early recovery. It's *structural rigidity*. Once you have a recovery plan, don't deviate from it. Practice rigid honesty in all your affairs. Be rigid about attending your recovery meetings and therapy appointments. Be rigid about your abstinence from your addiction. In your addiction, you likely had flexible structure or maybe no structure for how you lived your life. For sustained recovery, you must change this old way of living. At least for a while, live in a rigid recovery structure so you don't return to the chaos of addiction.

Shame

Shame is the hurt that comes from thinking that you've

done something dishonorable, improper, or ridiculous. It's accompanied by feeling disgraced by yourself or another person. Shame also comes from fear that your personality flaws and defects will be found out by others and exposed for all to see.

There is healthy shame and toxic shame. Healthy shame is when you feel negative emotions over an action you took or for hurting someone. That feeling tells you that you went against your personal or accepted social values, and it signals to you that you need to make amends and rectify the situation.

Recovering Intelligence

Toxic shame must be carefronted, processed, & resolved.

Toxic shame is when you allow yourself to be defined by a weakness over which you have no control. It dictates that your weakness is your identity. Toxic shame tells its holder that not only are their actions defective, but they are defective as a person as well.

To diminish your shame, start by openly sharing your flaws and defects with a trusted person. Develop healthy boundaries by learning to say no. Acknowledge that you are okay as a person, even though you said no. If you are dealing with core, toxic shame, find a professional to work with, if possible.

State Learning Disability

People who drank constantly still learned new skills while intoxicated. Skills learned while under the influence may not be remembered when sober and may need to be relearned. What did you learn while under the influence that has become a part of your life?

Style

Style is your manner of presentation. This is especially important if your presentation is connected to: 1) your addiction, a sub-group culture, or to being highly social; or 2) your personality and sense of self.

Examine how you want to present yourself to the world, your community, and your family. Create a new recovering style in your behavior, dress, and attitude; embrace a different appearance, one more positive and friendly, yet real.

Taking Other People's Inventory

Unwanted judgments about another person's program can undermine their recovery. Your opinions can appear to be helpful, but they may be more about distracting you from looking at yourself and your own program of recovery. Codependents are masters at taking other people's inventory because doing so feeds into their need for fixing, rescuing, and controlling. Ask for agreement before you give feedback toward someone else's recovery program, and then refocus on yourself. (Find *Codependency* in the Index.)

Vocational Issues

You work for money but also for personal satisfaction. Personal satisfaction comes from how you perceive your work. Focus on the gratifying aspects of what you do.

After your recovery foundation is strong, you may want to explore how you're going to earn a living until you retire. Does your career pay you adequately and give you personal satisfaction? If unemployed or wanting to change careers, network with your recovery community. Consider taking the career-oriented strengths assessment, StrengthsFinder 2.0, to help figure out the best vocational path for you.

Workplace Issues

It's important for your workplace to be supportive, or at least not toxic, to your recovery. It's not supportive if there is drinking at lunch, free donuts, no enforcement of smoking laws, or gambling activities, if those are your addictions. If your workplace undermines your recovery, ask for support. Change the situation, your job, or even your field of work. Your life is more important than a job.

Some workplace environments are required by law to assist or promote the rehabilitation of employees who have an addiction problem. Many companies have an Employee Assistance Program (EAP). If you have EAP staff available to you, make use of their confidential services; they are connected to resources and can get you the help you need.

PHYSICAL ASPECTS

Consider: **"In My Experience...you don't want poor sleep, extreme stress, and bad nutrition."** (See APPENDIX 7.)

Aftermath

Even if only from stress, your addictive behaviors have hurt you physically. High-quality exercise, nutrition, relaxation, sleep, etc. is required for maximum regeneration. For substance abusers, your brain and nervous system needs high-quality nutrition. Complete rejuvenation can take months to years.

Brain

Your brain is you! Your mind uses it to function. It's 60% fat and cholesterol, weighs about 3 pounds, and is the consistency of Jello. It has the ability to grow and adapt forever. If you damage your brain, you don't get another. Would you abuse your car engine and expect it to last?

Because of addiction, especially to substances, your brain has permanent changes to its reward system – the way pleasure is processed in the nucleus accumbens. Your addicted brain will try to manipulate and fool you into using again. This is because the brain has adapted itself into believing that its highest form of pleasure comes from you using. It will overrun your willpower, undermine your resolve, and sabotage your recovery. This is why you need a rigid recovery structure, a solid recovery foundation, and wise recovery support. With a solid recovery program, a lot of effort, and maybe the help of skilled professionals, you can nurture your brain and body back to health and

Recovering Intelligence

Your brain is vital, so keep it safe. Treat it right & feed it well.

rewire it for success.

The main problem in overcoming addiction has to do with how the brain processes information. The old, emotional, instinctual part of the brain, the limbic system, can communicate to the rational part, the frontal cortex, but the rational brain has a difficult time communicating back to the limbic system, which is much more reptilian, pleasure-seeking, and survival-focused. This is why you need to override your instinctual brain by practicing new, recovery-focused behavior. The good news is that your brain has the ability to change and grow as a result of your experiences and the new behaviors that you practice. This ability is known as neuroplasticity.

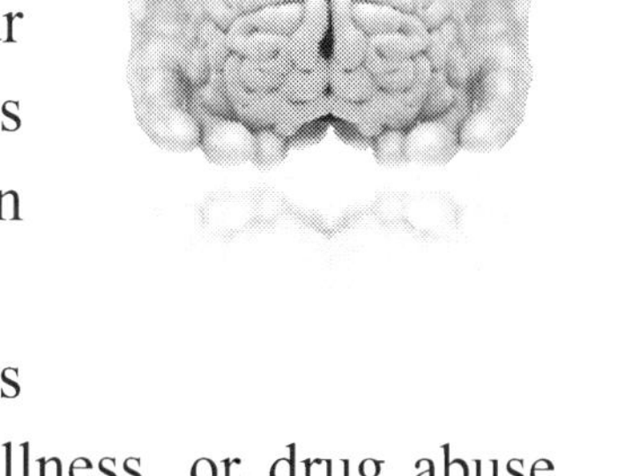

Brain Injury: Brain injury is generally due to a concussion, an illness, or drug abuse. Many people have had some level of brain injury and never realized it. Even minor accidents can cause an injury. For example, bouncing a soccer ball on your head can do damage. Be mindful to take care of your brain. Remember, your brain is you!

If your addiction has been to drugs, your brain has been neglected, abused, and even traumatized. Depending on your drug(s) of choice, your neurotransmitters were firing off between 40 and 2000 times their normal rate. This not only depletes them, but it can cause anxiety, depression, an inability to feel pleasure, and other mental health issues.

Brain trauma changes the structure of how the brain

Recovering Intelligence

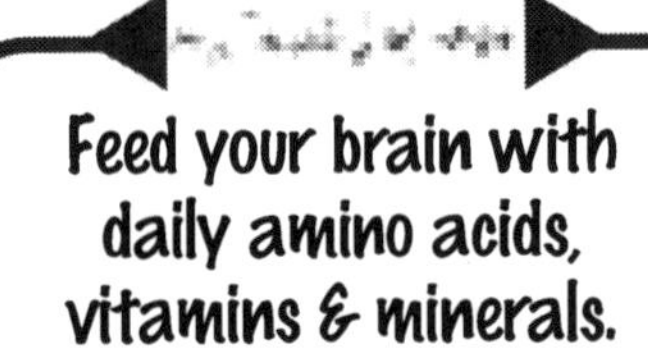

works. After a trauma, your brain can become overly sensitive and overreact to stimulation. Stimulating situations often become difficult to deal with. Many self-medicate by turning to drugs for relief and become addicted in the process. If this happens to you, seek professional help.

<u>Brain Healing</u>: Brain damage apparently can be helped, even reversed, through nutrition, mental exercise, therapeutic work, spiritual intervention, and Hyperbaric Oxygen Therapy. Get your blood flowing by exercising, drinking alkaline water, and reducing stress.

Amino acid supplements work like brain food, especially amino-nutritional blends. (See APPENDIX 3 & 10 and always consult your physician.)

The stomach is called your second brain because it produces more brain chemicals than the brain does. Consider taking digestive enzymes to help it function correctly.

Set yourself up for success by using a reminder system like the Red Dot Check-In System. It will assist in reminding you to support your brain in its recovery.

<u>Brain Training</u>: There are many options to help you develop your brain. Investigate computerized exercise games, acupuncture-based tools, and any common brain-stimulating activities, such as crossword puzzles. Doing new activities will generate new brain pathways and challenge your brain to grow and stay fit.

Note: If after 6 months clean you believe your brain still isn't working right, consider nutritional supplements, a nutritional consultation, and neurological tests, and even a (SPECT) brain scan, especially with drug addiction. (See APPENDIX 10.)

Illness

Illness is usually caused by disease or by stress. Increase the quality of how you treat your body, including learning to deal with stress, and you will become healthier. Some people seem to have more physical illnesses after they enter recovery than before. Generally, this is an illusion based on having neglected your health while you were in your addiction. It could also be the stress you experience due to how you relate to being in recovery.

Even if you feel healthy, it's possible you have a physical condition that has not yet presented symptoms. Blood tests may be in order, including the test for hepatitis and HIV. Also consider testing your blood for heavy metals and toxic substances, especially military veterans. Early testing is a smart decision for taking the best care of yourself. (See APPENDIX 10.)

Recovering Intelligence

Treat your body well & it will become healthier.

Nutrition

Everyone has a different opinion about what healthy eating is, but most people agree that what you eat has a significant impact on you and your life. Whatever you consider healthy eating to be, put it into practice. Consulting a nutritionist and even testing for food allergies will help you set up a food plan and decide which foods need to be eliminated from your diet.

According to experts, the average diet is inadequate or unhealthy to some degree. This is the source of many food addictions and physical illnesses. Additionally, toxins and pollutants, which block the proper digestion of food and the nutrition with it, can cause health complications.

Stabilizing Foods:

- Protein: 25-30 grams per meal
- Low carbohydrate vegetables: 4 cups a day
- Fat: Saturated 0-9, 0-3 GLA
- Higher whole carbohydrate foods: Limited

Your food plan should include fresh vegetables; fruits; honey rather than sugar or an alkaline substitute; fish, especially young fish like sardines and salmon; and more poultry than beef. Keep your intake of sugars, even fructose, minimal and carbohydrates, including whole grains, limited. Avoid fat, processed artificial foods, sugar, nicotine, and caffeine.

Processed foods have less nutrition and more chemicals than whole, fresh food. Organic foods have the most nutritional value and usually less toxins. A consistent and moderate style of eating will offer you stable and balanced energy levels. When making healthier food choices, research alternative ingredients to match your taste. Bake instead of fry; drink flavored water instead of sugary beverages. (Find *Nutrition* in the Index.)

Consider:

- Water: Flushing your body of toxins is very important, especially for substance abusers. Drink water daily, from 50 ounces to half your body weight in ounces (200 pounds = 100 ounces). But depending on your weight, drinking too much water can cause your body's electrolytes to be thrown off.
- Vitamins/minerals: It's believed everyone should take daily (cold-pressed, food state) multivitamin, mineral, and Vitamin C supplements.
- Nutritional supplements such as Omega 3 and antioxidants are valuable. There are also compounds specifically formulated for people in recovery from drug addiction.

A full nutritional work-up is desirable, especially if you have not been able to maintain abstinence, which could be due to food allergies, heavy metals, etc. Most people seldom know if they have issues like food allergies, nor do they know the negative effects these issues have on their life. You may blame your symptoms on other sources, and then rely on over-the-counter medications to subdue the symptoms, thereby putting additional substances into your body. If you think you might have a food allergy, stop eating the suspected food and consult an appropriate professional, such as an allergist or a nutritionist. (See APPENDIX 3.)

Physical Conditioning

Physical exercise is excellent therapy for general health, well-being, happiness, and stress reduction. Aerobics, building muscle tone, and developing balance and endurance

Recovering Intelligence

> Exercise increases your health, quality of life, self-esteem, & produces feel-good endorphins.

are all desirable for overall conditioning. Train at your chosen exercise for about 30 minutes, three or more days a week. Stretch before and after to prevent injury.

Get a physical exam from your physician before beginning any exercise routine. Recovering drug addicts, especially cocaine users may have developed various health problems that should be cleared before exercising. Exercise will increase your endorphins, which are neurotransmitters that naturally relieve pain. It will also accelerate the detoxification of fat-soluble drugs such as marijuana and PCP.

Physical Touch

Regular physical touch may increase your emotional and physical health. A pat on the back, a hug, and holding hands are all healthy and positive forms of communication. For many, physical touch feels good, relieves stress, and rejuvenates the spirit. Be aware of your emotional and physical need for touch, and attempt to have those needs met. Be clear that physical touch is different from sex. Some people don't like physical touch, so it is important that you ask a person before touching them. Try to receive a daily hug, handshake, massage, or just a pat on the back.

Prescription Medication

Prescription medications that cause euphoria or pleasure

should be prescribed limitedly, and you should use them with caution. Their potential for abuse and addiction is great. There may be effective and safer alternative options. Sometimes, the safer options are homeopathic and nutritional, especially amino acids, rather than the traditional medical and psychiatric options, but there can be issues concerning the quality of over-the-counter (OTC), unregulated nutritional products. Carefully research any product that is advertised as "natural."

Recovering Intelligence

Physical Touch: It feels so good & it's good for you. Do it a lot!

Sex

Sexual fulfillment is a powerful human need. In early recovery, particularly the first year or two, new romantic relationships are likely to cause problems and will distract you from your recovery. Consider waiting before entering a new romantic relationship. Use self-soothing or pleasuring activities instead. If you choose to be sexually active, be emotionally and physically cautious, such as the use of contraceptives, for the safety of both you and your sexual partner. Make sure the situation doesn't undermine your recovery.

If you fall in lust or love, a chemical response called the Love Sex Cocktail, which activates the neurotransmitter PEA, will make you feel high, especially when you're with or picturing the person. This

experience tells you the person is the right one for you, even if they aren't. The high will last about one to two years unless it is disrupted, so be very careful!

When you do choose to get involved in a relationship, or if you were already involved in a quality relationship before starting your recovery, make it a high priority but second to your recovery. Be careful you aren't using sex to avoid emotional intimacy or your recovery.

As you build your recovery, you will become more capable of emotional intimacy, which will enhance your sexual relationship. Professional guidance can be helpful. If both partners are in a 12-Step recovery program, consider joining Recovering Couples Anonymous.

Sleep

Experts say that you need 8 – 8½ hours of sleep a night. Sleep problems are quite common in addiction and recovery.

They are caused by poor sleep habits you have developed in order to cope with using dreams, emotional issues, brain chemistry imbalance, and possibly a brain or physical condition. Practice good sleep habits; let your body catch up on needed rest.

Don't take addictive sleep medications, because after even limited use, withdrawal from them can be difficult. Such medications block Rapid Eye Movement (REM) sleep and will stop you from dreaming. When you do withdraw from these medications, to compensate, REM will be more frequent, so you'll dream more for at least a week. Find *Detoxification* in the Index.

Solutions for Sleep Problems –

- Behavioral options include:
  - » Breathing: Take slow, deep breaths in through your nose, and exhale through your mouth. With each inhalation, count to four, hold for four, exhale for four, and repeat. This is called four-square breathing. It will distract you from other thoughts. Repeat 3 times.
  - » Progressive Relaxation: The practice of tightening and releasing all large muscle groups, from your feet up, is progressive relaxation. Tighten each muscle group for about 3 to 6 seconds, then release. Focus more on your head, neck, and face muscles, especially those around your eyes, by scrunching them together.
  - » Music: Play a meditation, New Age, or any kind of soft music or sounds from nature. Consider headphones or a speaker pillow.
  - » Stretching: Try slow, mild stretches for 5 minutes, just before you go to bed. Focus on your upper body, especially your shoulders and neck.
- Focusing:
  - » Focus with eyes open or closed; it's a personal choice.
  - » With eyes open:
    - ◊ Read slowly, maybe a hard-to-read book.

        - ◊ Stare at any one visual point. If your mind wanders, bring it back to your point of focus.
        - ◊ Don't multi task.
    - » With eyes closed:
        - ◊ Slowly count backwards from 100.
        - ◊ Focus on your slow breathing.
        - ◊ Meditate.
- Medical options: If you decide briefly using a medication is your best and only option, discuss their potential for addiction and abuse with your physician, especially if you abused drugs.
- Nutrition:
    - » Some holistic professionals recommend taking an amino acid supplement as the best option to induce sleep. Many people seem to be helped by taking certain foods and supplements.
    - » Foods: carbohydrates: unsweetened cereal, jasmine rice; crustaceans: shrimp, lobster; fish: halibut, salmon, tuna; raw garlic; tart cherry juice; dairy products: cheese, eggs, milk; meat: elk, dark turkey; nuts: almonds, pistachio, walnuts; flax seeds; chamomile tea with honey; vegetables: leafy greens like kale.
    - » Supplements:
        - ◊ Melatonin or serotonin, which converts into melatonin at night.
        - ◊ GABA, an amino acid, is a natural relaxer.
    - » An elevation of the stress hormone cortisol can play a part in insomnia. Apparently,

phosphorylated serine (not phosphatidyl), taken four hours before your cortisol levels rise, may help. Follow the directions on the bottle. To monitor its effectiveness, request cortisol level blood tests from your physician.

» For women, hormones can interfere with sleep. If you have tried the above suggestions and they haven't helped, discuss sleep interference with your physician.

Stress

Stress is your internal response to stressors in life. Major life stressors can include loss of a loved one, trauma, chronic pain, occupational stress such as work overload, and substance abuse. Stress causes many problems, including harm to your immune system.

In active addiction, you probably used to numb out your stress. In recovery, you MUST find a way to deal with your stressors, because the weight of stress is a major cause of relapse! (See *Stress Into Relaxation* in the Index.)

Toxins

There are toxic people, substances, and situations. Toxins are harmful or poisonous. They can be found everywhere, but you can reduce your exposure to emotional and physical toxins. Eliminate or reduce your association with toxic people – those who criticize, blame, and shame you. Practice reducing or neutralizing your response to their negative words or energy. Even with people you must interact with, like a boss or an in-law, there are ways to reduce the toxic effect they have on you.

Toxic People: When you're around toxic people, they can cause you to feel bad about yourself or your situation, draining your energy. Toxic people know how to push your buttons. Their complaints and manipulations can provoke anger and anxiety, if you allow it. In early recovery, it's important to stay away from the toxic people in your life and to focus on folk who are supportive of your recovery, strengths, and desire to change.

It can feel very scary to separate yourself from the familiar, even from toxic people and situations that you know are hurting you. People who tell you they are, "only trying to help you," or who encourage you to keep participating in your addiction. Toxic people can hold you as an emotional hostage if you allow them to. Reducing toxicity in your life requires setting boundaries about who you will allow in your recovery support circle.

In response to toxic people, consider the following:

- Ask for feedback from objective, valued others.
- If you are a sensitive person who is strongly affected by and takes on another's negativity, stay away from the toxic people in your life who cause you to feel negatively about yourself or your recovery.

- Learn strategies to protect yourself and neutralize the negativity.
  - » Pay attention to when you start feeling negative. To offset this, talk to yourself using positive affirmations, or physically separate yourself from the person or situation.
- Accept that you can't win. Even if you could, accept that it isn't worth it, and drop out of the "game."
- Carefront toxic people and their behavior, but only if you really want or need them in your life and believe they are open and capable of responding positively.
- Be pleasant and polite when you have to interact with them, but have a plan in place for emotional protection and support.
- If you choose to disconnect from a toxic person:
  - » Disengage and don't reengage; hold your boundaries, and if possible, eliminate them from your life. If you do interact, be pleasant, solution-focused, and outcome-oriented.

Toxic Substances include mind-altering substances, environmental pollutants, toxic products, medicines, and certain foods, even water in some geographical areas. Consider:

- Body: Cleansing your body of allergies, heavy metals, pesticides, etc. is important for long-term health and longevity.
- Cleaning Products: Use products marked, "100% Non-Bio Toxic," "100% Biodegradable," and "Safe

for Human Consumption."

- Environmental: Become aware of the many toxins in our food, water, air, and in the ground.
  - Other: Eliminate nicotine and caffeine. These substances can produce a "high" that mimics that of mind-altering chemicals.
- Foods: Reduce or eliminate fructose corn syrup like that in soft drinks, artificial sweeteners, and all processed foods and sugars. They are all toxic.
- Water: Get a good filter system for drinking water.

Toxic Situations are those that are high risk for relapse, those in which people around us are participating in an activity that goes against our value system, or those which elicit negative emotions. Practice neutralizing the toxicity of these situations or seriously consider leaving the situation altogether.

SUMMARY

This chapter contains a myriad of issues most of us face in addiction recovery. You'll want to acknowledge your issues and extinguish those which are self-created. If you don't, they will have a negative impact on your recovery. Do a personal inventory looking for:

- Addiction support issues
- Anger Issues
- Anxiety Issues
- Behavior issues

- Belief and attitude issues
- Family of origin trauma or history of abuse
- Family and relationship issues
- Interpersonal issues
- Mental health and emotional issues
- Personality style or defense style issues
- Physical, medical, or nutritional issues
- Secondary addictions
- Social issues
- Stress or stress-connected issues

If you can't deal with an issue yet, set yourself up to remember that you want to deal with it, as soon as possible.

Use this chapter to formulate your list. What causes you the greatest problem or most disruption? Is there one issue that requires immediate attention? Take one issue at a time, address it, discuss how to tackle it with your support group, find a solution, deal with it, and let it go. If you can't deal with issues yet, set yourself up: 1) to remember that you'll want to deal with immediate issues as soon as possible, and 2) if you have dealt with an issue, maintain that status.

Remember, dealing with the wreckage of your past is about progress, not perfection – one day at a time, even one baby step at a time.

Chapter 6

Continuing Recovery: Personal Growth

Chapter 6: Continuing Recovery – Personal Growth Table of Contents

PERSONAL GROWTH

Personal growth will improve your awareness, expand your identity, develop your strengths, enhance the quality of your life, and help you create **Your Recovering Future™**. The course you take to evolve as an individual can occur at any time and any place, be it a formal event or during a fun and playful activity. Embrace the gift of personal growth, and you will discover what a full life means to you.

MENTAL-EMOTIONAL HEALTH

Like the rest of life, living through addiction and recovery will bring with it many intense mental and emotional experiences. In recovery, it's time for you to:

- Get to know and use your character strengths, positive traits, and personal intelligences.
- Learn to feel, identify, and deal with your emotions.
- Open up and develop your mental awareness.

To be able to experience positive emotions, you must be willing to feel the negative ones. This is because the same channels that carry pain also carry excitement, joy, and love. Your addiction may have numbed your pain

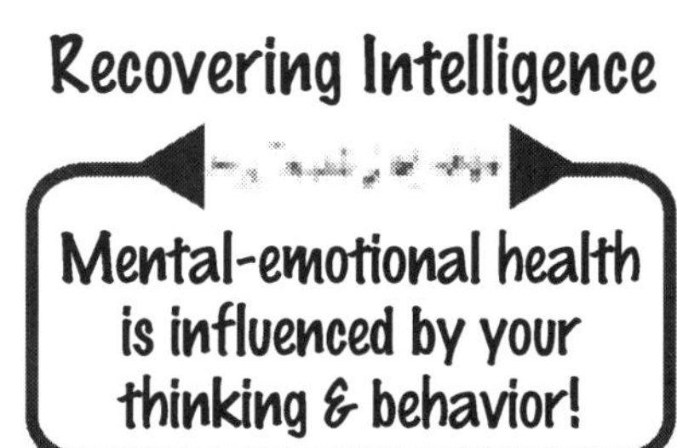

for a while, but it also kept you disconnected from your other feelings. At the beginning of your recovery, you'll experience those painful emotions and sensations that you have become an expert at numbing. Learn to identify and share them appropriately. A growth-oriented recovery program will make it easier for you to deal with emotions, process your pain, and move you toward healing.

As you open up and start exploring, make and grow a list of desirable activities you think would benefit you. Do you need to adjust your eating habits, add an exercise program, eliminate a secondary addiction, become a meditator, or maybe enlist a mentor? Recovery is mostly a mental and emotional process, but improving your relationships and your physical and spiritual health will promote your wellness.

It's important to note that while changing your lifestyle, your emotional health might feel worse before it gets better. This is normal. Change happens slowly and not always in a forward direction. Strive to stay motivated and build momentum.

In recovery, a healthy curiosity is valuable. This may be unsettling because, for many of us, unhealthy exploring led to us engaging in our addictions and other problems. But living your healthy recovery will help you resist the temptation to indulge in negative behaviors and keep you focused on exploring and learning new, positive ways of being in the world. Be curious about how you'll move through the recovery maze and create **Your Recovering Future™**.

Consider: **"In My Experience... you don't want your emotions to dominate you."** (See APPENDIX 8.)

Mental and Emotional Conditions

A mental and emotional illness is commonly known as a mental health issue. Many mental health issues involve brain chemistry imbalance and genetics. Others can be influenced by poor nutrition and negative behavioral patterns. Below is a review of some disorders that can be amplified by addictions, especially drugs. Symptoms of anxiety, depression, and psychosis that are drug induced will fade by 6 weeks. Be alert to any evidence of the following syndromes so that you can find assistance with how to best approach your recovery and personal growth.

Recovering Intelligence

Take mental illness very seriously - seek help & listen to informed others.

- Attention Deficit Disorder (ADD) is a brain condition that presents several different clusters of symptoms. The major symptoms are restlessness, impulsiveness, and distractibility. Thus, one's ability to focus is usually impacted. Hyperactivity may also be involved.
- Bipolar is a mood disorder characterized by episodes of high energy (manic) and low energy (depression). Moods swings may also include oversensitivity, irritation, and inaccurate thinking. If your mood swings disrupt your life, consider psychiatric medications.

Nutritional products could also potentially be effective.

- Conduct Disorder is a repetitive pattern of behavior where the rights of others or social norms are violated with aggressive, cruel, and destructive behaviors. Primarily a diagnosis for adolescents.
- Depression is a common feeling. Clinical or Major Depression is more debilitating and is accompanied by symptoms of hopelessness, immobility, inadequacy, sadness, and lack of interest or vitality. Suicidal thoughts can be present.
- Learning Disabilities are neurological conditions that interfere with a person's ability to store, process, or produce information. Having a learning disability is not related to high or low intelligence.
- Panic Attacks are sudden feelings of intense fear or anxiety. These feelings are accompanied by palpitations or an accelerated heart rate, sweating, shaking, shortness of breath, and chest pain. These symptoms usually peak within 10 minutes.
- Panic Disorder is defined as recurrent, sudden, and unexpected panic attacks.
- Personality Disorders are deeply ingrained, poorly adaptive patterns of behavior and personality style. They often cause personal and work problems.
- Phobias are persistent, irrational, and extreme fears of an object or an activity, which leads to avoidance.
- Post-Traumatic Stress Disorder (PTSD) is caused by an unusual and serious traumatic event, such as a major accident, an attack, or a natural disaster.

Symptoms include reliving the event, reduced involvement with others, and autonomic arousal, such as being hyper-alert and having an exaggerated startle response. PTSD can present itself when there is a threat of or an actual physical injury to yourself or someone close to you.

- Psychotic or Thought Disorders: Psychosis is a moderate to extreme disconnection from reality. Schizophrenia, the most well-known in this group, is a genetic brain condition with symptoms like loose, disconnected thinking and hallucinations.

If you suspect that a mental health issue is affecting you and/or your recovery, seek professional treatment. There are a variety of effective treatments for almost all disorders. You should be well served by psychotherapy and other medical options combined with personal support and feedback from your recovery and mental health community, self-help groups, family, and faith community.

To monitor your mental health, consider keeping a journal or a log to write down your response to specific situations, including your behavior, attitude, and feelings, as well as any triggers you are aware of. See if there are any patterns that may clarify or explain the issues you're having.

Eliminate or reduce your intake of sugar, processed foods, caffeine, and nicotine. To repair, balance, heal, and sustain your brain's health, try amino acids, nutritional supplements, and quality foods.

Neurotransmitters' Effect on Mental-Emotional Health

Food, drugs, sugar, caffeine, fat, protein, exercise, and sleep all influence your brain's production of neurotransmitters, which play a crucial part in your mental-emotional health. It's important that you have a working knowledge of how all these substances interact in your brain. (See APPENDIX 3.)

Emotional Feelings

Humans appear to have innate primary emotions. The negative ones are anger, disgust, fear, sadness, and shame. The positive ones are enjoyment, love, and surprise. All other emotions are variations or a blend of these.

In recovery, you need to understand and work with your feelings, monitor the level of your emotional intensity, and gain control of your emotional life. Feelings are a feedback system; they are not good or bad, and they aren't the experience itself. Although your initial feelings toward recovery might be fear, this doesn't mean recovery or people in recovery should be feared.

Recovering Intelligence

A feeling isn't good or bad; avoiding feelings can work at first, but often hurts you later.

If you block your feelings because they are uncomfortable, you will lose valuable feedback and miss out on critical emotional development. Some people become stuck at the emotional and developmental age they were when they started using. The typical result of this

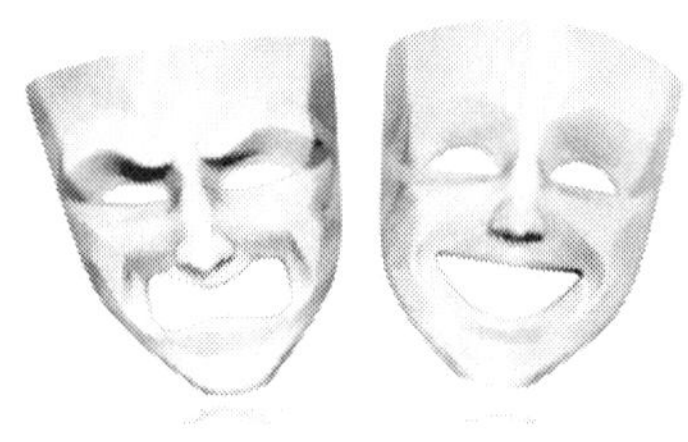

is significant immaturity and emotional limitations. In recovery, we learn how to facilitate emotional maturity.

When you are connected to your emotions, some perceptions can feel legitimate, even if they're not. If you act only from your feelings and ignore rational thinking, you can get stuck in those feelings and use emotional logic to make poor decisions. Your feelings (and your heart) should be felt and honored, but then use your intelligence to balance your emotions with logic, especially when making decisions. This is the most effective strategy. Further, when making important decisions, ask for feedback from valued others.

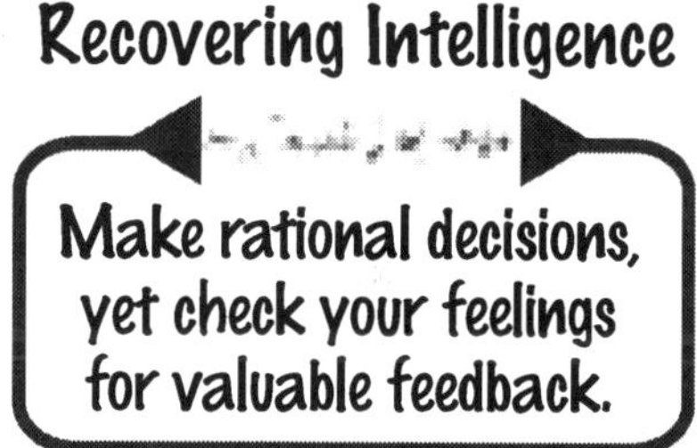

Intense Feelings

Intense feelings can put a lot of pressure on your body and brain. They can lead to emotional flooding which may overwhelm you and undermine your recovery. Drama, emotional relationships, and extreme activities can produce intense feelings. Consider whether you can or want to handle these situations.

Feeling Bad

Addiction is the only disease that tells the sufferer they don't have a disease. All thoughts that promote this lie are called *stinkin' thinkin'* (ST). Stinkin' thinkin' may be due to depression, poor nutrition, or adverse events, but usually it's mostly from your negative thinking patterns.

Negative Feelings: Negative feelings aren't bad; they are feedback about something that is wrong or not working. Pay attention to your negative feelings. Write them down and review them. Discuss them with trusted others. Keeping track of negative emotions may lead you to finding a solution to challenging situations. Covering up or blocking negative feelings may create a set-up for relapse.

Negative feelings, like anger, are often a cover for deeper, more painful emotions. Consistent self-focused work such as personal check-ins, reframing your thoughts, and receiving feedback from trusted others will help you access and process important emotions. If this doesn't improve your emotional life and relationships, consider professional help.

False Moods: Some nutrition-based addiction experts believe that poor nutrition can cause negative moods. There are four false mood types caused by a lack of specific nutrients, leading to underproduction of the neurotransmitters serotonin, catecholamines, GABA, and endorphins.

It has been found that low serotonin levels lead to obsessiveness, worry, irritability, sleeplessness, and eventually depression. Reduced amounts of catecholamines cause feelings of apathy and lack of energy. GABA is required for relaxation and release of stress, so with reduced GABA you feel wired, stressed, and overwhelmed. Depleted endorphins will contribute to tears and oversensitivity.

Because these moods are created by low neurotransmitter levels, they don't necessarily reflect your mental-emotional state. If you suffer from negative moods, consider increasing your nutritional intake of the appropriate amino acids.

"Act As If" and "Fake It 'Til You Make It" are strategies for offsetting stinkin' thinkin' and overcoming negative feelings about not getting what you want in life. They are catch phrases to remind you that imitating confidence will produce success until that confidence becomes real and natural. If you smile and think optimistically, you will feel better, and you will positively affect others, who'll in turn affect you. Here's how "Act As If" and "Fake It 'Til You Make It" can have an effect on negative emotions:

- Anger is a common, hurtful, and intense emotion. It's based on a belief you have been offended or wronged, but it's often a cover for deeper, more painful emotions. To "Act As If" when you're angry allows you to detach from the situation so you can consider your options in dealing with your anger. You can "fake" acceptance (not agreement) of what the other person said or did, giving yourself a chance to disconnect and talk out your thoughts and feelings with someone you trust and value.
- Contempt, disgust, and ridicule are opinions aimed at someone or something perceived to be inferior or unworthy. Manage such thoughts. Pretend that the person or situation you find disgusting doesn't

actually affect you. "Fake It" until the emotional power of your judgments gradually fade and you become more centered. Look at yourself and then look at the target's good points. This does not mean you can't have boundaries or standards regarding the behavior of others. It simply means that while you are moving away from negative thinking, put your contempt, disgust, and ridicule in a safe container until you can think about your judgments and how they serve or hinder your recovery. Where does empathy fit in?

- Drama distracts you from and undermines your recovery, and it can become an addiction in itself. In the drama triangle, people become victims, persecutors, or rescuers. If you stop playing the victim, the persecutor has no one to hurt, and the rescuer has no one to save. "Act As If" means not entering the game of giving advice, making suggestions, or saving someone from the consequences of their bad decisions. Exiting from someone else's drama, and accepting them for who they are, even if you have a great idea for them, assists you in detaching. "Act As If" it's none of your business, that YOU can't solve their problem... and in truth, that IS the TRUTH!
- Embarrassment is a brief and intense emotional experience of acute self-consciousness when a socially or professionally silly or unacceptable situation is witnessed by others. Embarrassment

proves your humanness, so accept, embrace, and make fun of it. "Fake It 'Til You Make It" enables you to acknowledge your blunder without having shame attached to it.

- Emptiness, at its worse, feels like a dark, bottomless, and emotionally painful internal pit. Fill this pit with healthy feelings, people, and experiences. Nothing outside of yourself can do it for you; only you can do it. You must open up and allow yourself to fill up with the positives of recovery. To fill up your emptiness through "Act As If," tell yourself that there is no man, woman, material item, amount of money, or addiction that will fill that seemingly empty space like your recovery will. And "Act As If" you believe it! Emptiness may be a symptom of depression. (Find *Depression* in the Index.)
- Fear is the most powerful negative emotion, but fear also helps you avoid negative situations. If you indulge in fear, you can become consumed by it, and it will block out positive experiences. You can create things to be fearful about by mentally traveling into the future and playing the "What If" game. When we indulge in this line of thought, we make up fearful scenarios that we believe COULD happen. What if I relapse? What if my car won't start? What if I can't get a sponsor? Stay in the present. "Act As If" the present is all you

have – second by second, minute by minute, day by day. It's not a lie. THE PRESENT is all any of us have.

- Guilt, remorse, and self-directed resentment are very similar terms. Guilt is self-blame for supposed inadequacy or wrongdoing. Remorse is moral anguish and bitter regret arising from repentance for past misdeeds. Self-directed resentment is the experience of being angry or hating yourself as a result of a real or imagined offense. To "Fake It 'Til You Make It," you must stop beating yourself up about the past and accept that you did the best you could at the time. You will have many opportunities to atone for all of your misdeeds.
- Sadness is anguish and grief accompanied by feelings of gloom and misery. Sadness zaps your energy and possibly directs you toward isolation. Sadness can evolve into depression. "Fake It 'Til You Make It" does NOT imply that you should ignore your feelings. Rather, it supports the idea of not focusing on your gloom, but instead, involve yourself in service to others.

Negative feelings can be reduced or eliminated by "Act As If" and "Fake It 'Til You Make It." In addition, they can further be diminished by:

- Feeling and talking about such emotions.
- Choosing to reframe the situation more positively.
- Disconnecting to refocus on something you want.

The venting of negative feelings can feel good and be

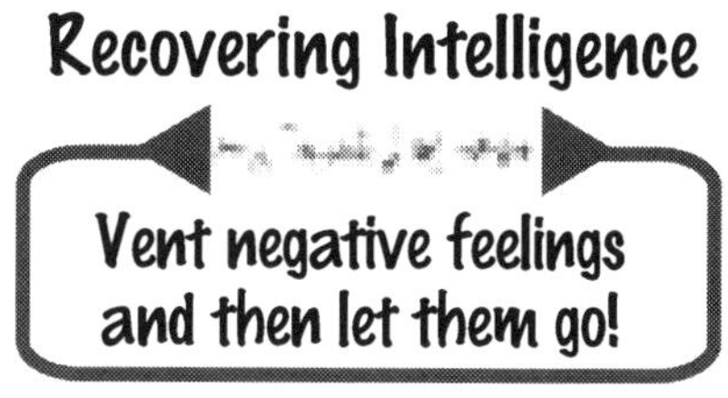

healthy, yet it can cause them to spread. Learn to cope using the following: accept, distract, reframe, focus on the positive, and let go. If you feel emotional while you're doing these tasks, that's good. Process those feelings, and they'll likely lessen and resolve. This will improve your emotional health.

Positive Communication Techniques:

1. Communication – Use communication to vent and process negative feelings by talking about your emotions and your experiences with trusted others, or with the person you have allowed to upset you. Use assertive statements starting with, "I feel," "I think," and "I want," or "My experience is..." If you start your sentences by focusing on the other person with the word "you," that person is likely to become defensive.
2. Creative Activities – Activities such as:
    - Art: Acting, drawing, sculpting with clay, etc.
    - Music: Playing, singing, writing, or conducting
    - Writing: Journals or letters
3. Acting Out/Striking Out – Release your feelings with activities such as:
    - Hitting with padded gloves or kicking a punching bag (40 lbs. or less), hitting pillows, hitting tennis balls, or hitting baseballs at a batting cage.
    - Screaming into pillows in a way that others

won't be disturbed.

- Crying while watching a tear-jerker movie to process and release your emotions.

You need to process your thoughts and feelings about upsetting situations, or you will stay stuck in your emotions.

Consider: **"In My Experience . . . you don't want to over-focus on the negative, your problems, or what you think you are 'losing' in recovery."** (See APPENDIX 8)

Positive Emotions

Recovery is an exciting time in your life, especially when you try to maintain positive emotions as you work through your plan. Positive emotions energize and motivate, and they generate even more good feelings. If feelings of thankfulness, joy, and desire do not come easily to you, focus on learning skills to develop and nurture them. To sustain overall happiness, you need to have three positive experiences for every one negative experience (3 to 1).

Recovering Intelligence

Positive emotions lead to a happier, healthier, & more successful life.

Many of us have spent too much of our lives listening to

our "itty, bitty, shitty (IBS) committee," which tells us we have little value. Quiet that IBS committee by acknowledging the positive emotions that you possess, even those that have been buried by your addiction. You can tap into any positive emotion when you need it! These include:

Courage is the ability and willingness to confront fear, pain, danger, uncertainty, or intimidation. A courageous person doesn't deny fear but acknowledges it, breathes, and moves through and pass it. Acknowledge how brave it was of you to enter recovery. Accept how brave it is of you to talk in your recovery groups. Recognize you have courage!

Desire is an extremely powerful positive motivator. Desire is self-perpetuating. Having desire creates an urge to have more desire. Recognize that your hope for recovery will propel you towards your goals and into **Your Recovering Future™**. Open up to and connect with your ambition to change your life by creating a quality long-term recovery.

Happiness is the most favored emotional state. It's the personal goal of many. Pleasure is delightful, but it isn't happiness. Pleasure is fleeting, and it's found in the external. Happiness is an internal experience and comes from being engaged in positive emotions and activities you enjoy. Happiness is heightened if the activities are purposeful ones. Find *Positive Psychology* in the Index.

Harmony is about agreeableness. Strive for personal harmony rather than discord, interpersonal harmony rather than conflict, and harmony with nature rather than disharmony. Connect with your complete self, your relationships with others, with nature, and with your Higher

Power.

Intimacy is an interpersonal relationship that involves physical or emotional closeness. It's created through feelings of familiarity and connection with others, but it can also exist with yourself and with your Higher Power. In recovery, we often share intimate details about ourselves with trusted others. Creating interpersonal relationships through sharing will help you fill the void you experienced from letting go of the intimate relationship you had with your addiction.

Deep intimacy is found only in close relationships. It takes time and experience with another person to develop deep intimacy. If you are single and starting recovery, it is suggested that you don't get involved in romantic relationships for at least a year. This is because there is usually a hidden hope that the feeling of love will offset the feeling of loss that evolved from not being able to participate in your addiction. New relationships will derail your recovery. Take your time and build a solid recovery foundation first.

If you were in an existing relationship when you started recovery, you might feel like you want to flee, but unless the relationship is toxic, you need to stay right where you are to practice new relationship skills. Deal with the wreckage of the past by creating more intimacy in your relationship. Some level of deep intimacy usually develops when you

Recovering Intelligence

Practice emotional intimacy with friends by slowly opening up.

share a difficult emotional experience. Practice sharing and being vulnerable. It's vital to understand that though deep emotional intimacy is hopefully part of your romantic relationship, sexuality is not the same as deep emotional intimacy.

Intimacy can be wonderful and nurturing, or scary and destructive. To have an intimate or deep emotional connection with another person, you must be willing to explore your feelings and share them. Go slowly with the sharing process, so if the person doesn't return your desire to deepen your relationship, the situation doesn't become too uncomfortable. Breathe and relax; it should get easier with practice! If you can find the courage, it's worth it!

Love is a life force that starts from within. Beginning with self-love, the energy of this life force radiates out to others, directly or indirectly. It's the comforting, hopeful joy that soothes pain, makes problems okay, and makes life worth living. To fully experience love, you must give love, open up to love, and receive love. Attempt to give yourself and others the accepting love we all want. Spiritual models generally believe love comes from The Source. People who believe in this model gain enormous value, wisdom, strength, and hope as well as the advantage that comes from connecting to the love coming from The Source.

Secrets

You're only as sick as your secrets. Do whatever it takes to get these secrets out of you and into the light. Tell a friend or your spiritual leader what they are, work with your coach or counselor, or do a fifth step with your sponsor. How you choose to share your secrets is up to you.

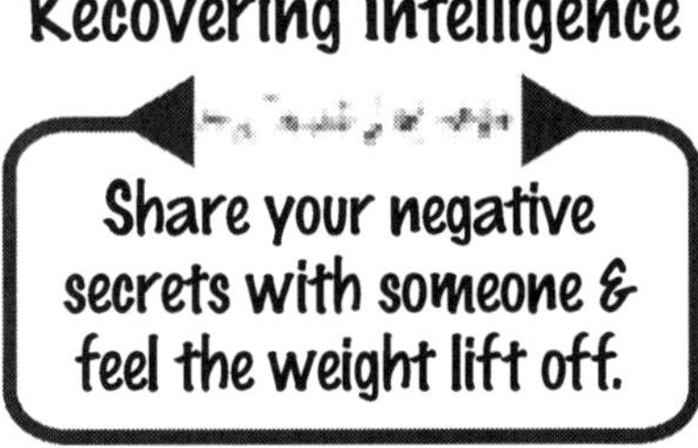

You may have old secrets buried in your subconscious from your childhood. When you are ready, face your history until you are conscious of these secrets. Stop repressing, ignoring, or defending them. Repressing your secrets will continue to damage you. Becoming conscious of them allows your secrets to come into the light where they can be seen for what they are and heal.

Trust

Trust is the first building block of human development. To trust, you must learn to have confidence and faith in yourself first, and then in important others and in your Higher Power. Put your fears aside, be courageous, and choose to trust your recovery core, those close individuals who support your recovery, so that you can get the benefit of their resources. None of your recovery core will be perfect, and they may not be able to give you all you think you need, but trust they'll do the best they can. If someone falls short, turn to someone else. Recovery is an individual commitment and a group effort.

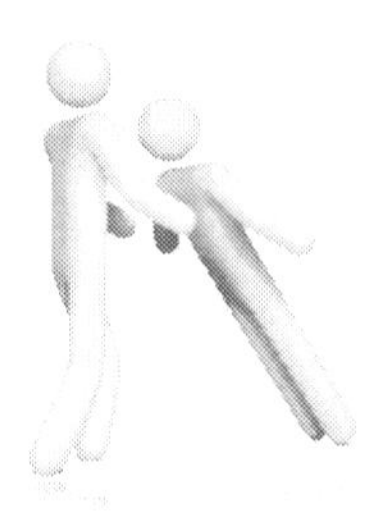

Using Your Mental Resources

You have many mental resources, such as courage,

curiosity, forgiveness, hope, love of learning, joy, and many others. Your personal strengths are also a mental resource. Some resources are fully available to you, and some need to be developed. Focus on using your mental resources to help you build **Your Recovering Future™**.

PERSONAL GROWTH

A commitment to your personal growth is necessary for building a quality recovering lifestyle. Once you have made a commitment, growth will come quickly as you deal with past and present issues and create **Your Recovering Future™**. Take your time and ready yourself for big shifts. This does not mean you have to experience a burning bush that presents itself to you with miraculous energy, a sacred light, or a flaming heart of purity, love, and clarity. If you are like most people in recovery, you will first experience many subtle shifts that lead into bigger ones. Be sure to honor each one, because it has manifested from your hard work and perseverance.

Addiction Patterns and Support Behaviors

It's mandatory to discover and change all of your addictive patterns and rituals, as well as the behaviors that support them. If you don't, they'll trigger you and pull you into a relapse. Examples of using rituals and how to change them are:

1. <u>Alcoholic</u> Ritual: Every day you stop to socialize at your local bar after work. Change: Find desirable sober social activities to participate in at the end of your work day.
2. <u>Codependent</u> Ritual: Picking up empty bottles after your spouse's drinking bout. Change: Sit, feel, and observe. Let the alcoholic in your life do their own clean-up.
3. <u>Shopaholic</u> Ritual: Going to store sales for fun. Change: Take a vacation from shopping, and go to the movies, library, gym, etc. instead.

Assertiveness

Assertiveness is a form of behavior and a presentation style that excludes anger or aggression. It's characterized by a confident declaration or affirmation without need of proof. Confidence, strength, clarity, and appropriateness are all components of assertiveness. Being assertive enables you to say how you feel and what you want by expressing yourself in a kind and respectful manner. Practice relating what you want with assertive statements:

"I would appreciate a call when you are going to be late for dinner. Can you do this?" (Wait for the answer and accept it! There is no need for further explanation or discussion.)

"I feel upset when you call me names. I want you to stop. Are you willing to do so?" (Accept the other person's answer. There is no need to comment. YOUR job is to decide what

YOU are going to do if this person won't stop calling you negative names.)

"When you overspend on the family budget, I feel angry and disrespected. I need to see a change in thirty days. Otherwise, I am going to separate our finances." (NO further discussion is necessary! Just be sure you can follow through on what you say.)

Role-play in a mirror or in person with a friend until you feel ready to launch your assertiveness. Consider taking an assertiveness training class. It will help you immensely with your communication skills.

Boundaries

As you get to know yourself better, you'll develop a clearer, healthier identity. This will involve your understanding of who you are and what is acceptable and not acceptable to you. These are your boundaries. Setting boundaries is necessary. Before recovery, you may have allowed yourself to be manipulated by others. These people may resist your boundaries, but if you stand firm, they will eventually believe and respect the limits you have set. Discovering your boundaries is often the most difficult with family, close friends, and associates. This is because, when pressed, it is easy to abandon your "rules of engagement," thus making your boundaries seem negotiable when they're not.

There are many types of boundaries. Food, gift giving, sex, touch, and gossip are but a few. Once you have established clear boundaries, it can be very difficult to keep them. If, for example, in the past you have gossiped with other family members about your Uncle Henry, they will expect you to continue this behavior. However, if in recovery you decide that gossiping is a character defect that you want to overcome, it can be quite challenging to convince your family members that you are no longer going to discuss Uncle Henry with them. They will prod and question and maybe even insult your decision. If you falter, you have just trained them that when you set a boundary, YOU don't respect it, so why should they? (Find *Boundaries* in the Index.)

Control

In your active addiction, you turned your life over to the chaos that addiction brings and the way it entices you to behave. YOUR ADDICTION was in charge! In recovery, regaining control of your life can be challenging. Remember, addiction is the only disease that comes with a voice that tells us it is okay to harm ourselves. And it has so much control over us, we believe it!

So how do you put some control back into your life? Control is about discipline. First, whatever that addict voice tells you to do, DON'T DO IT! Second, practice new behaviors so often that they become automatic. Third, don't put yourself in risky situations! It will provoke your addict voice to tell you it's okay to use. Fourth, SLEEP! You are healing your brain so it will be able to learn those new behaviors. Fifth, eat three nutritionally balanced meals a day, with limited sugar and carbohydrates. Last, do only ONE thing at a time! Multitasking is not your friend! Incorporate all of the above into your recovery program.

Recovering Intelligence

In every human interaction, there are control issues; manage them!

Control also involves domination and authority. This could mean that you try to over-control people or situations. This drains your energy and wastes your time. Others will feel pressured, manipulated, and resentful. Let things be as they are. People, places, and situations outside of yourself are beyond your control. Work an organized program, and the things around you should gradually fall into place. Choose to believe that with the help of your resources, you can create the recovering life that you want.

Developmental Stages

Healthy people grow and develop on a consistent emotional level. The following is a brief, general example of the stages of growth experienced as a person ages. In your addiction, you have probably not passed through these stages of maturation. In recovery, be patient with yourself as you catch-up to your chronological age group.

- General: As you pass through the stages below, recognize the validity or uselessness of many of your childhood and family of origin beliefs.
- 20s: First attempt to build the "good life." The focus

is on roles, career, and an intimate life partner. In addiction, our focus is on partying, using, drinking, eating, buying, etc. We are intimate with our addiction, not other people.

- 30s: Realities become clearer. Life commitments are made, deepened, or broken. In addiction, we have broken many commitments, and we deny the reality that our addiction is harmful to our life.
- 40s: Reassessing old dreams. Gender roles may change, and self-discovery increases. In addiction, the only self-discovery is due to the consequences of practicing our maladaptive behaviors.
- 50s: Life roles are accepted, embraced, or released. Life purpose is recommitted. In addiction, our life role has been as the "poison container" (the person who gets blamed for all ills that befall those close to us.)
- 60s and older: Major life changes. Career ends at some point. Finding other creative outlets and relationships that are more important. Desire for more purposeful activities. In addiction, we experience remorse and grief for a life that has been dedicated to numbing out. We feel we have missed something and, indeed, we have. We have missed OUR LIFE! But it is never too late to throw addiction to the curb and begin anew.

Dreams

Dreams are sequential images, emotions, ideas, and

sensations that occur involuntarily in the mind during certain stages of sleep. Everyone needs to dream to be healthy.

You may have using dreams that produce vivid and intense images about the use of your favorite drug, or about relapsing. Upon waking, you might think you have relapsed and experience annoyance and shame for the strong cravings these dreams arouse. Using dreams are normal, but they can be confusing and upsetting for some people. They usually diminish after 6 months of recovery but can be experienced throughout one's life.

Dream Study: Upon waking, write down or make a voice recording (and transcribe ASAP) what you can remember about your dreams. Think about your dreams several times throughout the day. At night, as you're drifting off to sleep, ask your unconscious mind for more information and clarification about previous dreams. Watch for symbols and themes that show up often as they may provide interesting and useful information. When finding meaning in your dreams, know that your own personal interpretation is the most profitable. Very soon after you start studying your dreams, you'll remember more of them.

Recovering Intelligence

Analyzing your dreams is easy & free. Just ask, "What does it mean?"

Milestones

You've encountered many milestones – landmark experiences that have shaped your life. Milestones give you good insight into how you became who you are in this moment. Review your life milestones. Take an inventory regarding what you want to incorporate into your life that you have missed. Figure out how you can make use of what you learn now and in the future. Review:

- The pivotal people in your life, positive and negative
- Your positive and negative choices
- The defining moments

Personal Education

Even if you understand a lot about recovery and healthy living, you can always learn more. This doesn't require school, just the real world. Be curious, listen, read, explore, ask questions, and keep an open mind about education and growth. Practice lifelong learning. Doing this will help keep your brain astute and assist you in living a longer, happier, and healthier life.

Success Acknowledgment

While moving forward and becoming successful in your recovery, it's valuable to remember, acknowledge, and build upon your personal achievements. Reflect internally on past successes to imprint what it felt like for you when you triumphed and reached your goal. What did you feel emotionally and in your bodily sensations? Allow

yourself to savor the sounds, images, tastes, and aromas that went with your accomplishment. This information provides you with the contents of your success response – how you feel when you achieve your goals. What goals have you set for your future? Imagine the feelings and sensations of success as you work toward those goals. This exercise not only acts as a motivator, but it will also provide your brain with a format for goal attainment.

SPIRITUALITY

Spirituality can be defined as, "the search for the sacred." It is about reformation, finding a transcendent dimension, and connecting with a Higher Power or The Source. In our active addiction, we have worshiped at the feet of our substance and turned to it in times of happiness, grief, anger, and uncertainty. In recovery, we MUST replace our worldly "God" (addiction) with a Higher Power. We MUST discover the spiritual nature within us that has been drowned out by our addiction.

While many spiritual people belong to a religion, spirituality is not the same as religion. The word *spirit* comes from the Latin word *spiritus*, which means *soul*. It is related to another Latin word, *spirare*, which means *to breathe*. Through a spiritual practice, we give, "breath to our soul."

How do you do this? It may be through private prayer, yoga, meditation, quiet reflection, or even long walks. Or participation in an organized religion, faith-community, or connection with nature. Such activities remind you that you are not alone; you are not separate from The Source, however you define it. Don't let words or labels get in the way of connecting to your version of spiritual recovery. After all, you didn't let labels deter you from bonding with your addiction, so popular excuses like, "I don't believe in God," or "I'm not spiritual," no longer apply.

Spiritual Development

There are many ways to develop your relationship with spirit. All spiritual paths, from the mainstream religions to creating your own spiritual practices, have positives. For those in recovery, a common choice has been to combine several different types of spiritual ideas or practices.

Recovering Intelligence

Spirituality is about your connection to your Higher Power - the universe.

As divinely inspired as all spiritual paths may claim to be, all are created by humans and are vulnerable to charismatic leaders. Be careful of being psychologically controlled by another's desire to be right or to exert power and control over their followers. Give yourself time to step back and give serious thought to situations in which you may be asked to do things that you don't want to do, or to believe that there is only one way for you to be spiritual – their way! Ask the opinions of trusted others. Be Careful!

Higher Power

Quantum physics states that everything is energy. If so, then spirit is energy. Belief in spiritual power brings peace, contentment, and happiness, as well as a much larger perspective toward the value of life.

The term Higher Power from AA is a good title for The Source. Feel free to designate your own title. Your heart-connection with your Higher Power is what's important. Some people start by seeing their Higher Power as their recovery or their self-help group. Others view it as the universe or God. Whatever you believe, it is essential that you recognize your Higher Power as a valuable resource; embrace it and let it benefit you.

Higher Self

Your Higher Self describes an eternal, omnipotent, conscious, and intelligent being who is your real self. It is thought to be who you *really* are. It connects your physical self with your Higher Power. Your Higher Self is always available to you, and if you allow yourself to put faith in it, you will be amazed by the gifts it gives you. Ask to connect to your Higher Self and open up. Let go of your ego and your fears. Meditation is an excellent tool for learning to connect with your spiritual being. Religions and spiritual paths have their own names for the Higher Self. Christianity calls it the soul. Use what is desirable to you.

Spiritual Evolution

People from many theoretical and scientific backgrounds – astrologers, channelers, historians, mystics, and quantum physicists – have declared that our planet is going through a spiritual evolution, which they define as a shift into a higher vibrational frequency. While the contemporary scientific community has not yet validated this construct, those who follow this line of thinking believe that fully manifesting to a higher vibrational frequency will be a cosmic event. This idea of spiritual evolution expands beyond all prior knowledge of what reality is.

Spiritual evolution is a big paradigm shift for most people. Some beliefs are:

- You are spirit and are part of The Source.
- You get what you focus on and it expands.
- If you ask The Source, you will receive.
- The essence of life is happiness, joy, and love.
- You are here to experience and learn; what you find exciting, likely has a purpose!
- Be what you want to become. To become loving, you must act lovingly.
- Change is constant, except for the above ideas.
- Be responsible for who you are and your actions.

Note: This is a very simple and brief introduction to a deep and complex topic that has many interpretations.

Values

Values are a set of principles or standards by which you consistently live your life. They are the structure for your moral code. Living by your values provides a foundation for your integrity. Your values come from your family, formal education, peers, society, media, and spiritual training.

> **Recovering Intelligence**
>
> **Living your values will eliminate conflict & build your integrity.**

During active addiction, your values are usually discarded and replaced by rationalizations justifying any unacceptable behavior you adopted in order to participate in your addiction. Your old values can become confused, weakened, and even lost.

In recovery, you need to reconnect with the values you have lost and develop new ones. You can learn new values in your church, recovery community, and any other place in which integrity is regarded as an asset. Living your personal, moral, social, and spiritual values will confirm your sense of self.

Value Conflicts: A conflict can occur between what you believe and how you act, or your beliefs and the beliefs of others. Conflict causes tension; you'll want to reduce or eliminate this tension as soon as possible. You can do this by clarifying what you believe good values are and then acting in ways that support those beliefs. Attending a party where you will be socializing with your using buddies will cause a value conflict between your addiction and your sobriety. Don't put yourself in situations that lead to a value conflict.

Value Clarification: Now is the time to re-evaluate your values, rebuild your personal integrity, and start living in a way that matches who you are and who you desire to become. You'll know your values are okay when you don't feel the tension of conflict between your behavior and your values. Replacing your addict belief system with new values is not easy. But YOU can do it!

In order of importance, make a list of things you believe take priority in life. Next, reorganize the list according to how you actually live your life, including what you focus your attention on. Compare the two lists. If they don't match, take action to change your behavior so that it is congruent with your prioritized values.

SUMMARY

Your commitment and the actions you take toward your mental-emotional health, personal growth, and spirituality will change your life. You'll become more aware and in control, happier and healthier, more connected, and at peace.

Personal growth in the areas of mental and emotional health helps you:

- Achieve more tasks, goals, and milestones.
- Identify illness, accept it, and compensate for it.
- Enjoy a healthier, more balanced, successful life.

- Work with feelings and your feedback system.
- Identify your social-emotional intelligence, which is vital for thriving.
  - » Become more optimistic, and therefore, happier and healthier.
  - » Be aware of your emotional intelligence, which will benefit you by:
    - ◊ Enabling you to build, broaden, and savor positive emotions.
    - ◊ Assisting you in identifying negative emotions so you can feel, acknowledge, cope, respond, and let go of them.
  - » Aiding you in developing social intelligence, which is vital for relationships.
- Personal growth comes by choosing to open up to learn new ideas and options. Then you will:
  - » Naturally move through life's developmental stages.
  - » Shift your addictive patterns to healthy ones.
  - » Take control of your life's goals, milestones, and dreams.
  - » Develop assertiveness, and create healthier boundaries.

Connecting with your spirituality and The Source offers:

- Additional invaluable resources and perspective.
- Connection to yourself and who you really are.
- Connection to your values and integrity.

Chapter 7

Continuing Recovery:

Relapse

Chapter 7: Continuing Recovery – Relapse
Table of Contents

RELAPSE: AVOIDING THE USING ENVIRONMENT

With all addictions, the call to relapse can be compelling. Addiction is the only disease in which your brain tells you it is okay to do something that will harm you. Because we have let our addict brain control our thinking for as long as we have indulged in our addiction, it is a formidable challenge to start paying attention to the wise, rational part of our brain that exists to protect us from poisoning our body, mind, and spirit. You don't have to relapse! But if you do, there are techniques that will help get you back into your recovery. This chapter is dedicated to educating you about relapse, how to avoid it, and how to escape its permanent clutches if it temporarily lures you back into your addiction.

Abstaining from an addiction will be easier if you keep yourself away from all aspects of your using past. This means keeping yourself away from people, places, things, and situations which might tempt you to relapse or spark enticing euphoric memories of being in your addiction. If you have to re-experience your past using environment for

Recovering Intelligence

A clean environment will support your recovery; ask for support.

any reason, be careful. Set yourself up for success by relying on your core support group and staying conscious of positive escape plans. (Find *Positive Escape Plans* in the Index.)

Cut off using connections that could sabotage you by:

- Setting boundaries about who you socialize with.
- Telling your family and friends what support looks like to you; describe to them ways in which they can support your recovery.
- Changing your phone number.
- Firmly informing your past using associates of your commitment to recovery.
- Avoiding involvement with active users, even if they are work associates, neighbors, or parents of your child's best friend.

Prepare yourself against tempting situations:

- Know and practice what you will say until it's easy.
- Mentally rehearse how you will act, feel, and respond to different scenarios of a situation that could tempt you to relapse.
  - » Role-play with people in your core group.
  - » Practice managing your feelings. Visualize if you would feel scared, shaky, or angry and devise a plan about how to de-escalate your emotions.
  - » Practice deep, slow breathing.

You may have little choice but to continue living in an

unhealthy neighborhood, relationship, or family. You can build the structure you need to handle these situations by:

- Building a positive, healthy support community.
- Focusing your time on recovery.
- Making a geographic move.

Healthy Options For Avoiding the Using Environment

Whatever the situation, you can choose to focus your mental and emotional attention on positive, healthy options that will support your recovery.

Community: If your neighborhood has temptations or if you associate it with your using rituals, spend as little time there as possible. While a geographic fix doesn't always work, consider if moving out of a toxic, using environment will assist you in practicing a recovery lifestyle. As you weigh your moving options, remember that you always take yourself and your issues with you wherever you go. Can you create or find a healthy local recovery community without moving?

Home: If your household is chaotic, respond with good communication skills that are calming. Listen to music or meditate. Suggest family meetings or counseling. Offer ideas and ask others for suggestions to improve the situation. The structure of a 12-Step meeting could put some peace and order into your life.

Interpersonal: If all your friends are users, you need to end those relationships and make new friends by visiting and participating in an established recovery community. As you look around at the personalities that make up your recovery community, it's possible to put together a surrogate family for yourself. An "adopted" uncle or grandmother can provide comfort and guidance in times of challenge. Sharing your story and learning of the life experiences, hopes, and strengths of others in recovery seeds a thread of common experiences, providing an opportunity to bond. Share your history and also the story of **Your Recovering Future™**.

Giving back and being of service to others is often a sign of a strong and generous recovery. It allows you to get outside yourself and your personal struggles. You may want to freely offer to do a task at your local recovery meeting, or do volunteer work through a fellowship, your church, or with a community agency. You could also contact your local volunteer bureau.

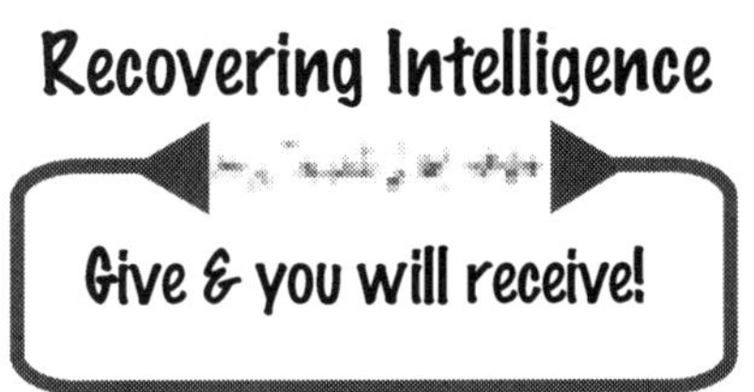

RELAPSE

Most people don't want to think about relapse, and yet it's essential to do so. Recovery is not 100% certain. It's important that you have a working knowledge of how to prevent, work through, and move past a potential relapse.

Relapse is a part of the disease of addiction, and during recovery, many will have one or more relapse events where they use again. The answer is to work a solid program.

The two things that can cause a relapse event are:

1. <u>Triggers</u>: Due to their effect on glutamine.

2. Stressors: Due to the hormones that are released.

Note: Relapses start long before you use or participate in your addiction.

When we use drugs or participate in behavioral addictions, the neurotransmitter dopamine is produced by the brain, and we feel better, happier, elated, sedated, excited, etc. Because dopamine is pleasurable, the reward center of the brain increasingly seeks it, making the release of dopamine highly addictive.

In most individuals, the brain has the ability to balance out its chemistry. Initially, a minimal amount of a drug or a short period engaging in a certain behavior is satisfactory, but the brain quickly adjusts and craves more. This is how tolerance develops.

The urge to participate in our addiction grows stronger with tolerance. The amount of a substance or the time needed for our behavioral addiction increases with such speed, we are often not aware that our addiction has taken over our thinking and our behavior! Tolerance affects both the mind and the body. Because the brain adapts so quickly to producing certain amounts of dopamine in order to "feel better," we not only develop an obsession to feed its pleasure center, but our body also develops a physical need to feel as good as it does when we are using.

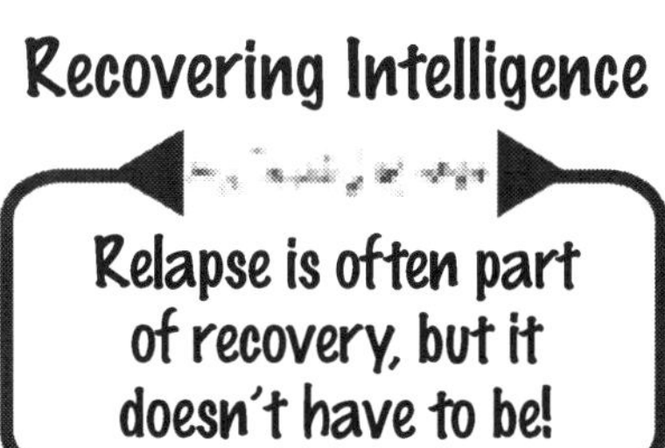

As you continued in your addictions, pathways were worn between the emotional part of your brain and your pleasure center. The consequence are that when you feel your emotions, such as happiness, anger, or stress, your "I want to use" or "On" button gets triggered.

Concurrently, dopamine neurotransmitter sites are stimulated to such a degree that they can become depleted, leaving us feeling depressed, anxious, bored, exhausted, and emotionally spent. Our addict brain tells us that to feel better we must use... and indeed, after using, we usually DO feel better. With enough practice, the chemical/emotional/behavioral connections between pleasure and mind-altering substances or addictive behaviors are PERMANENTLY changed in our brain's reward system so that our greatest pleasure comes from using.

Because it's embedded into the reward system, the brain's chemical reaction to an addiction starts unconsciously, well before we recognize it as an addictive response. This is the reason why many people relapse as a result of stress and pressure. To try to prevent relapse, you must remain aware of how you are feeling and train yourself to stay relaxed.

The biological functions behind relapse create an unhealthy emotional state of mind, the stinkin' thinkin' wherein your brain tries to rationalize your addiction. This is known as the mental state of relapse and includes relapsing beliefs, attitudes, thoughts, feelings, and behaviors. In the mental state of relapse, options decrease and stress increases. You can slide in and out of mental states of relapse.

A relapse event does not occur suddenly but after a long

period of mental and emotional relapse. There are usually some warning signs, but your lack of awareness creates the illusion that relapse is sudden. However, despite being in a mental state of relapse, a relapse event doesn't have to happen. There are methods to prevent it. If it does, it doesn't have to continue to a disastrous end. It can be interrupted at any point, even before hitting absolute bottom. Research has shown that if you immediately return to your recovery program, future relapse events will be much less likely to occur. Similarly, analyzing the reasons for your relapse event can make you and your recovery stronger.

Recovering Intelligence

Why specifically do you want recovery?

The Relapse Process

The process of recovery involves changing the behaviors and thoughts that enabled your addiction and practicing new lifestyle choices that support your recovery. If you resist change and growth, you will become emotionally and cognitively stuck in your addiction. Your mental and biological triggers will tell you that you want and need to use. Your relapse warning signs will become more obvious – if not to you, then to your recovery support system. Ultimately, you will act on what your addict brain tells you: "It's okay to use! You need to use! Nobody will know, and if they do, screw them!" This is known as a case of the "F___ its." The "F___ ts" are alive and well in every relapse.

Choose to step off the relapse slide. Stop the excuses and use your resources to get back onto your recovery path. If you do get back on track, you will probably stay there until you have to again confront the issues that propelled you to relapse. If you face your fears and process these issues this time around, instead of avoiding them through use, you will grow and move on. If you don't, you will again move back down the relapse slide. Some people will go through this cycle many times.

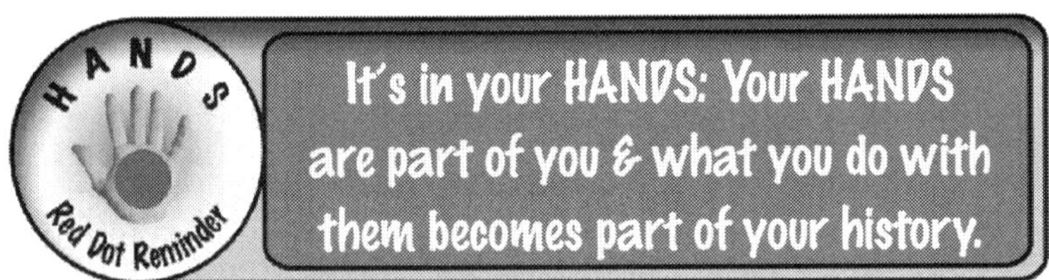

Note: One day clean and the next day using is just continued use, not a relapse. To relapse you need to have clean time and a commitment to your recovery.

Triggers and Cravings

Cravings are the result of the automatic pathways in the addict's brain that connect body and mind. They are the heart of many relapses. You can be triggered by any number of things, but it is not until you focus on your triggers that cravings set in. Cravings are generated by the body's hyper-alert system and by obsessing over how nice it would be to use or participate in your behavioral addiction "just one more time." Avoid *euphoric recall*, when you allow yourself to get stuck while remembering the pleasant high of using.

Recovering Intelligence

Manage cravings with less stress, the right nutrition, & relaxation!

Many people experience intense cravings caused by internal or external triggers. When cravings are at their worst, especially with drugs, the dopamine in your brain can cause you to unconsciously receive the message, "I must use to survive." If you don't use, the cravings will pass, usually within 15 minutes. Distract yourself. You can do anything for 15 minutes.

If you're lucky enough not to have cravings early in your recovery, respect the possibility that you may have them in the future. Be prepared. Cravings can be helped with nutritional compounds and medications.

PAWS

Post Acute Withdrawal Syndrome (PAWS) is a set of symptoms occurring after withdrawal from substances, especially alcohol, opiates, and benzodiazepines. Symptoms include depression, anxiety, irritability, mood swings, thinking problems, difficulty forming new memories, and a general focus on the negative. They occur at regular intervals of 3, 6, 9, 12, 18, and 24 months.

PAWS can blindside you and your recovery. It occurs in 75% of people recovering from long-term drug use and other

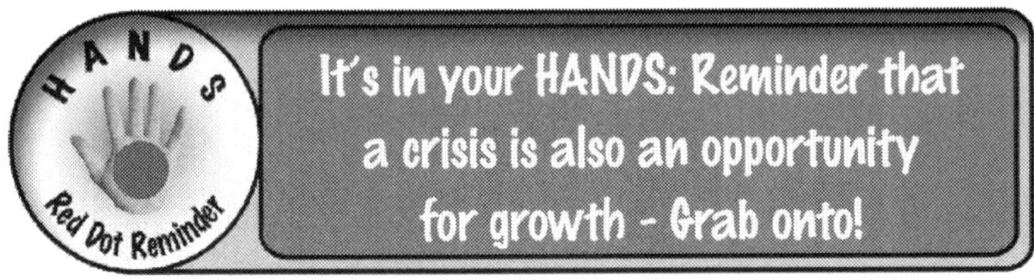

addictions. It can possibly be stimulated by psychotropic medications. Stress, strong negative emotions, or triggers can increase the intensity of PAWS. Sometimes, symptoms may occur for no apparent reason. Nutritional and/or cognitive behavioral therapy are your best treatment options.

Self-Sabotage

Deliberate destruction of your recovery is a prominent element of relapse, be it conscious or unconscious. Awareness, commitment to recovery, and written relapse prevention plans will stop self-sabotage.

Stuck Points

A stuck point is anything blocking your growth process and the progress of your recovery, like dealing with low self-esteem, emotional trauma, the breakup of a relationship, or

the loss of a job. You will come up against these barriers throughout your recovering life. If you deal with them successfully, you become more capable of warding off the next stuck point. If you don't deal with them, you will move into psychological relapse, stop growing in your recovery, and put yourself at risk of a relapse event. Facing a major stuck point is called hitting the wall. When you realize you are stuck, confront the situation using your resources. Attempt to resolve it or accept it, and move on.

Symptoms of Relapse

Relapse symptoms are the negative, inaccurate, and anti-recovery beliefs, attitudes, thoughts, feelings, behaviors, and situations that you were involved in during active addiction. As soon as you are aware of such symptoms, understand that you are dealing with a physical, mental, and emotional relapse. Refocus on your recovery to reduce or eliminate relapse symptoms. Examples of symptoms include:

- Beliefs:
  - "I can't change who I am."
  - "I'm not ready to change."
  - "I can't live without..."
  - "Life wouldn't be worth living without..."
- Experiences:
  - Skipping one or more meals.
  - Regular participation in extreme activities.
  - Isolating yourself from recovery activities and your recovery community.
- Emotions: Depression, anxiety, fear, and not doing

anything to deal with your emotions.

- Tactile (Touch): Self-injuring by cutting and/or burning.
- People: Not staying in contact with your support group and being in contact with using acquaintances or old using buddies.
- Places:
  - » Choosing not to go to your home group.
  - » Showing up at the old places where you used to use.
- Smells:
  - » Savoring aromas that are a byproduct of using.
  - » Being around tantalizing odors that trigger using memories.
- Special Dates or Events:
  - » Staying at an event after you're triggered.
  - » Attending a party where people are using.
- Sounds: Continuing to listen to druggy or antisocial music or the tunes that you listened to when you were using.
- Taste: Eating too much. Indulging in foods that trigger you, such as sugar.
- Time: Spending hours of unfocused time alone, especially if you are bored or isolated.
- Thoughts: Focusing on using or on past memories that incite resentment. Remembering the "fun old times" when you were active in your addiction.
- Vision: Picturing being with your ex or with your old using friends.

Triggers

A trigger is anything that starts or accelerates a physical or psychological response to use. You have no control over triggers. They can remind you of a past negative event or trauma, or a pleasant past using experience, thereby provoking you to use. Triggers can be:

1. Externally activated by an event, person, place, situation, or time period.
2. Internally activated by a thought or feeling.

Recovering Intelligence

Triggers: Internal & external spontaneous things that you can't control.

External and internal triggers release dopamine in the brain and incite emotions that make you want to use. You can be triggered in as little as 0.032 of a second of exposure to the stimulus, before it even enters your awareness. Triggers cause pre-using brain chemistry called the *kindling effect*, which readies your brain for using.

Recovering Intelligence

A strong connection to your desire for recovery can stop triggers!

The stimulus that triggers you also tricks you into believing that participating in your addiction is as important as or more important than anything else. The limbic system in the brain, the ancient survival system that tells you to "Go," activates your addiction before the rational part of your brain, the "Stop" and think system, can weigh the consequences of the impulse. The two normally can work together, but when the mental path for the "Go" becomes dominated by the process of addiction, the "Stop" system needs help.

The medicine baclofen appears to slow down the brain's "Go" response, giving you the extra time and opportunity to make better decisions. There are also techniques and tools for slowing down the "Go," such as tapping, snapping a rubber band worn around your wrist, and holding ice cubes in your hand until the "Go" fades. A nutritional option is L-glutamine, which stabilizes blood sugar, thus reducing cravings caused by low blood sugar. A quick drop in blood sugar is an aftereffect of indulging in such products as sugar, processed foods, nicotine, and caffeine.

Since triggers can appear suddenly, it's important to be prepared by staying aware of your thoughts and feelings and alert to what is happening around you. Set yourself up for success by having pre-planned strategies ready to use when responding to triggers.

Hot Triggers: Be aware of triggers that cause intense stimulation, discomfort, or drain you of your energy. In early recovery, it's especially important to eliminate those people, places, situations, and sensory triggers that you find to be particularly alluring. Develop a plan of action BEFORE you find yourself facing a hot trigger. Your recovery plan must include activities that do not mimic any component of your using behavior. Schedule fun activities with recovering

Recovering Intelligence

External Triggers: People, places, things, situations, & times!

people, and have many familiar recovery tools ready in case you are blindsided and find yourself in the middle of a hot trigger.

Consider: **"In My Experience... you don't want to be unprepared, especially for the sudden or unexpected triggers."** (See APPENDIX 7.)

External Triggers: An external trigger is an event, person, place, situation, or time period that arouses an addiction. Sometimes, we don't even realize that our addiction is being energized by something external. For example, if you are on your way to the grocery store, and you have to walk by a bar to get there, you might unexpectedly find yourself triggered by aromas wafting out the door.

Processed food and sugar are powerful triggers because they shoot up your blood sugar levels and give you a small boost that can feel like a mini stimulant. Sugar affects mood, and sugar cravings mimic cravings for alcohol and other chemicals. Take stock of what you eat. Food from the drive-through doesn't nourish the recovering brain. Prior to eating, be aware of how hungry you are and what you are feeling. Don't eat because of your feelings.

Sex and new relationships can be another common external trigger. They take the focus off our recovery and the issues we need to fix. It is recommended that you make no changes to existing relationships, unless they are abusive, and that you don't create new, romantic relationships for at least 12 months.

There are many other external triggers in your everyday environment that, once discovered, may surprise you. The behaviors you have repeated while practicing your addiction have become hardwired. They are automatic. You must learn what they are. Pay attention to them, write them down, and avoid them.

Once you have made a list of your external triggers (and you can keep adding to this list), create a plan that will enable you to separate from them. You can do this by separating physically, or if a trigger is going to be a constant in your life, by learning a way of detaching from it in a positive manner. Meditation, yoga, or passive martial arts are good options. Practice "breaking" the negative connection by separating and detaching until you know you can neutralize your response.

To assist you in making your External Triggers List, consider connections that are paired with using:

- Environment: Sunny Sundays, rainy or snow days, or other bad weather, very hot or cold days, the longest nights/shortest days of the year, tornados, hurricanes or earthquakes.
- Experiences: Seeing others living an addictive lifestyle, dating, driving, intimate dancing, specific foods, someone flirting with you, being stimulated by someone's attire, a recovery discussion that

focuses on your ex-drug of choice, visiting relatives who drink or use, special events, unexpected extra or loss of money, positive and negative work interactions, and scenes from various media that depict using, drinking, and smoking. Also, anything that tries to promote the "benefits" of addiction, like advertisements show the positives of drinking, eating, shopping, smoking, loveless sex, etc.

- People: Ex-using friends; aggressive, exciting, irritating, negative, toxic, or unhappy people.
- Places: Bars, cars, drive-in theaters, home, school, where you feel stressed, past or current workplaces.
- Aromas: Specific scents connected to your addiction, chemicals, cigarettes, foods, matches burning, perfumes.
- Special dates or events: Anniversaries, birthdays, celebrations, successes, failures, concerts, crises, funerals, holidays, meals, office parties, Valentine's Day, and weddings.
- Sounds: An excited announcer's voice, slamming doors, a cigarette lighter clicking open, a pop-top can being opened, a specific person's voice or song.

Recovering Intelligence

Internal Triggers: Feelings, thoughts, memories, & chemistry.

- Time periods: Free time, weekends, after work, late night, pay days, vacations, and other times you engaged in your using rituals.
- Images: Advertisements, seeing your substance

of choice being used, an ex-using partner, money coming out of an ATM.

Internal Triggers: Occasionally, thoughts and feelings may lead to relapse. Even if you're not aware of it, an external trigger can leave an imprint on your internal emotions, causing you to entertain using thoughts that incite a desire to participate in your addiction.

Examples of internal triggers include:

- Thoughts: Euphoric recall about using, rationalizations about why you should use, minimizing the consequences of your addiction.
- Emotional feelings: Anger, anxiety, boredom, depression, loneliness, celebration, and stress.
- Physical sensations: Anxiety or tingling, dry throat, fabric, money, physical pain, skin on skin, tiredness, taste of mouthwash.
- Taste: Flavors that were present in your addiction.
- Imagery: Picturing using behaviors, remembering images of dreams.

If you know something will be a trigger and you choose to engage in it without support, you are already in mental-emotional relapse. This can happen very easily and quickly. Instead, prepare yourself against triggers by practicing responses like:

- External Triggers:
  - » "No thanks."
  - » "I'm in recovery. I hope you're doing well. Bye."
  - » "I'm on my way to... (a medical appointment). Take care."

- Internal Triggers:
  - » "That's what I'm feeling, but I don't have to act on it. I can choose to... (act differently)."
  - » "It's not true; it only feels that way."
  - » "I'm leaving this situation now and calling..."

Mental Relapse Style

Mental relapse styles often evolve from your using styles and rituals. Whenever you turn away from a healthy recovery approach and towards self-sabotage, you are acting similarly to the way you did when you were active in your addiction. Your mental-emotional relapse starts long before you are aware of it. It can precede a physical relapse, by months before you realize what is happening and refocus on your recovery. Sometimes, you may wonder how you could have stayed so unaware for so long. That's why setting yourself up to remain conscious of your feelings, thoughts, and actions is so important. The following are examples:

> **Recovering Intelligence**
>
> Awareness of relapse behaviors can keep you in control of your style!

Avoidance:

- In addiction: You avoided facing problems, conflicts, and your feelings by using.
- In recovery: You confront your problems one at a time and often seek out guidance from those in your support group about how they overcame avoiding their issues. You learn to take on your challenges and let go of the outcome.

- In relapse: You shy away from your personal issues, your problems, conflicts, and debt. Ignoring your feelings is part of avoidance. Remember, avoiding your feelings doesn't eliminate them. Rather, avoiding feelings allows them to run you, often in negative, erratic, and out of control ways.

Comparing:

- In addiction: You compare yourself to others to see how you measure up. Your addict brain tells you that YOU DON'T MEASURE UP, and this leads you to reactivate your addiction so you won't care. Additionally, you make up stories about how others have a better life than you do. Others appear happier, more successful, and have more money, possessions, etc. Comparing yourself to others cultivates envy and jealousy – great reasons to use! But larger than all these comparisons is the one you make by scanning your surroundings and looking for all those "NORMAL" people who are drinking, shopping, gambling, etc. without negative consequences! They can easily walk away from those activities which, for you, are impossible to stop! These comparisons all provide fuel for indulging in your drugs and addictive behaviors.
- In recovery: You disregard what others have. You focus on your own talents, friends, the promises of working a recovery program, and how you can make yourself a better person. You use your resources, goals, and values to compare your behavior to your

potential. You develop an "attitude of gratitude." You practice self-compassion and self-forgiveness.

- In relapse: You return to comparing yourself to others, and you develop resentments about why YOU aren't a "normie." You slide back into your addiction as your primary relationship and become closed to the tenets of recovery. You reject feedback, because those who are trying to support your recovery, "Don't understand me and my issues." (Find *Defenses and Defended into Openness* in the Index.)

<u>Defending:</u>

- In addiction: You don't trust, you won't listen, you negate all feedback that doesn't support your addiction, and you are closed to any conversation that challenges your actions. You avoid, avert, head off, prohibit, and obstruct any intervention to your using practices.
- In recovery: You become open to feedback about behaviors, thoughts, associates, and practices that enable your addiction. You ask respected others for their opinions and really listen to them, and then you make use of what you learn.
- In relapse: You return to putting up barriers against any opinions and activities that could challenge your closed and limited thinking and stop you from moving towards your addictive lifestyle.

<u>Entitlement:</u>

- In addiction: You assume that whatever you desire,

you should have; whatever you want to do, you should do; and whatever you want from someone, they should give you. These assumptions promote your addiction. Your arrogance about what you deserve feeds resentment about how unfair the world has been to you. All the reasons you feel about why YOU should have things others have, without earning those things, serve to provide what seem to be valid rationales to numb out with drugs, alcohol, shopping, gambling, food, working, etc.

- In recovery: You realize that you are only entitled to what you earn; you learn to take advantage of and be grateful for your opportunities. You let go of arrogance, grandiosity, and envy, and you embrace humility, gratitude, and acceptance.
- In relapse: Entitlement provides you with the mantra, "I want it, so I should have it." Your focus returns to what everyone else does or has. You look around recovery rooms and become envious that others are living "the promises of the recovery program," but you are not. You want it to be easy and simple. You forget that grandiosity and entitlement are cornerstones of addiction.

Escape Plan:

- In addiction: Your escape plan is any strategy that assists you in participating in your addiction and any anti-recovery strategy that can be used if the situation arises. Examples are: keeping old medications, the coupon for the big box of chocolate, the special bottle of wine, or the phone numbers of old using friends.

- In recovery: You develop positive escape plans. Examples are: having a strategy for dealing with difficult situations, having solid support when experiencing hard times, and replacing all concentrate on how your job, friends, family and church life isn't working.
- In relapse: You set up situations that increase the likelihood that you will chose negative escape plans. An example: keeping using paraphernalia (your favorite X) as a decoration or as a positive reminder.

Mental Focus:

- In addiction: You obsess on the negatives instead of the positives in your life. You perceive the negatives as good excuses to indulge in your addiction. You concentrate on how your recovery meetings, treatment group, or sponsor isn't working, won't work, or isn't good enough, thus fueling your addiction.
- In recovery: You acknowledge the negatives, but you dwell on the positives. You open up to and let in all of the benefits that your recovery has brought and will bring you. You learn to look on your addiction as the blessing that led you to take a deeper look into your truer self.
- In relapse: You return to concentrating on the negatives in your life: your unpaid bills, your bad luck, the faults of those around you, and how you

are misunderstood – things you feel are great reasons to return to active addiction.

Other notes to consider:

- Mental-emotional relapse states indicate a lack of motivation for working through issues or stressful events. This can be seen in one's resistance to engaging in the process of recovery.
- Possessing paraphernalia (your favorite X) that was involved in your using is a relapse behavior. Even items only indirectly associated with using can trigger you. If the item isn't really needed, eliminate or replace it. Examples:
  - » Possessing things: A smoking jacket, fat clothes, druggie music, clothes with a sales tag, or carrying much more money than is needed.
  - » Same activities/locations: Listening to the same music, hanging out at the casino, socializing with the same using people, or reading sales flyers.
- Romancing your using is when you only focus on the positive aspects of using.
- Telling or listening to war stories can feel fun and exciting, but they usually don't include the negative consequences of your actions. Think about the negative consequences at least as much.
- Testing your willpower needlessly is a bad idea, especially in difficult or dangerous situation. Don't try to prove your motivation for recovery,

that willpower overcomes triggers, or that being in a good recovery program will protect you.

Consider: **"In My Experience... you don't want to prove anything connected with your past addiction or your current recovery."** (See APPENDIX 7.)

RELAPSE WARNING SIGNS

The STOP Signs of Recovery

User Relapse Warning Signs

Here is a partial list:

- Confusion and helplessness
- Defensiveness
- Hopelessness, self-pity, and depression
- Inaccurate thinking, racing thoughts
- Irregular exercise or sleep patterns
- Faltering in your program
- Isolation and loneliness
- Negative attitude
- Obsessiveness, compulsiveness, and impulsiveness
- Out of control thoughts, feelings, and behaviors
- Poor planning or an inadequate daily structure

Codependent Relapse Warning Signs

Here is a partial list:

- Emotionally disconnected and experiences of mood

swings

- Focus on the external, especially the addict's behavior to identify, stay aware of, and deal with your triggers.
- Negative attitude, defensiveness, fears, guilt, self-pity, and resentments
- Not using your structure or your support group
- Other abusing behaviors
- Poor boundaries
- Poor self-care

Family Relapse Warning Signs

Here is a partial list:

- Defensive, rigid or closed behaviors
- Agreements are not kept
- Members stop working their program
- Immature or acting out behavior
- Starting or increasing another addictive behavior
- Negative and destructive behaviors return
- Refusal to participate in the family process

USER RELAPSE TRIGGERS TO SYMPTOMS

A trigger becomes a relapse symptom soon after your brain has been stimulated by a sensory image. If you don't try to reduce or eliminate the symptom caused by the trigger, you are choosing to engage with the trigger.

The key to preventing relapse is to identify and stay aware

and deal with your triggers and their symptoms. This allows you to take the appropriate action to remove yourself from the situation. Examples are:

1. You run into an ex-using buddy in an area you wouldn't have expected to see him or her.
    - This trigger becomes a relapse symptom when you stop and interact with him or her.
2. While getting a ride home from a meeting, the driver says she is going to make a stop at a store sale. You're triggered to shop, as this is your favorite store.
    - This trigger becomes a symptom if you don't explain the situation and talk about options.
3. At a family gathering, someone starts telling war stories about you two using together.
    - This trigger stimulates euphoric recall when you don't stop the situation or walk away.
4. At a social event, an attractive person catches your eye and starts to flirt with you.
    - This trigger becomes a symptom when you respond and engage by flirting back, knowing this will cause problems.
5. In a social situation, a person jokingly forms sugar into lines pretending they are going to snort it.
    - This opens the door to relapse when you don't take care of yourself by turning or walking away.
6. You run into an ex-lover who is still using.
    - This trigger becomes a relapse symptom when you don't walk away but instead engage with your ex-lover and think about hooking up.

7. In a social situation, someone you want to impress suggests participating in your addiction.
   - This trigger becomes a symptom when you don't clarify you won't be participating.

RELAPSE PREVENTION STRUCTURE

There are three steps in relapse prevention:

1. Identify your relapse triggers, symptoms, and style.
2. Decide how you will deal with them and practice until you know that you can handle them.
3. Stay aware of your relapse attitudes, feelings, beliefs, thinking, and behaviors, and the consequences.

Your approach needs to include:

- Telling your support group about your triggers, symptoms, and style.
- Asking for and getting an agreement from your support people that they will strongly carefront you, if need be. As part of the agreement, settle on an acceptable carefrontation approach, one that they are willing to do and you are willing to respond to. 
- Clarify what the response of your support group will be if you reject their attempts to help you. Ideally, your negative response will mean your support group will disconnect until you respond positively.

Responding to Triggers

You can control how you respond to triggers. Learning to handle your sensations and emotions, especially the negative ones, will make dealing with using thoughts and feelings much easier. Identify what you're feeling and thinking in the exact moment you are triggered. Be aware of what's going on in your life in general. Recognize that unfamiliar sensations can be uncomfortable and easily mislabeled as negative, even when they're not. If you breathe deeply while observing yourself, triggers will be easier to process.

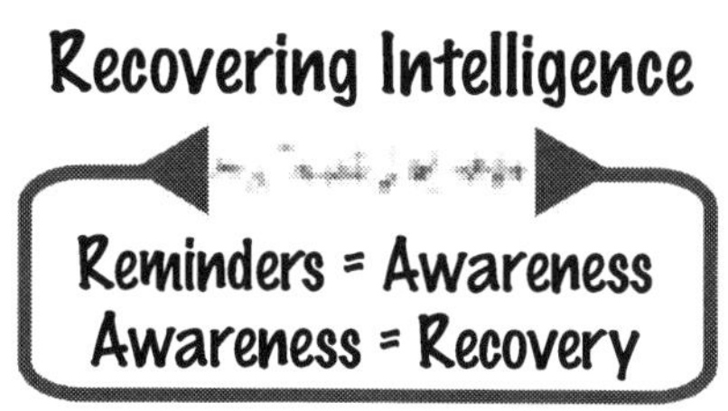

You want to neutralize all hot triggers so that they can't provoke you into using. Practice responding to potential triggers. Practice as often as it takes until your recovery responses to become automatic. (Find *Recovery Strategies* in the Index.)

In response to a trigger, affirm, breathe, meditate, pray, relax, and refocus on recovery. Use your tools. Reminders are one of the best ways to set yourself up for success, such as friends who will carefront you, visual red lights and dots, changing the type of music you play, or "One Day at a Time" signs. They remind you that you're in recovery and need to pay attention to how you're doing, and they help you to stay committed to your decision for a better future.

<u>Things on which you can focus</u>: Until you can reach additional resources, have at least one thing that will always

pick you up, calm you down, put you back on your road to recovery, and give you a reason to live. It should be something as certain as the sun rising and could include:

- Connections: Recovery or inspirational reminders, your kids' names, remembering the negative consequences of using or why you want recovery, or your connection with your Higher Power.
- Places:
  - » Positive: Your fellowship or church; being in nature or any place that would provide you with a very healthy, positive experience.
  - » Negative: Court or jail; facing your family.

Positive responses include:

Breaking State: Once triggered, breathe and break the mental emotional relapsing state you're in by disconnecting from it. Shift into the state of recovery by taking action.

Recovering Intelligence

Prepare: Break the state that's been triggered, & refocus on recovery.

Now M.O.V.E.:

- Move:Breathe, walk, exercise, etc.
- Observe: Acknowledge that your current reality is that you are in recovery.
- Visualize: Focus externally on anything non-using such as your shoes, the weather, and other people.
- Effect: Take recovery action immediately, and it will have a positive effect on your abstinence.

Full Circle Thinking is connecting the euphoric recall of using to the consequences. Think through the outcome of participating in your addiction. What would happen next? How would those results affect your life? Repeat this circle of questioning until you come to the reality that you would be lucky to end up back where you are in recovery, and you'd be worse off than you are now if you relapsed. This is often called *playing the tape out*.

Recovering Intelligence

Play the tape out & truly connect with the consequences of using.

Options Card: Have at least two effective go-to options available for when you're triggered or off track:

- Phone numbers.
- Powerful reasons for your recovery
- Review them daily. These will refocus you when you're triggered and/or hurting.

Recovering Intelligence

Your Options Card: 1) Support group phone #s & 2) Your motivation for recovery!

Phone numbers: Have the phone numbers of seven support group members and call one daily, on the same day each week. This telecommunication support group could include your sponsor, mentor, professionals, spouse's cell, treatment program, minister, and warm hotlines.

Positive Escape Plan: When a situation becomes too difficult to deal with, have an escape plan you and others have pre-agreed to, so that you have a way out of your dilemma. For example, have a pre-agreement with your spouse to leave a wedding if it gets too stressful.

Reframing is looking at something from another

perspective, which helps your recovery by giving you additional options and solutions. Reframing a trigger by viewing it in a different light can keep you from acting out.

Thought Stopping: Say to yourself, "Stop It!"

- Out loud with volume: Yell the words loudly, gradually lowering to a whisper as you repeat them.
- In your head: Silently "yell" the words in your head gradually lowering to a "whisper" as you repeat them.
- Practice until the words are mentally wired in, and even a silent whisper gives you a strong stop response.

Relapse is a frequent part of recovery for those who choose to turn towards the familiar, the temporary high, the darkness of despair, and the illusion that the addiction will work this time. Their reward will be continued insanity or worse. If you choose to stay aware, take personal responsibility, turn towards the light of hope, and use your available resources, you will get the better life that you want.

If, despite your supreme effort, you find yourself using, tell yourself that if you continue to use, the consequences will get much worse. Look into a future of continued active addiction and physically and emotionally, feel all the negative aspects of it. Imagine the reactions of others, and also recognize all you will lose. Ask yourself if it will be worth it to continue using. If not, reconnect to your recovery.

If relapse has been a problem for you, you may need intensive work. Find a qualified professional to help you deal with it. (See APPENDIX 10.)

SUMMARY

Relapse is a process whereby one's recovery thinking gradually evaporates and all the addictive thinking that support active use, return. You will regularly move in and out of mental-emotional relapse states. If you work a solid program, it's likely you won't ever have a relapse event, despite the occasional relapse state of mind. And if you do experience a relapse event, you'll usually recover from it much quicker.

The key is to be prepared for life's big and small issues, and especially for your hot triggers. You do this when you:

- Set up and live your quality recovering lifestyle.
- Set up and know your relapse prevention structure.
- Choose and use recovery tools and strategies.
- Stay aware: set up reminders and an options card.
- Know and manage your triggers: internal and external.
- Role-play and mentally rehearse your responses.
- Know your relapse symptoms and deal with them.
- Learn to reduce and manage the stress in your life.
- Shift your mental relapse style to a recovering style.

If you are triggered, your response will be to:

- Avoid the person, place, or situation that is triggering you. If you can't, breathe and manage your feelings.
- Connect with your resources especially your support group.
- Use your tools and strategies: options card.

No one is immune from a potential relapse event. Until you have made the mental-emotional shifts necessary in recovery, relapse is more of a possibility. Once you have processed and let go of issues – traumas, negative beliefs, and attitudes – and committed to **Your Recovering Future™**, using isn't as likely.

Breathe Deeply & Slowly &
Remember Why You Want Recovery!

Chapter 8

Marriage & Family Recovery

Chapter 8: Marriage & Family Recovery Table of Contents

MARRIAGE & FAMILY RECOVERY

The family of an addict has a lot to deal with. It's particularly difficult to live with the uncertainty of an addict's future. Will the addict in your family really stop and commit to recovery? Will your family free itself from secrets, destructive reviewing of past behavior, inconsistency, and verbal attacks? Will the family regroup into a healthy unit? Though it's normal to have questions, part of family recovery work is finding the tools, strategies, and support to develop or restore healthy balance to the family system.

FAMILY ADDICTION

Every birth family (family of origin), current family (partner and children), and extended family (close relatives and friends) has a system of relating, a way in which they interact. No matter how uninvolved or young they are, all family members have roles they play, which they learned from the family or adopted in response to it. Addiction can disrupt the balance of the family system and change the roles of the members. If the system finds a renewed

balance through consistency and health, it's usually because the family enters recovery, including counseling.

Family members attempt to have their needs met and cope with life the best they can. When there is addiction in the family, some may deny the problem and their part in it. This is referred to as ignoring the pink elephant in the room – which means that a big issue that everyone knows about, is not being addressed. Addicts in the family are totally caught up in their addiction, and the rest of the family refuses to deal with it directly, at least at the start. This is sometimes compared to being at war, but the enemy isn't a person. The enemy is the addiction or the addicted brain. This war probably started years earlier with certain behaviors that escalated to addictive behaviors.

A family with addiction often has issues like rigidness, mental illness, or child abuse. Addiction controls the family's life and causes an unhealthy family system to develop. As the system gets sicker, it focuses on surviving and becomes more rigid and closed to outsiders. Hiding family secrets, like the addict's using, a codependent covering-up, or a child never bringing friends home, these become normal. The family will defend itself by denying reality, the family's issues, and the need for change. When the family's

Recovering Intelligence

What are your family's secrets? Expose them & begin healing.

defenses are really strong, they refuse to acknowledge the pink elephant in the room by routinely talking and walking around it.

Over the years, family members try small, bigger, and then extreme things to curb or stop the addict's behaviors. The family system will permanently change for the better only when it becomes so disrupted that it must. The motivation for permanent change can occur when something inside of the system alters, like a family member moving away or dying, but usually it starts because of outside pressure. Examples include:

- An addict's work behavior leads to a manager's Employee Assistance Program referral.
- A child's intense acting out alerts authorities.
- An addict's behavior causes legal problems.

Choose to move your family's system towards health.

FAMILY RECOVERY

Due to a history of problems, all family members need to be in recovery. Even if a member is healthy, recovery is a chance for them to review their lives and consider their futures. The more family members that are involved in the family's recovery, the better the results are for everyone. It might be desirable to include extended family members and even very close friends, especially if they interact with your family on a regular basis.

Complete involvement cannot be expected for young children, severely handicapped individuals, or very elderly family members. It would be very beneficial for all family members, as individuals, to review this book.

By the time you start recovery, your current family and your family of origin can be torn apart, drifting, or stuck. Some changes can happen quickly, but it can take a long time to reconnect and heal deep wounds. One sad consequence of addiction is that some relationships may never heal.

Recovering Intelligence

Family members must engage in the recovery process.

Your family system must be observed, gently disrupted, and moved towards healthy functioning. The goal in recovery is to increase your family's:

- Feelings of being safe
- Openness and flexibility
- Nutritional health
- Ability to communicate and relate
- Ability to align as a unit, yet get individual support for each member

Your family will resist change and will have good and bad periods. You must expect these fluctuations. If you stay in recovery, balance will be restored. It's difficult for a

Recovering Intelligence

Healthy families are open & flexible; they explore, feel, trust, & talk.

family to change itself by itself. If it's possible, get help from a trained professional who can give valuable feedback and constructive suggestions for desirable changes.

Although your first priority as a recovering addict must be personal recovery, you also need to actively participate in the family's recovery. This can feel intense at times. If you breathe, relax, and stay focused on the goal, you can do it.

Family of origin: If you grew up in a very dysfunctional family where addiction was present, you qualify as an Adult Child of an Alcoholic (ACA). You likely have emotional scars that you will need to explore and work through. If a parent or sibling chooses not to change and wants to stay stuck in their dysfunction, you may have to build a new family of choice with people who act like a mother, father, or sibling.

It will be beneficial if your family of origin, other relatives, or close friends are healthy enough to be positive, but be careful. Everyone needs to be open and look at their previous beliefs, attitudes, and roles, and learn to stay aware of and handle their emotions. Together, hopefully your family can gradually develop a safe, healthy, and happy future.

Starting Recovery

Much of what you have learned so far, your family can apply towards their recovery. Explore the level of motivation and commitment of each family member. Some family members and sometimes the entire family is toxic and unwilling to change. Others are unsafe due to abuse issues. In recovery we must decide how to relate or not relate to our families. Decide to set your family up for success by building a solid program structure. Consider including:

- Couple or family counseling or treatment program
- Personal counseling for all members
- Family meetings and separate parent meetings
- Family activities and separate parent activities
- Writing down agreements and commitments
- Strategies or guidelines for dealing with chores, conflict, issues, vacations, etc.
- Exploring and changing family rules and roles

As you're ready, share your deeper feelings and dreams with each other, which might help bond you together.

Note: As the addict starts to get well, the family may begin to confront him or her about their anger, pain, worry, and other emotions.

Guidelines for Recovering Addicts

A partial list:

- You've likely been self-destructive, irresponsible, and untrustworthy, so expect that your family will question your motivation and commitment.
- Encourage your family to learn about recovery and your personal recovery challenges, especially relapse.
- Ask your family to actively participate in your recovery during treatment and in social activities.

- Open up emotionally and reconnect with your family (if it's safe). If they aren't instantly responsive, be tolerant and patient, steady and consistent. You need to prove things to yourself first anyway.
- Ask to spend one-to-one time with each family member, and be okay if they hesitate or decline.
- Find balance between relying on your support group and your family.

Guidelines for Family Members

A partial list:

- Understand recovery isn't easy; there may be setbacks. It's a time-consuming lifetime process about living a clean, quality life. Living a recovering life is a time-consuming and lifetime process, yet so desirable compared to addiction.
- Educate yourself about addiction recovery, especially family recovery. If the addict is in a treatment program, be involved as recommended.
- Develop a recovering home environment:
  - » Eliminate all addiction-related items and everything associated with them.
  - » Change or remove items that are triggers.
  - » Reduce stress, tension, and pressure.
  - » Clarify and communicate your needs, expectations, and limits. Stand up for yourself and the family. Set and achieve goals. Carefront issues and negotiate agreements.

- Personal work: Develop an awareness of and a commitment to dealing with your recovery and other issues, especially your codependent, communication, and boundary issues.
- Personal growth: You and your family need rest and fun. Everyone needs to focus on increasing their happiness, personal strengths, and self-development.

Guidelines for the Recovering Couple

A partial list:

- Practice kindness, apologizing, and forgiveness.
- Let go of your fears, and let down your defenses.
- Spend quality time together. Learn to engage and be emotionally intimate with each other.
- Socialize with other healthy recovering couples.
- Recognize and stop negative behaviors and interactions; rework them into positives.
- Develop your identity as a healthy couple.

Attitudes

Family members may hold beliefs and attitudes about addicts, recovery, psychology, or spirituality that oppose recovery. Overall, a family's attitude will be a negative or a positive force. Negative labels such as sick, pathetic, crazy, or loser will be destructive. Positive attitudes like wanting to help a loved one's recovery from a disease or to improve

Recovering Intelligence

Examine your attitudes & hold on to the healthy ones.

the family's ability to deal with life are constructive. What are your family's attitudes about recovery?

Balance

Your family system attempts to stay balanced as members take on roles and follow rules developed to maintain cohesion. The recovery of any one family member may throw off the balance of other family members. As a result, other members may unconsciously try to reestablish the original balance of the addicted system. These attempts may be as subtle as a call for help at an important treatment time, or as obvious as planting triggers (alcohol, food, money, etc.) for the addict to find, hoping for him or her to use, thereby keeping the addicted family system alive.

In recovery, while evolving a healthier balance, you should consciously, yet carefully, push the growth limits of your family system. Once you have some stability, you will also want to bring your own life into balance by focusing less on fixing the problems from your addiction and more on improving your and your family's lives.

Children

Children are victims, and they suffer a lot. They often assume the family's problems are their fault. It's very important that children get a strong, consistent message that they are not to blame for the family's problems. They

need to know that it's okay to be a child, they are loved, and you'll be there for them. Have them be as involved in recovery as possible through Alateen or a similar support group, keeping in mind each child's age and emotional development.

Codependents

Codependents are people who are close to the addict. They try to act in helpful ways; however, their actions keep the addict using and the sick family system alive. They are not the healthy ones, and once in recovery, they may have more problems than the addict. Many family members, especially spouses, feel the label of codependent (co) is a stigma. This makes them feel guilty. They need to let go of labels and focus on their growth and happiness. Generally, codependents have had more control over their behavior than they'd like to admit, but it's still essential for them to be in recovery. If they became healthy, the family system will change for the better. In the case of spouse codependents, recovery offers a chance for a couple to grow and stay together.

Codependency usually starts in childhood, so kids are also codependent and are affected by the family's addiction. They should be encouraged to work through their feelings about the past and their fears about the future. Children adopt roles, such as the sick

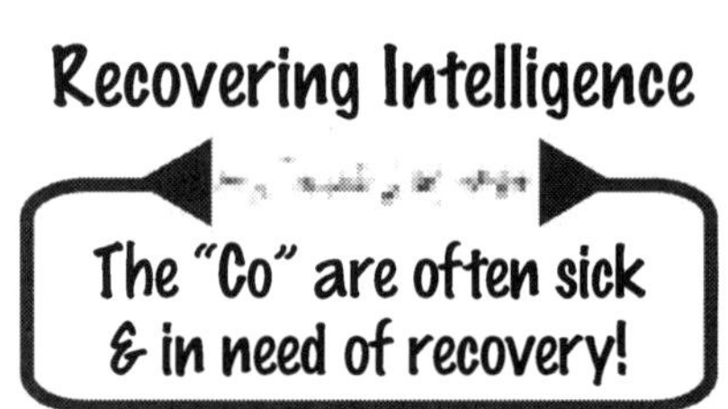

or rebellious one, to take the heat off the addict. If children don't resolve their issues now, they will carry them into their adulthood, possibly causing years of trying to work out their family of origin issues in adult relationships.

After building a recovery foundation, codependents need to rediscover themselves and explore their early years and how those years connect to current issues, patterns, and feelings. They need to learn to express their truth about what they like, need, and want.

Commitment

Many important commitments will be made throughout recovery. Some will be unique to your family, but there are two very fundamental ones.

The number one commitment of a family should be healthy recovery for all of its members. Each member needs to accept his or her addiction issues and be willing to dedicate the time necessary for successful recovery. Without this commitment from all family members, the family as a whole will struggle. The number two commitment is to develop the family unit by building quality relationships with each other.

For those in a relationship, plan to commit to at least one month of active relationship recovery for every year of active addiction before you make a

decision to end your relationship. There are exceptions, such as either partner's unwillingness to start recovery, physical or emotional abuse, and major disagreements about appropriate behavior or life values. In these situations, commitments should be reconsidered, even if there are children.

If your spouse refuses to go into counseling, tell him or her that you want professional help with your personal issues; ask him or her to join you for support. If he or she still refuses, go alone for yourself and your relationship.

Each parent should commit to providing a safe and supportive environment for their family and to be a role model for their children. They should take their children seriously, value them for who they are, and help them to become healthy, happy, secure, and well-adjusted people.

As each family member works through recovery issues, they should keep in mind their commitment to their own recovery, the addict's recovery, and the family's recovery. All three are integral to success.

Conflict

> **Recovering Intelligence**
>
> Pick your battles. You can win the battle but still lose the war.

Conflict can be a normal part of relating to one another. How you deal with it decides the health of your relationships and the happiness of those involved. Acknowledge and manage your ego, power, and control issues. Learn to agree to disagree and let things go. An open, caring, and *we*-focused style to resolving conflict will improve your relationships. A controlling, rigid, *me*-focused approach will damage them. It's quite likely that unresolved issues will always exist in a relationship; let it be okay.

Resolving Conflict: Learn how to argue fairly without an abusive tone, especially when you end the conflict. Set up a structure with rules to remain respectful, keeping in mind your desired outcome. (See APPENDIX 10.)

Coupleship

Coupleship is about building, rebuilding, and maintaining a primary relationship, hopefully one that's happy, healthy, and mutually beneficial. This takes opening up, trusting, caring, healing, bonding, and growing. To become a very intimate couple, you must attach, bond, and merge; these are important aspects to a relationship. You'll want your partner to positively influence you. You want to develop an identity and agree on relationship values and on the approach you'll use to create these.

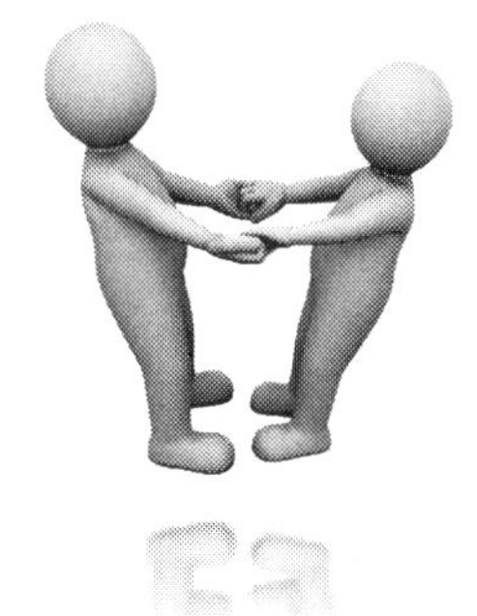

The four most toxic coupleship behaviors are:

- Blocking: Stopping or delaying interactions.
- Contempt: An attitude of utter disgust or hatred of

your partner.
- Criticism: Telling your partner about his/her faults.
- Defensiveness: Protecting oneself.

Family Defenses

Your family has built defenses that have become a part of how it functions. The family's defense system is comprised of the defenses of each individual member, starting with the parents. Old defense systems are loyal to no one. They can be represented as negative attitudes, such as:

- "We're fine as we are!"
- "I've done enough!"
- "It will never get better, so why try?"
- "If only (a specific person) would change, we would be good!"

Your family must become aware of the illusions of its dysfunctional defense style. The goal in recovery is for each member to open up and share their feelings so they can work through and release the pain of the past and make a change. Family members need help in developing a system with healthier defenses and boundaries. If parents lead by example, children may feel safe to follow. So parents, take a deep breath, and lead your family and all its members into healthier, happier, and more successful futures.

Recovering Intelligence

Family Recovery Rule #1: Open up, connect, trust, talk, & feel.

Family Education

Educate all immediate and extended family members about your addictions and your family's addicted system, and recovery from both. Recovery will include dealing with your family's defenses, roles, rules, and style. There are many resources on the web that will help you in educating your family about addiction and recovery – groups such as Al-Anon, Nar-Anon, CODA, addiction treatment programs, and private psychotherapists or coaches. There are also many books, workbooks, audio CDs, DVDs, YouTube videos, and literature available. Get information online and from local resources. Keep exploring until you find the resources you need.

Family Roles

We all have played, do play, and will play a variety of public and private roles.

- Public roles: Addict, money earner, parent, etc.
- Private roles: One or more roles in your addicted and recovering family system that help it work.

Roles are played to keep the family in balance. The problem is that roles don't allow people to honestly be themselves. Many of the following family roles are similar; you may find yourself switching roles or playing more than one role. Which role(s) do you identify with?

- Addict (Identified Patient): They and their addiction are the focus of the family. This pulls the family's focus, time, and resources away from deeper issues, member's needs, etc.

- Caretaker (Enabler/Rescuer): Controls, minimizes, seeks responsibility, focuses on others' issues and consequences, avoids self-focus. Looks good and helpful, yet pushes the addict towards his or her addictions.
- Hero: Approval-seeker, overachiever, successful, which keeps the focus off the system. Like the Caretaker, this role looks so positive, but the motivation often is not personally fulfilling.
- Lost Child: Escapes the family: avoids, is indifferent, reserved, silent, solitary, and withdrawn.
- Mascot: Attention seeker, comic distracter, keeps the focus off the family's addiction, even if negatively.
- Scapegoat: Angry, defiant, acts out, sullen, taking the focus off of the family's addiction.

Think about the ego-based roles you are playing in your relationships. Roles are not you; they are a script you play out. Explore them more deeply. You may have outgrown some roles, and other roles that have developed over time may be unhealthy. Knowing who you have been, who you are now, and who you want to become is essential for improving your life and your family's life.

Family Rules

All families have spoken and unspoken rules about what is okay and what is not okay. With family addiction comes the "don't talk, don't trust, don't feel" rule. An example of a common rule is, "If you don't confront me on my issues, I won't confront you on yours."

Explore your family's rules and become clear about what they mean, even the unspoken ones. Write them down and talk about them. Decide which ones you want to change, and change them. Start using your new ones. Leave them posted in a visible place. Pay attention so the old rules don't slide back into use.

Generational Families

All families inherit genetic, psychological, and behavioral traits. Knowledge of those belonging to your parents and past generations will be very helpful. Research indicates that issues can carry on for many generations. Be the person who breaks your family's generational links to addiction and other negative traits, for yourself and for your family.

In Your Primary Relationship

Recovering Intelligence

Emotional intimacy is the vehicle for connecting sexually & spiritually.

Healthy people aren't desperate for a primary relationship to make them whole or happy. But they do want to have the joy and fulfillment of being in a loving, mutually beneficial relationship with another healthy person. Open up to your desire to stand side-by-side with your partner, pursuing goals and sharing a full life together.

You'll want to be there for each other with mutual love and respect. You'll have room to grow your relationship, making it healthy, safe, intimate, and passionate, but the ultimate goal in recovery is to have a solid relationship and to help heal each other's past wounds. At this level of intimacy, you'll have the privilege of experiencing your partner's deepest fears, wounds, hopes, and dreams. This can be unpleasant, painful, and scary – and a blessing. To successfully live through the amazing adventure of an intimate relationship, you must push through the expected issues, and live with the ones that may never get resolved.

When one person is emotionally available and the other isn't, the available person can feel abandoned. If the unavailable person wants to be available, they must dig deeper.

Consider: **"In My Experience... you don't want a relationship goal of being right or getting your way, but of being fulfilled, happy, and successful."** (See APPENDIX 7.)

Physical connection is important. People need physical stimulation, touch, hand-holding, massages, etc. Sexual connection is vital for emotional, physical, and spiritual health. Both people need to agree on the amount, level, and style of their physical-sexual-emotional relationship.

Issues In Relationships

There will be many relationship issues to overcome and

grow from. Most of these issues can wait until the family has become stabilized, reconnected, and has started to heal.

To work through relationship issues, first look at the problem behind the issue so you can see the solution. Don't deny or defend during the exploration process, but first, LISTEN, and then share openly, honestly, yet kindly.

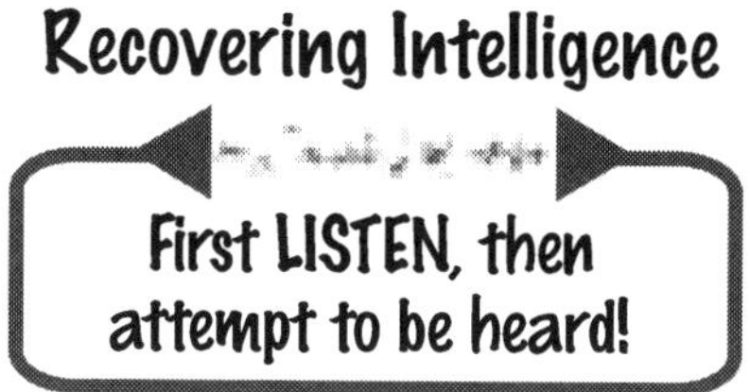

Second, assume old issues will return and new issues will arise. Pay attention so that when they do, you'll see them and can face them. Pay special attention to the yellow flags, and a lot of attention to the red flags:

- Abuse: Current abuse must stop, even if it means moving to a safe place. Physical abuse is never acceptable. Emotional and verbal abuse is hurtful to everyone. The abuser needs to become more responsive to the feelings of others and educated by looking at the consequences of his or her behavior. The abused person needs to stop tolerating abuse and do whatever it takes to be safe. Past abuse issues must be processed and healed.
- Boundaries: Assume that your family has boundary issues that need to be improved. Healthy boundaries will help everyone function better. Keep your personal limits strong and flexible; support other members to do the same. Family members should practice

saying, "no," to each other. (Find *Boundaries* in the Index.)

- Despair: Confronting your past history, and working on moving through these issues will reduce, or even reverse, your despair.
- Disappointment: Your life will have disappointments, broken promises, and unfulfilled expectations. Accept this reality, release these disappointments, and focus on being grateful for what you do have now, and will have in the future.
- Distrust: Hurt needs to be healed and trust rebuilt, if possible. This will take an unknown period of time. Healing begins with constructive actions, not empty words.
- Embarrassment: Everyone makes mistakes and feels embarrassed occasionally. Laugh at your humanness, and be okay with yourself. The better you feel about yourself, the less of a problem this will be.
- Fear: Fear is a response that motivates you to act in a dangerous situation. While fear is a healthy response, an excessive amount of fear isn't. Don't mistake anxiety for fear. Respect and challenge your fears, and move through or around them. Don't let fear stop you.
- Guilt: You can't change your past actions, so release the guilt you feel over them and acknowledge your commitment to not repeating such acts again. Accept your humanness.

- Identity: To start, the whole family's negative identity must be shifted from sick and addicted to partially functional and recovering. Then onto happy and fully functional.
- Intimacy: The level of emotional intimacy in your close relationships indicates their quality and depth, as does the physical and sexual intimacy in your primary relationship.
- Isolation: Feelings of fear, guilt, and shame cause addicted families to put up walls to guard their secrets, thus isolating themselves to hide the family disease. These feelings and patterns may continue into recovery. Safely talk about family secrets with members or trusted others, including your feelings about your situation. Never isolate!
- Power and control: All human interaction has power and control issues. Whether you try to claim power and control, are neutral, or give yours away – accept and deal with the truth that the only real thing you have control over is how you deal with your part in the process of interacting. Develop cooperative relationships.

Consider: **"In My Experience... you don't want to excessively focus on external power or controlling other people."** (See APPENDIX 7.)

- Resentment: Your resentment can be about small things, like your partner won't immediately pick-up after him or herself, or huge things, like your family won't talk to you. Promote an open discussion with those who are feeling resentment and attempt to clear the air. Everyone needs to admit and take responsibility for their actions. Hopefully, this will get rid of the pink elephant in the room.

- Secrets: We are only as sick as our sick secrets. Sick secrets are anything that causes family members extreme embarrassment, humiliation, or shame. They pull you down and sabotage your family's recovery. What are your family secrets? Would they cause any family members to feel bad if others knew? Expose them to caring others and let them heal.

Recovering Intelligence

A sick secret needs to be revealed & discussed so that you can heal.

- Suspicion: Leave the past in the past, and trust others based on their behavior and the facts.
- Trust: Start rebuilding the trust of others by learning to trust yourself. Walk your talk, and keep promises. This will show yourself and others that the new recovering you is trustworthy.

Parenting

Recovery gives you a chance to make your children a high priority in your life. You need to learn how to:

Recovering Intelligence

Recovery gives you & your children a second chance!

- Be the authority: guide and teach them.
- Be a role model: help them develop their boundaries, a sense of self, self-worth, strengths, values, etc.
- Take care of them: recognize their physical and practical needs.
- Open up and be emotionally close to them.
  - » Ask them about their life and listen.
  - » Have weekly one-to-one time with each child.
  - » Make amends in a way that is desirable, understandable, and will be helpful to all.
  - » Acknowledge your love and gratitude for your children and that they are a blessing.
  - » Give them affection, love, and support.
  - » Without offering a drug history, share with them that you have an addiction. Be age appropriate; consider whether or not certain information will really help them.

Relationship Building

You need to show by your behavior that you want your relationships to work. Do this by acting in positive ways and not acting in negative ones. Practice the following:

- Acknowledge appreciation, gratitude, kindness, and thankfulness: Positively acknowledge your family as often as possible. Relationships flourish at a ratio of five or more positive experiences to every one negative (5 to 1) experience.
- Act loving: Do things you know your partner and kids will like, love, or will help them in a way they

will value. If you don't know what these loving things are, ask them.

- Apologize: Acknowledge the negative behavior that you regret doing, and state that it won't happen again. Communicate how sorry you are.
- Be Emotionally Available: Share your feelings, and listen to others. Being emotionally honest and vulnerable makes healing and growing together possible.
- Practice Empathy: Attempt to actually feel what others are feeling. Offer to help. With hope, this will make them feel special.
- Engage: Actively interact with your family through quality time, in real and playful ways, individually and as a whole.
- Forgive: Forgive yourself and others when mistakes are made. This doesn't mean you forget what happened, as that may cause the wrongdoing to continue and re-injure. Stay aware of past mistakes so you don't repeat them.
- Heal: Relationships heal in response to apologies, amends, forgiveness, and quality behavior.
- Be Grateful: Experience your feelings of gratitude, and share those feelings with your family and friends. Consider writing a letter of gratitude to very important people and keeping a gratitude list.
- Create Identity: Build or reinstate a positive identity as a couple and as a family.
- Share Intimacy: Share deep thoughts and emotions.

- Address Issues: Stay aware of and carefront all unhealthy patterns and negative outside influences, old or new.
- Be Kind: Kindness improves relationships; lack of kindness deteriorates them. Be kindhearted and practice random acts of kindness.
- Listen: When someone is speaking, actively listen, keep eye contact, acknowledge the speaker, and share your thoughts, feelings, and opinions if asked.
- Practice Reconciliation: Attempt to settle all disputes or conflicts, or agree to disagree.
- Show Respect: Respect the beliefs, opinions, and decisions of others, even if they totally disagree with yours.
- Be Safe: Develop a sense of safety with each other.
- Be Supportive: Be available and ask your partner and children what they need. Then offer them the support they ask for, unless it involves acting negatively.
- Know Your Tools: Use your recovery tools when needed.
- Develop Trust: Show your trust and trustworthiness.

Strategies

You need to implement successful strategies to help your family become healthier and happier. Define your family's most valued goals. What are your family's strategies for

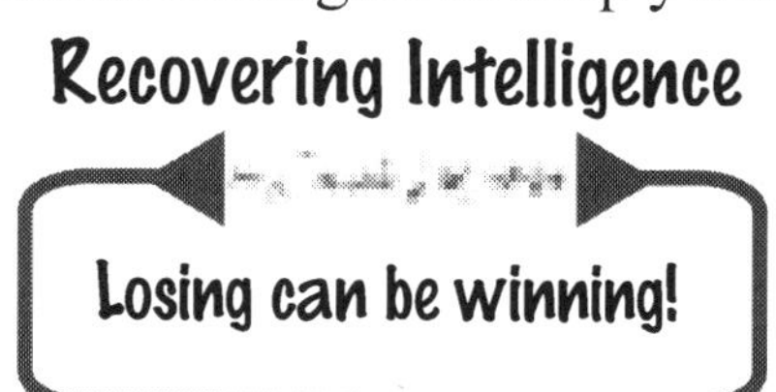

finding options, solutions, and for meeting their goals? Do you need to adjust, evolve, or replace any of your strategies?

Be careful that ego, power, and control issues don't cause problems and hurt everyone in the process. An example of a positive strategy for dealing with ego is "Winning the War." A mature person accepts that it's sometimes necessary to lose a battle – letting go of an issue, forgiveness, etc. – to win the ultimate victory of maintaining a functional and desirable relationship. Hopefully, it's more important to be happy than to always be right.

Recovering Intelligence

Each family member & the family as a whole needs support.

If your strategies aren't working, try different ones until you find the strategies that work, or at least work better than what you have been doing. If you're unable to establish successful patterns, read a self-help book and actively put the suggestions to use or get professional help.

Support System

Early in your recovery, you may find the support of friends and family to be invaluable. Along with your usual needs, you'll have new recovery needs. Your using friends and codependents will eventually disappear. It's a time to reaffirm positive existing relationships. Maintain a quality connection with your current family and friends if possible. Reach out to the recovery community and start new relationships with those who understand recovery. Seek out couples for social support with whom you can associate, share feelings, and talk through situations.

RELATIONSHIP RECOVERY APPROACHES

Recovery approaches that are focused on your family and relationships will feel awkward or strange at first, but with practice, they will become easier. If you use the following resources, your family will grow and prosper.

Communication

Open and honest sharing can be difficult, especially with a history of family addiction. Yet, it's the foundation of quality relationships. Most couples don't communicate effectively. Learn to communicate using recovery tools to help you. Take it slowly; attempt to be as kind and supportive as possible while still sharing your truth. Grow comfortable discussing how you're feeling. Listen. The biggest problem in interpersonal communication is not listening to the other person.

Defensiveness makes communication very difficult or even impossible. You can be calm, pleasant, and communicative and still be defensive. Be very honest with yourself whether you are truly being open and responsive. If you can't agree when you're carefronted, respond with, "I'll think about that." Then think about it, and sooner or later, let others know your thoughts. Breathe as you do this!

Suggestions for better communication:

1. Listen actively – Pay attention to what the speaker

is saying and genuinely think about it. Wait three seconds before responding to them.

2. Keep eye contact – Look the speaker in the eye for the same amount of time they look at you, somewhat longer when you are the one speaking.
3. Use "I" statements – "I" statements are powerful and can't be disputed (although someone may try) because they come from your experiences. Using "I feel..." "I think..." or other "I" statements takes personal responsibility.

Family Meetings

Weekly family meetings use an agreed upon structure and are for all family members old enough to participate. They are opportunities to vent feelings, carefront issues, and share the joys of each member's life. All issues from the week are put on the table. None are pushed aside. Parents use judgment about the subject matter.

Family Outings

Family outings are drug-free, social time spent together. Cooperatively decide in advance what the family's activities will be – what will happen and how much money and time will be spent on specific things. Remember to cooperate, compromise, be kind, and have fun.

Immediate Recovery Plans: Family Contract

You and your family members need to write up and sign a clear and specific dated and signed contract among yourselves and others. This can be an important turning point in your family's motivation to be in recovery.

Intimate Family Experiences

Emotionally intimate experiences, where deep thoughts and feelings are shared, are very important between parents and their children. They can happen individually or as a group. Intimate family experiences allow families to become closer, really get to know each other, connect, and develop personal relationships. They also show your kids how to connect with others. It's best to share during a favorite activity, like around the fire during a camping trip.

Positive Reinforcement

Random yet consistent acts of kindness, where feelings of value towards another person are expressed, positively reinforces family members. Expense isn't important; it's the thought that counts. This can be a personal note written on a Post-it or greeting card, cooking a favorite meal, or taking the family out for a special dinner or activity.

Pre-agreements

A pre-agreement is a planned arrangement to initiate a specific action in response to a situation, usually one that's turning excessive, extreme, or out of control. It's a basic back-up plan. When a specific action or situation arises, a pre-agreement of how to act would go into effect. For example, if anger escalates to an uncomfortable level, anyone can call a time-out or wave a white flag, and all parties will walk away and return after a pre-agreed amount of time.

Recovery Goals

All family members of an addicted family system need to participate in recovery. The goal of the family unit should be to:

- Support all members' recovery and their personal health, growth, and happiness.
- Listen to every member and practice empathy, support, and encouragement.
- Use family recovery and relapse prevention plans.

Family recovery goals: The goal of most families is to develop a healthy family system comprised of open and honest communication. Family recovery, spiritual values, and financial stability are examples of other worthwhile and obtainable goals. With the input of all family members, including children, decide what your most important family goals are, and set up a structure to achieve them. Blend family goals with the goals of each member. Encourage self-development, and explore personal needs and roles.

Sharing positive, loving, and intimate feelings while experiencing the joy of recovery will replace the criticism and pain that may have occurred during addiction. As your family's recovery builds, the negative intensity of addiction will decrease, and healthy interaction will become common.

FAMILY RECOVERY PLANNING

Your family's recovery plan clarifies its recovery structure as well as specific life needs, both in the process of recovery and beyond. All family members need to develop an individual recovery plan for themselves, separate from the family recovery plan, which can still include some of the personal needs of family members. Follow the format offered in earlier chapters of this book, starting with *Defining Your Personal Recovery*. Design a plan that will fit your family's needs as a whole.

Codependents should pay close attention to the following strategies:

- Boundaries and setting limits: Explore and clarify who you are and what you want for yourself and your family. Set clear, strong, yet flexible boundaries so your family will have structure.

- Clarify your family goals: Parents need to discuss the family's goals with each other and then with their kids, as age appropriate. Make your short-term goals support your long-term ones.
    - » Relationship goals: Determine goals that will support recovery for family members.
    - » Family: Decide what kind of family you want. One that is independent? One in which all

members get their needs met?

  » Children: How do we help our children flourish?

- Codependents' personal recovery: Codependents must let go of responsibilities that are not theirs, especially those belonging to the addict. They need to take responsibility for their own life and realize their feelings, wants, and needs are important. This is accomplished through self-discovery and learning to feel, trust, and share their feelings and their truth.

Recovering Intelligence

Codependents must focus on themselves & their addiction(s).

- Communicating: Family members need to share their feelings, wants, and needs with each other; to think and share in ways that encourage communication, growth, intimacy, and trust.
- Support Groups:
  - » Couples: Find the support of other couples who are in recovery. Consider Recovering Couples Anonymous (RCA) if both partners are in a 12-Step program. In RCA, couples work through the steps together with a sponsor couple. Also, look for a support or treatment group through a church or recovery program, or start your own.
  - » Children: Children may benefit from a support group. Look for a professionally run group.
- Family recovery structure: Build an approach that will move your family forward; include your

recovery plan, family meetings, and support.

- New family rules: After reviewing your family rules, change them to shift your family towards health.
- Recovery tools: Really learn and understand the recovery tools presented in this chapter and Chapter 3. Then put them into practice regularly.
- Relapse prevention:
    - » Codependents: The relapse symptoms of a codependent are different from an addict, but the prevention process is similar. All family members should know their relapse symptoms and have specific agreements about how they will respond, solve their issues, and get back on track. (Find *Relapse* in the Index.)
- Relationship counseling: If relationship counseling is started within the first six months of recovery, it should be limited to surface issues: cognitive, behavioral, and practical. Focus can include communication, a crisis, lack of a family member's involvement, and the family's recovery goals.
- Successful strategies: Look at the strategies you are using. What works and what doesn't? Ask trusted others for their feedback.

SUMMARY

Families feel the pain and wreckage of addiction perhaps even more than the addict does. This can create a big challenge for the family and the addict to reconcile and heal. In an effort to keep their balance and their sanity as they move forward, families attempt to cope with the insanity of addiction by developing an addicted family system of "don't trust, don't feel, don't tell."

All family members:

- May resist self-examination and healthy change.
- Need to play healthier roles and stabilize the family.
- Must choose to open up, trust, feel, and talk.
- Must choose to support only healthy behavior.
- Need to develop and work their personal programs.
- Must shift their sick roles to healthier versions.
- Need to be patient and kind, and act courageously.

Codependent family members need to:

- Stop trying to control and fix others' behaviors.
- Focus on their own feelings and behaviors.

The family must:

- Set up a successful approach and use it.
- Stabilize and practice clear, open communication.
- Be educated about addiction and recovery.
- Wake up to reality and engage in recovery.
- Expose the family's secrets and let them heal.
- Support a safe, open, and healing environment.
- Consciously change their rules to promote health.
- Shift the closed family system to a healthy open one.
- Be encouraged to use their strengths and live fully.
- Become playful, supportive, trusting, and intimate.
- Shift from despair to hope, and faith.
- Develop a healthy family identity.

- If a good effort doesn't work, get professional help.

The children must:

- Be supported and encouraged to be healthy.
- Know that what has happened is not their fault.
- Be given time, love, support, and connection.

The parents must:

- Be role models and lead the family.
- Have their own structure, plan, time, and goals.
- Build and nurture their intimate relationship.

If the family is very ill and unable to shift, healthier members must find a family of choice, people who want to act like their family.

Thriving Beyond Addiction™

Conclusion

THRIVING BEYOND ADDICTION™ SUMMARY

If you have thoroughly read this book, you have been offered a lot of information, concepts, strategies, tools, and other resources. You were introduced to three new concepts:

- The Red Dot Reminder Check-In System for raising your awareness of your recovery and life in general, increasing your options and control over your life.
- The concept of **Recovering Intelligence™**, which contains emotional intimacy, resiliency, social, spiritual, and interpersonal intelligences. This is the knowledge and skills you need to effectively create a successful recovering life.
- The vision of **Your Recovering Future™**, reminding you how important it is, in the present, to move toward your ideal recovering lifestyle. Imagining what your future will be if you stay in recovery can help you create such a clear and desirable image, you'll do what it takes to reach it.

Remember the ideas discussed in this book. Weave them into your life, one at a time. Easy does it! Ideas such as:

- Always remember the truth about your addiction.
- Attend self-help programs on a regular basis.
- Be curious!
- Be happy and enthusiastic about your life! Go for the life you want!
- Be honest about personal issues and challenges you're facing as a result of your past or personal style, even when it's painful. Discuss your options

with trusted friends or a professional.

- Become comfortable with the ideas, concepts, and definitions of words used in recovery.
- Breathe, deeply and slowly.
- Choose a recovery approach, but add your personal goals to meet your needs and desires; live your life in the successful structure you create.
- Choose to believe you will successfully complete your next recovery goal or milestone.
- Develop, use, and improve your written recovery, life, and relapse prevention plans.
- Develop and use your Observing Self (or Observer Self), especially in difficult situations.
- Don't defend against people who are on your side.
- Grow as much as possible, in all areas of your life.
- If you falter, get right back into your recovery. Review what happened and make adjustments.
- Learn: read, attend meetings, talk to others in recovery (from your particular addiction), etc.
- Learn and practice new healthy ways of thinking, acting, and relating with others. If not, you'll continue your old ways that supported your addiction.
- Learning about recovery is good, but getting involved is great! Recovery is a blessing!
- Listen; be curious, willing, and grateful.
- Make a list of your recovery tools and skills. Practice them until they are natural and effective.
- Practice and embrace strategies for mentally-emotionally staying in recovery when you encounter

high-risk situations. Have positive responses ready for when you become triggered or start to crave.

- Put aside your negative beliefs, attitudes, and assumptions about recovery and focus on the new and different options that will be offered. Remember, addiction is a FAMILY disease; all members of the family need to be in recovery.
- Review the quality of your nutrition. Consider adding amino acids or other nutritional supplements.
- Stay aware, focused, and motivated, yet relaxed.
- Set yourself up for success by "the action of now."
    - » Develop a style for completing important tasks; set reminders to yourself to do the tasks by a certain time or date.
- Take advantage of the powerful and valuable experience that the therapeutic group process offers.
- Trust your support group and the process that many have successfully used before you.
- Understand the three phases of recovery. Know which one you are in, based on your progress, not the length of your clean time; and what activities you're not ready for, such as starting a romantic relationship.
- Use your personal strengths daily.
- Realize that your structure strongly influences your outcome.

Quality recovery starts with self-awareness, embracing recovery, and building a solid recovery foundation. Sustained recovery continues because you invest in your new life, your health, and your personal growth. Remember how much time, money, and energy you spent sustaining your using lifestyle? Invest that much effort in recovery, and your life will change for the better, possibly even dramatically.

CONCLUSION

I hope this book has helped you understand the process of recovery. That it has inspired you to set yourself up to successfully develop your **Recovering Intelligence™**. And that it will help you cut through the maze of recovery and to create **Your Recovering Future™**.

Your future can either be a lifelong struggle with emotional pain, physical diseases, and spiritual longing, or it can be a life full of opportunities to grow into the best you can be. The life you will live is the one that you focus on, feed, and nurture. It's up to you. Everything is a choice; choose wisely!

I hope you'll accept your humanness, defects and all. That you'll embrace and use your strengths every day and love your ever-evolving self. One day, one hour, one minute, one second at a time, accept the challenges ahead. You'll be successful if you:

> **Recovering Intelligence**
>
> **You'll succeed one thought, feeling, & decision at a time!**

- Always remain aware of your most powerful motivation for why you want to be in recovery!
- Decide to do whatever it takes to succeed.
- Be patient! Because of all the years you practiced your addiction, thinking and acting like an addict became second nature. Give recovery your total commitment for ½ or even ¼ that much time.
- Embrace a healthy, growth-oriented lifestyle.
- Expect you'll come across periods of time when you are having problems with your motivation, you are ill, or life just isn't going well. If, at these times, stressors such as old friends call and invite you to drink or use, eat, gamble, play, shop, etc., replace old patterns by activating new ones. You'll tell yourself, "It'll be okay." Lean on your support system to get you past such times and situations, and return to engaging in your recovery.
- Follow the lead of others who have gone before you.
- Make use of every needed inner and outer resource.
- Open up to, focus on, and embrace the great life that recovery can offer you and your family.
- Use this book often.
- Use the accompanying **Thriving Beyond Addiction Workbook** for a fuller and deeper program.

Valued outside resources can make your life a lot easier, but recovery is an inside job. You are the only one who can look at your own reality accurately, handle your

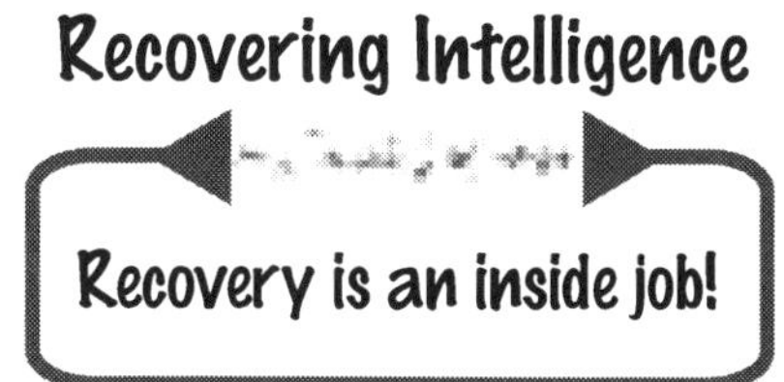

emotional responses, consider all of your options, make the right decisions, and take the best actions. You are the one who has to live with your outcomes.

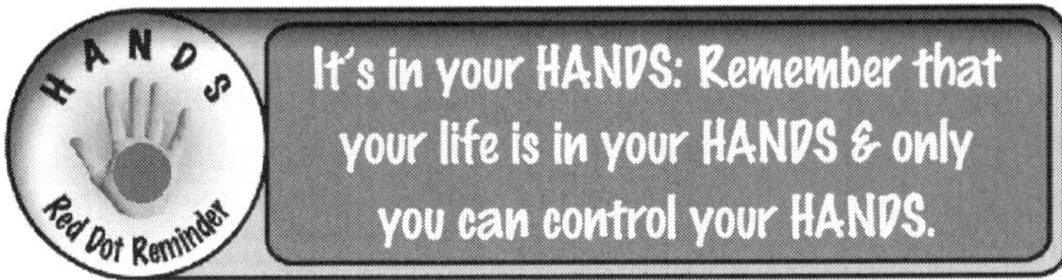

In the final analysis, it's your behavior that is the reality of your recovery and your life, not your words.

You can do this!
Keep breathing and keep walking towards Your Recovering Future™

Live fully, laugh often, love deeply, & celebrate your recovery
Good luck!

MY RECOVERING INTELLIGENTLY APPROACH

- **Learn: Read, listen, practice, stay present.**
- **Focus: On recovery, NOT on the "old days."**
- **Honesty: About your addiction.**
- **Recovery Program: Have it! Know it! Use it!**
- **Structure Your Life: Hourly... Daily... Yearly!**
- **Connect: With your thoughts and feelings, and with your support group, accountability partner, mentor, and your Higher Power.**
- **Consume: Quality nutrition.**
- **Awareness: Of old addiction thoughts and behavioral patterns.**
- **Tools and Strategies: Use recovery tools to support your strategies for recovery.**
- **Set and Achieve: Goals and milestones.**
- **Focus: On positive feelings, healthy living, and spiritual openness.**
- **Assess: Mental, emotional, physical, social, and spiritual growth.**
- **Create: A relapse prevention plan.**
- **Amends: Make them to family and friends.**
- **Foster: Supportive relationships.**
- **Nurture: Social-Emotional Intelligence.**
- **Keep: A clear vision of My Recovering Future™.**

= Your Quality Recovering Lifestyle

Thriving Beyond Addiction™

APPENDIXES

Thriving Beyond Addiction™
Appendixes
Table of Contents

APPENDIX 1: BEFORE RECOVERY CAN START

ADDICTION EVALUATION

You have an addiction when using causes significant life problems, and yet you continue to use. Using has become the problem, but it still feels like a solution. Addiction is a biological, emotional, mental, social, and spiritual based disease. It creates excessive negative behaviors that you can't control. Addictions especially flood the brain with neurotrasmitters. These cause the brain to be rewired so it eventually believes, "I must use to survive." Even when you aren't using, you're thinking about it. If you think you may have an addiction issue, you do.

Underneath the misuse of substances, destructive behaviors, and codependency, are emotional feelings that are pushing your addiction along. Coping with your addiction is difficult, but you must move past your issues and build a positive emotional life. A major factor in addiction is avoiding negative emotions. In recovery, connect with all of your feelings and with your heart.

In the beginning, your addiction likely did help you avoid negative emotions, or at least it seemed to help, but now it has turned on you. You may have sworn off using for a period of time, believing time off would solve your addiction problems, only to find the same issues reappearing when you started using again. It's time to look at and accept the reality of your using before the dues become even heavier, or it's too late. If there is no problem, prove it to yourself and abstain from using for six months or longer.

Addictions are common. Stop asking, "Am I an addict or not?" And ask, "How is addiction affecting my life?" or "To what degree is my behavior negatively affecting me and my family?" You may also be addicted to the process, to the experience, and to the behaviors of addiction. These include stimulation, scoring, obtaining, preparing, using rituals, social interactions, and a sense of belonging.

The key to the self evaluation below is to be honest. Avoid rationalizing your responses. The following quiz should only be a starting place.

Addiction Self-Evaluation

Answer Yes or No:

_____ Has anyone asked me or commented about my using?
_____ Do I use more, or more often, than I plan on?
_____ Do I feel negative emotions about my using?
_____ Do I hide or sneak my using from others?
_____ Do I cover up my using or the consequences?
_____ Do I have fewer close friends than I used to?
_____ Do I continue to use despite negative results?
_____ Do I think about using for hours before I do it?
_____ Has my using caused me to act undesirably?
_____ Has my using decreased my desired activities?

_____ Has anyone confronted me about my using?

One yes answer should be a concern; three or more and you should seriously consider that you have an addiction issue and explore recovery; six or more and you have a problem. Start recovery immediately.

PRE-TREATMENT

Hitting Bottom

Major motivation for recovery occurs when you have hit your bottom, which is the point in time when you experience the reality that you have an addiction and that it is hurting your life and the lives of your loved ones. When you hit a bottom, the negatives of your behavior become real, your defenses break down, and denial is gone. You are left with the consequences that your addiction has caused in your life. Connecting as fully as you can to this awareness will motivate your need for change. Everyone has their own *enough* level, which is their bottom. You can raise your bottom by looking at your illusions, and reconsidering the mythical value that using has in your life. Let the reality of your using sink in. Connect with your healthy self and with those who care about you.

If you are fortunate, you will have hit your bottom early in your using career. If you say, "I'm not that bad, yet," good! Why would you want to get worse or get that bad? Hitting bottom is not completely negative. It's a crisis, but like any crisis, it's an opportunity to experience change and growth and become better. Choosing to continue your addiction can lead to many problems, such as jail, illness, loss of a job, loss of money, damaged relationships, and ultimately death.

Brain Scan: A brain scan is a powerful reality check. It's very hard to deny that there's a problem while looking at an image of the physical damage that has resulted from your behavior. This can be expensive, unless you can get medical insurance to help with the cost. Find *Brain Scan* in the Index.

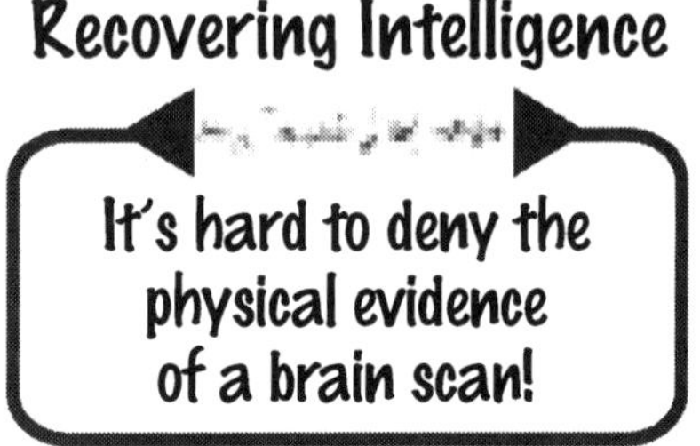

Intervention

An intervention is a method for family and friends to give caring and supportive confrontation to the addict in their lives. In this collective group, the possibility of increased defensiveness, avoidance, manipulation, and hostility is reduced. The goal of an intervention is to awaken the addict to their need for help, and get them committed to recovery immediately. Traditionally, this involves an addict consenting to treatment in a residential program. For many, this isn't the right fit. The person may be motivated to participate in a less intense option, it would be financially difficult, job restraints or there are no residential programs for his or her specific addiction.

The theme in an intervention is concern, and the approach

is carefronting the addict with facts about how their behaviors have effected those participating in the intervention. If the addict is able to relax his or her defenses, and accept the truth, they may be rescued from hitting a lower bottom.

A well-done intervention is a loving, yet manipulative process. The motivation for an addict to recover comes partly from their relationship with the carefronters; the possibility of loss of support, family, or a job can be very persuasive. Often, once an addict has realized their need to change, recovery will take hold.

The phases of an intervention are:

1. Family, friends, employer, etc. who are concerned about, and important to, the addict need to agree to participate. A group of eight people is about right. Ideally, get a professional interventionist, who will hold one or more pre-intervention meetings.
2. At pre-intervention meetings, the following issues will need to be discussed and a plan finalized:
   - Each participant needs to understand the intervention process. They need to vent their negative feelings towards the addict and decide on a personal experience they will share with the addict as an example of why they are concerned.
   - It's vital to break through any denial the participants may have about the confronted person's addiction. Usually the addict's addiction has been

enabled by well intending family members. This must be addressed and an agreement has to be made to stop rescuing, fixing and saving the addict from the consequences of his or her behavior. Furthermore, the participants must get past their negative feelings about the addict, their using, and the intervention process itself.

- A decision must be made to determine whether an intervention is going to happen, who is going to participate, and what the group will expect the confronted addict to do. Anything less than a strong, clear, and solid group agreement is likely to sabotage the intervention.
- A plan must be agreed upon as to how to get the addict to the intervention location and other details that need to be arranged.

3. The intervention experience:
   - One or more participants will bring the confronted addict to a home, doctor's office, treatment center, or any desirable location. This may need to be done under false pretenses.
   - The designated facilitator will briefly share the reason for the meeting and ask the addict to agree to listen until everyone has shared. Hopefully, the addict agrees to listen. If not, a prearranged response needs to be initiated.
   - Each participant, in pre-agreed order, will share for up to five minutes one specific using-related incident that was difficult, embarrassing, hurtful,

or scary and their feelings regarding the incident.

- The participants can share their feelings and hopes for the addict to accept help and live a healthy life. This is not a debate about whether the addict has a problem; it's a monologue of why the addict needs help.
- The facilitator shares the group's decision and expectations for the addict and attempts to get an agreement with the addict.
- If no agreement is obtained, a second, less intense option can be offered with a consequence rider. That is, if the second option doesn't work, the first option will be carried out. For example, if the addict refuses residential treatment but agrees to out patient care, if the latter is unsuccessful, then residential treatment becomes the only option.
- If neither option is accepted, then it's time for the participants to share their response to that decision. Until recovery is started, participants will break off their relationship, separate from marriage, be severed from work, etc. If the confronted still doesn't respond, end the intervention and put tough love into action.
- If the addict returns to using, a second intervention may be necessary. This last and final intervention sets up what the addict must do to continue having any contact with family and friends.

Intervention is a very hard experience, and not everyone

agrees that it's the best approach.

Community Reinforcement & Family Training (CRAFT)

CRAFT is a cognitive behavior model for dealing with alcoholism that aims to achieve abstinence by eliminating the positive benefits of drinking and increasing the positive benefits of sobriety. CRAFT has several parts and is designed to build up motivation to quit using:

- Helping the addict initiate sobriety.
- Analyzing the addict's using patterns.
- Increasing positive benefits through reinforcement.
- Learning new coping behaviors.
- Involving significant others in the recovery process by teaching them skills.

APPENDIX 2: ADDICTION: CAUSES & TYPES

CAUSES OF ADDICTION

Understanding the causes of addiction can stimulate you to want to recover from it. There are many models of how addiction originates.

Bad Habit Model: In this model of addiction, bad habits develop as a benefit of pleasure, comfort, and security. These habits have been influenced by negative environments. Habits can be stopped by changing behaviors, repairing relationships, and utilizing strength of will. Although this model offers useful ideas, it's not the best answer for recovery.

Brain Addiction Model: According to experts, about ¾ of drug and food addicts, and likely many other types of addicts, have brain chemistry issues, specifically:

- Mood chemistry deficiencies: Inherited or triggered in response to stress.
- Poor regulation of blood sugar: Inherited or made worse by bad diet.

Recovering Intelligence

Bad moods & irregular blood sugar cause cravings; amino acids curb them!

Both negative moods and irregular blood sugar result in cravings. This is what 12-Step programs and the disease model call an allergy. It's the essence of the cause behind addiction. Increasing the health of neurotransmitter activity in your brain with good diet and nutritional supplements will decrease negative symptoms and increase emotional and physical well-being.

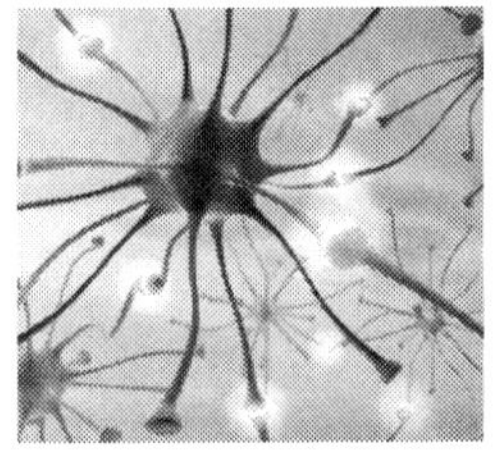

The process of addiction of all substances and behaviors, from liking to wanting to needing, occurs in the pleasure circuit of the brain. You experience pleasure from an experience, so you repeat it increasingly until your tolerance develops. As time passes you need more intensity or frequency for the same amount of pleasure to occur. Eventually, your liking becomes needing – not for pleasure, but to not feel bad and to be able to function. This process changes the addicted brain permanently. The neurobiology behind the addicted brain model is gaining visibility and acceptance in recovery communities and the scientific world.

Disease or Medical Model: This model believes some people have a genetic predisposition for drug or alcohol addiction which causes them to establish a lifelong, incurable physical allergy. Evidence appears to validate this.

Loss of Choice Model: A new theory states that in some addicted brains, the region of the brain needed to make good decisions is more vulnerable to addiction and addictive behaviors. As abuse grows, this region becomes more emotionally detached, and its decision making ability is reduced. Eventually, the natural yet inaccurate brain hardwiring that results from your addiction overrules all else, and you use, no matter the consequence. You believe that you need to use in order to survive.

Drugs, including sugar and addictive behaviors to a lesser degree, cause large amounts of brain chemicals, especially dopamine, to flood through your brain and control your thoughts and behaviors. Chemical floods produce new addicted pathways that start small then become large canyons, while normal pathways become weaker. These changes may become permanent.

Moral Model: This model describes addiction as an immoral behavior by people who make sinful choices due to having bad character or those who violate social and moral codes. The addict is unworthy of sympathy and should be punished.

Personal Issues Model: Core childhood issues or traumas may lead to negative patterns and emotions. If you don't explore your personal issues, they will undermine the quality of your life, and you won't maintain high-quality recovery. This is at least part of the cause of addiction for many, and a big part for some. As such, if you have unresolved issues or traumas, accept that resolving them may need to be a part of recovery. Denying issues will continue to cause pain. Please note, doing deeper work in early recovery deserves caution, leaning to contain core issue may be a better approach.

Psychological Model: All addictions – except alcohol, drugs, and maybe sugar – are obsessive compulsive issues rooted in personality and character flaws. Some can be helped with medication. From this comes the Personal Issues Model.

Spiritual Model: Separation from your spiritual connection causes a void. This leads to the desire to replace that void with something that makes you feel good or feel numb – this often leads to an addiction or addictive behavior.

TYPES OF ADDICTION

There are two types of addiction: addiction to substances and addictive behaviors.

Traits of Addiction

Many addictions and addictive behaviors have similar traits, such as:

- Acting in response to negative emotions or negative situations.
- Doing more than you want to, need to, or can handle.
- Being emotionally disconnected.
- Feeling compelled to act.
- Feeling a rush or a high, which is followed by a lack of pleasure and the need to maintain using to keep from feeling negative symptoms.
- Shame and guilt.
- Feeling big, proud, and empowered; or small, self-conscious, and out of control.
- External focus:
  - » Controlling people, places, situations, and things; not focusing on self.
  - » Looking outside of self for a fix of mood.

- Inadequate and inconsistent nutrition.
- Increasing energy, focus, and time involved in the practice of the addiction.
- Planning your life around your addiction.
- Lying to important others.
- Rewarding yourself by making using, an okay choice: "Because I need it, it's okay."
- Thinking about it a lot.

Addictive Behaviors

Addictive behaviors can be simplified as any behavior causing significant or regular harm, loss, or problems to the addict or someone close to the addict. The addict continues to use in spite of the negative impact on others or him/herself. The addict's behaviors are focused on the reward or high, not the depth or consequences of the experience.

It's necessary to recognize that the using behavior is the primary issue in addiction and occurs independently of other mental health issues, such as anxiety, depression, or mental illness. Poor impulse control is considered its own diagnosis but should not be ignored; it can lead to more serious addictive behaviors and other issues.

In order to be diagnosed with an addictive behavior, a person must have at least five of the following symptoms:

- Preoccupation: You have frequent thoughts about all aspects of using.
- Tolerance: You require larger amounts or more frequent using to experience the same rush.
- Withdrawal: You experience emotional/physical

pain that is associated with attempts to cease or reduce using behavior.

- Escaping: You use addictive behavior to improve your mood or escape issues.
- Chasing: You use to compensate for losses.
- Lying: You try to hide the extent of your behavior by lying to family, friends, or professionals.
- Loss of control: You have unsuccessful attempts to reduce the behavior.
- Breaking of boundaries: You break a personal, social, or legal limit in order to fulfill your desire.
- Rescuing: You turn to family, friends, or another third party for assistance.

RESPONSE TO ADDICTION

It's essential you have a clear and strong response to your addiction. Depending on the type of addiction and your relationship with it, this requires either abstaining or maintaining, or abstaining after attempting to maintain.

Abstinent Addictions: Abstinence requires total avoidance from the addiction. Consider the following:

- Drugs or Non-Prescription Medication:
  - » Alcohol
  - » Amphetamines
  - » Benzodiazepines

  - Caffeine
  - Cocaine
  - Ecstasy
  - Hallucinogens
  - Inhalants
  - Marijuana
  - Nicotine: Smoking or chewing
  - Opiates
  - Over the Counter Medications
  - Performance Enhancing Medications: Steroids, human growth hormones, etc.
  - Synthetic or designer drugs
  - Tranquilizers
- Gambling
- Pica: Ingestion of non-food materials
- Self Harm
  - Burning, Cutting, and Pounding
  - Suicide attempts
- Sex: Pornography, Internet

Maintenance Addictions: With some addictions aspects of the addiction are unavoidable or have some redeeming value. Your recovery approach needs a structured plan with specific limits. Some addictions may necessitate a brief period of abstinence, such as sexual abstinence when you are in recovery from a sex addiction.

- Beauty:
  - Cosmetic Surgery
  - Tanning: Tanorexia

- Codependency
- Collecting
  - » Cluttering and Hoarding
  - » Status: Art, cars, women, an entourage
- Competition:
  - » Sports: Watching or participating
  - » War: Against self or others
- Stimulation: From high risk behavior
  - » Criminal activity
  - » Drama
  - » Extreme activities: bungy jumping, hang gliding
- Extreme Exercise and Body Building
- Fame: Ego-acknowledgment, achievement, money, attention
- Food
  - » Overeating
  - » Binging/purging
  - » Dieting
  - » Eliminating: suppository
  - » Obesity
  - » Sugar or carbohydrate abuse
  - » Under-eating: Anorexia
- Gambling and Gaming
  - » Personal or Interactive
  - » Video: Units and online
- Money
  - » Saving
  - » Spending: For pleasure
  - » Spending: For effect, status, control, ego

- Power and Control
  - » Accumulation: Making, keeping
  - » Institutional: Organizational, religious
- Prescription Medication
- Relationship, Love, Romance
- Sex
  - » Personal, Interpersonal
  - » Video, Television, Movies, Porn
- Work, Personal Projects

Note: Categories are not clear-cut. Depending on the details, addictions could be in a different or more than one category.

Evaluating Addictions

Addictions and addictive behaviors are often defended by the addict. When you defend, it usually means you fear there is a problem. A healthy person doesn't need to defend an annual indulgent evening on New Year's Eve, an occasional cosmetic procedure, or hanging on to a tacky, old chair.

All regularly repeated, nonessential behaviors need to be explored for the degree of their addictive nature. For example, feeling compelled to jog daily for an hour may be a bit excessive, but feeling bad about yourself if you don't train every day for weekly triathlon events is clearly an addictive pattern.

Brain Chemistry's Role: The main role of the neurotransmitter dopamine is to signal the frontal lobe that a behavior is desirable, important, or better than most, which causes heightened awareness and a craving for more.

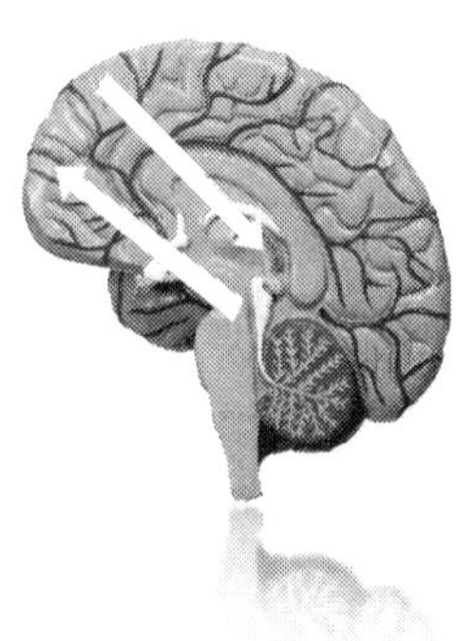

All natural pleasures produce dopamine, including drugs and addictive behaviors. Drugs induce a very large release of dopamine, which serves to intoxicate the brain into thinking that the experience was overpoweringly wonderful. And, indeed, perhaps it was. However, with enough use, the brain's pleasure center becomes rewired to believe that use of mind altering chemicals is the highest form of pleasure, and when triggered, your chemical response eventually becomes, "I must use to survive." This results in persistent using and a loss of control, even when there are significant negative or even disastrous results.

Positive Addiction: The term *positive addiction* sounds good, but if something is a true addiction, it's not positive. Some maintenance addictions, like exercising or dieting, have positive aspects, but can be unhealthy when done in excess. It creates an unclear gray area where addiction problems are compared to the added value of the addictive behavior, resulting in an almost equal balance of cons and pros. This is especially tricky when dealing with addictions related to everyday tasks like eating and working. If your behavior falls into this category, consider cutting back when possible and getting involved in another positive activity.

APPENDIX 3: NUTRITION

NUTRITION

Everyone's body, and especially the brain, needs the proper nutrients in the correct amount to work well. Neurotransmitters in the brain require specific nutrients to work effectively so information can be transferred from one brain cell or neuron to another. The most important food is protein, which is made up of amino acids.

If your brain doesn't have the amino acids it needs, you may be more vulnerable to addictive substances that mimic those amino acids. Mimicking in neurotransmitter sites promotes addictive responses in your brain. Taking enough amino acids is necessary if you want your brain and body to work right and to be less susceptible to addiction and mental health issues.

Your brain also needs many other nutrients to function properly. For example, the brain is two-thirds fatty acids and cholesterol, so you need to provide those nutrients for it to work at its best. Feed your brain and you'll have one less roadblock in recovery.

Note: Amino acid research started in the 1970s. Research in the mid 1980s showed that amino acid supplements increased the success rate of drug addicts in recovery. Yet, most recovery programs don't know about the body's amino acid requirements or use them in their recovery process. You may have to inform your treatment program of this essential resource for successful recovery.

Neurotransmitters and Their Effects

Amino acids are the building blocks of neurotransmitters. The following outlines the four vital neurotransmitters and their roles, including:

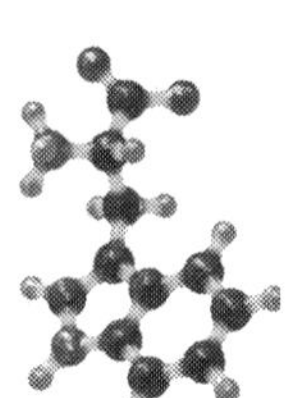

- The amino acids that affect them
- The symptoms of deficient amino acids
- The drugs and activities that are desired for a higher level of brain function

1. Endorphins: *The natural pain reliever*
   - DPA (D-phenylalanine) or DLPA (DL-phenylalanine – L form also stimulates) are used for the symptoms:
     - » Physical or emotional pain, including flooding
2. GABA: *The natural relaxer*
   - GABA (gamma amino butyric acid) is used for the symptoms:
     - » Anxiety, sleep problems, stress, or tension
3. Catecholamine: *The natural stimulators*
   - L-tyrosine is used for the symptoms:
     - » Apathy, depression, low energy, poor concentration

- » Lack of focus or motivation
- » Being irritable or stressed
- » Desire for stimulating or risky sports and activities like gambling and unsafe sex

4. <u>Serotonin</u>: *The natural mood elevator*
   - 5-HTP or tryptophan are used for the symptoms:
     - » Anxiety, depression, negativity, worry, or stress

Blood sugar balance is also a vital issue in addiction recovery because imbalance causes cravings. It can be helped with the amino acid L-glutamine.

5. <u>L-glutamine</u>: *Natural blood sugar stabilizer*
   <u>Hypoglycemic condition</u>:
   - Blood sugar instability is balanced with L-glutamine
   - The symptoms are:
     - » Blood sugar highs and lows
     - » Processed sugars and carbohydrates, caffeine, and nicotine influence blood sugar instability

Using Amino Acids (Check with your physician first)

- <u>Time of Day</u>: Follow suggested directions.
- <u>Dosage</u>: Start with the lowest recommended dose (or half dose) and wait 30 minutes for any potential allergic reaction, often only a headache. If no reaction occurs, continue. Take as directed on the bottle, even though some people say they experience relief of their symptoms by raising their dosage with no negative side effects. The absorption of amino

acids can be somewhat improved if you hold the powder under your tongue. There appears to be only one consistent side effect of taking too much of an amino acid: Reverse Syndrome.

- Reverse Syndrome: The symptoms you are trying to eliminate can return if you take a larger amount of amino acids than your brain needs or if you take them for longer than is needed. Allergic responses are unusual and might be eliminated by powdered Vitamin C.
- Response Time: The body usually responds to amino acids within 15 minutes. Some blends may take a few hours. The directions on the label may state that it can take a few days.
- Best Results: Take quality vitamin and mineral supplements and higher doses of Vitamin C. Ask your physician for general nutrient testing.
- Amino Repair Period: A 3 to 12 month period is usually required for amino acids to fully positively effect your brain, after which you won't need regular supplements unless your life becomes difficult.
- Duration: Take a supplement for three months then stop taking it and see how you feel. If your symptoms return, continue to use it. If you feel better, stop and see what happens.
- Amino Acid Intravenous Drip: In some cases, an amino acid IV drip is a highly effective detoxification method for all drugs, even opiates like methadone and Suboxone. It can be performed at an out-clinic,

but medically difficult cases need to be inpatient. It's not widely available in the US, but availability is increasing.

- Evaluation: Most of the time, your experience is enough to know the effect of what you are taking. If you don't get good results from amino acid supplements or if you have an allergic reaction, testing is the best approach. The only reliable test for neurotransmitters is examination of blood platelets (BP). Also consider testing for heavy metals and other substances.
- Experiential Feedback: If you aren't sure of the results you're getting, relax and pay attention to what you're feeling: maybe you're feeling relaxation, stimulation, or the relief of pain, or a negative mood or anxiety.

AMINO ACID THERAPY PRECAUTIONS

Consult a knowledgeable professional if you:

- React negatively to supplements
- Have a serious physical illness, particularly cancer
- Have severe liver, kidney, or ulcer problems
- Are pregnant or nursing
- Have Bipolar or other mental disorders
- Are taking mood-stabilizing medication

If you have:	Be cautious of:
• Melanoma, PKU, Grave's Disease	DLPA, DPA
• High blood pressure	L-tyrosine, DLPA, DPA
• Very low blood pressure	GABA, L-taurine
• Migraine headaches	L-tyrosine, DLPA, L-phenylalanine
• Bipolar tendencies	L-tyrosine, L-phenylalanine, DLPA, L-glutamine
• Asthma, severe depression	Melatonin
• A carcinoid tumor	L-tyrosine, DLPA
• Hashimoto's Thyroiditis	DLPA, DPA

Additional Nutrients for Detoxification

- For all addictive substances: General multivitamins and minerals, Vitamin C (up to 5,000 mg daily), Omega 3, and a pro-recovery diet are helpful. Amino acids vary with your situation. There are specific amino acid compounds blended to help your brain regenerate in early recovery.
- For liver detox: Vitamin C.

Testing

Tests help determine whether something physical or chemical is working or not working. There are tests that examine neurotransmitter and amino acid levels, as well as those pertaining to adrenal glands, blood sugar, food allergies, Vitamin D, the liver, pancreas, Pyroluria, and thyroid gland. Consult with a qualified professional.

Orthomolecular Medicine and Psychiatry

Orthomolecular medicine is the practice of preventing and treating disease by providing the body with optimal amounts of substances that are natural to the body. According to this field, Pyroluria is a blood disorder that appears to cause depression and contributes to many addictive, psychiatric, behavioral, and physical conditions. The established medical field currently disputes the concepts behind orthomolecular medicine.

DIET

Personalized Diet Approach

It's best if your diet is based on your nutritional needs. Ultimately, if you listen to the feedback your body is giving, you can determine the foods you were designed to eat. Are you tired, fulfilled, or starving 20 minutes after you eat? If you feel really tired, hyper, or sad soon after you have finished a meal, maybe you are eating the wrong foods for you. Also look into food allergies. You can get tested for food allergies, or just eat a suspicious food by itself and see what happens. Allergies to wheat and other products can cause relapse and physical problems, even death.

General Recovery Diet

- Fresh food is best; frozen is the next best.
- Protein: Eat meats three times a day in moderate portions; also consider amino acid supplements.
- Supplements: Take daily:
  - » High-quality amino acids until your diet improves
  - » Vitamins and minerals (cold press, food state)
- Fresh vegetables: All colors. As many and as much as possible.
- Fresh fruit: Equivalent 1 to 2 cups a day.
- All fats: Omega 6 and 9, but mostly Omega 3.
- Greatly reduce or eliminate all processed foods, processed sugar, and flour.
  - » Includes most cereals, packaged meals, and a lot of restaurant food.
- Eliminate all artificial sweeteners.
- No caffeine or nicotine.
- No foods you're allergic to.

It's especially important to follow this food program during the amino acid repair phase. This is usually a 3 to 12-month period, but varies with the person.

GENERAL MENU IDEAS

BREAKFAST	LUNCH	DINNER	PM SNACK
1/2 c. orange juice, 2-3 eggs with onion, green pepper, tomato, and one slice toast with butter	Tuna fish salad sandwich with lettuce and tomato, fake crab, macaroni salad, and an apple	Veggie chili, cornbread, big sweet potato, spoonful of yogurt, and a veggie salad with light dressing	One apple and a cup of tea with honey
Oatmeal or all-bran cereal (medium), milk, a tbsp of raisins, and a handful of nuts or seeds	Hamburger or veggie burger with lettuce and tomato, fake crab, macaroni salad, and an apple	Small baked chicken or tofu, med. baked potato with a spoonful of yogurt, and green beans or broccoli	One apple or two to three oatmeal cookies and a cup of tea with honey
Several reg. turkey sausages, 1-2 eggs, and one slice of toast or a piece of fruit	Soy protein drink: blueberries, yogurt, and ice; a few wholegrain crackers and nuts	Large baked squash, grated cheese, tomato soup, steamed carrots, and onions	Two pears, oranges, or apples and a cup of tea
Soy/whey protein drink: strawberries, sunflower seeds, yogurt, and ice	Big Caesar salad, turkey or chicken, med. sweet potato, and butter or sour cream	Small baked salmon, steamed green beans, and onions and brown rice	Two pears, oranges, or apples and a cup of tea

BREAKFAST	LUNCH	DINNER	PM SNACK
Peanut butter on toast and a cup of whole milk	Roast beef, steamed lima beans/onions, and big veggie salad with oil	Broccoli with cheese, large baked potato, chicken, and rice soup and apricots	Triscuits or wheat crackers with fruit preserves and a cup of tea
Cottage cheese, fruit and nuts, one cup of rice or almond milk	Baked fish (lg.) with butter, lemon, green peas, onions, and a big veggie salad	Spaghetti with sauce and veggie salad with chicken or tofu with light dressing	Several cups of popcorn with butter, vegetable oil, or hot sauce
Grilled ham and eggs and one slice toast with butter	Big veggie salad with avocado and tofu with dressing, squash, and cheese	Cajun rice and beans, veggie salad with dressing, and fruit with yogurt	One scoop of ice cream and half of a cantaloupe

Bread: The best breads are apparently sprouted grain, stone ground whole-wheat, rye, or pumpernickel. Though these are healthier options, you still want to limit your intake.

Sugar: Processed or refined sugar is addicting, and it is a contributor to diabetes, heart disease, high blood pressure, and obesity. All of those conditions damage your brain.

Salt: Salt is also addicting. Alkalizing mineral salt is supposed to be the better option and is very good for you, meaning you can use a reasonable amount and still be healthy. This product is expensive.

For further information, (See APPENDIX 10.)

Note: Consider:

- Steaming vegetables
- Baking fish
- Replacing butter, cheese, sour cream, salad dressing (oil), etc. with smaller amounts, unless...
  - » Using extra virgin olive oil or coconut oil
  - » Using almond, coconut, or rice milk
  - » Reducing Omega 6 fat
  - » Using organic products

For further information, (See APPENDIX 10.)

APPENDIX 4: DEFINITIONS

GENERAL DEFINITIONS

These general definitions are useful in addiction recovery:

A

Abstinence, Clean, Clean, Sober: Free of all mood-altering substances and addictive behaviors.

Addict, User, Abuser: A person who is using substances or practices any behavior excessively and consistently, in spite of negative consequences.

Addiction, Using, Substance Abuse, Behavioral Addiction: An addiction is an excessive behavior or a physical and emotional dependence. One feels compelled to indulge in the behavior or use, even after it has created major life problems.

Addictive Process: The process where one practices their addictive behaviors or substance abuse, in spite of negative consequences.

Adult Child of an Alcoholic (ACA), Addict or Dysfunctional Family: Someone raised in an addicted or chaotic family system. ACAs are characterized by lack of trust, fear of abandonment, and approval-seeking.

Alcohol, Drug, Mood-Altering or Psychoactive Substances: Substances that create a positive change in perception, mood, or consciousness, usually with a lot of pleasure.

Amino Acid Repair: The healing of brain and body through, amino acids (protein) and other quality nutrition.

Anchor, Trigger, Que: A memory of a person, place, situation or something that's wired into the memory and is experienced when stimulated.

Attitude: An expression of favor or disfavor towards something.

Automatic Negative Thoughts (ANTS): Negative thoughts, often based on lies, which become an automatic, declared as true, and damaging your self-esteem and self-concept.

B

Baseline: A starting point or personal standard that provides a point of reference for evaluating change. A new baseline can be created.

Behavioral Addiction: Any behavior you continue to participate in, in spite of negative consequences. See Process Addiction.

Behavioral Therapy: Therapy that focuses on reducing negative behaviors and increasing positive ones.

Belief: An acceptance that something is true and that things that in opposition to that belief, are not true.

Bond: A deep, emotional connection with another person.

Boundary: A physical, visual, mental, emotional, or spiritual border or limit: your resources, space, or time. A big issue in personal relationships, especially codependency.

Brain Scan: An image of one's brain taken with a fMRI, MRI, PET, or SPECT machine. It provides insight of brain functioning, helping with diagnosis and treatment.

C

Clinical: Assessment and understanding based on research and treatment of psychological or physical distress.

Clinical Training: Instruction in counseling and psychology: classroom and supervised internship, working directly with clients. Clinical training is the practical application of how to facilitate healing.

Codependent, Enabler, Rescuer, Controller: Anyone, usually a partner, whose "helpful" attitudes and behaviors enables the addict to continue to use. A codependent is addicted to pleasing, fixing, and rescuing the addict, and not looking at themselves. See also *CODA* and *Al-Anon*n.

Cognitive: Thinking or awareness of thinking.

Cognitive Therapy: Therapy that focuses on increasing the accuracy and focus of the client's thinking from negative problems to positive solutions.

Co-ing: Codependent behavior. See *Codependent*.

Consequence: A result that follows an action or a situation. Often used to mean a negative result.

Container: Mental imagery tool; an imagined container that holds an emotional issue until you're ready to deal with it.

Contempt: An intensely negative feeling or attitude towards someone or something as being inferior or worthless.

Co-occurring: Additional conditions that accompany the primary condition or issue.

Cortisol: A hormone produced by the adrenal gland in response to stress. It increases blood sugar and often leads to weight gain.

Counseling (Psychotherapy): The process of a trained professional working to assist a client in moving through personal issues and related feelings about current, past, and childhood issues. There are many styles; talk therapy is the most common. See also *Psychotherapy*.

Counselor: Usually a trained professional who may or may not specialize in addiction treatment. Counselors have a wide range of training. If in private practice, he or she will hold a private psychotherapy license. See also *Psychotherapist*.

Critic: An inner voice that attempts to help by pointing out your deficits, mostly judges and demeans.

Cross Addiction: A person dependent on one substance or behavior, trades that addiction for another one, often prescription medication.

Cue: See *Trigger*.

D

Defenses, Psychological: Psychological protection to cope with and reduce anxiety. There are various types of defenses, primarily unconscious. The most common is denial.

Defensive, Defended: Using one of many defenses as protection against change, criticism, vulnerability, or mental-emotional attack. Defenses can be used counterproductive.

Denial: A defense; the refusal to accept the truth, even in spite of feedback from people you trust.

Detoxification, Detox: The period of physical withdrawal from a substance.

Diagnose: The process of identifying and labeling the cause of a condition or situation.

DSM (Diagnostic and Statistical Manual of Mental Disorders): The psychiatric insurance bible for diagnosing mental illness; current version is DSM-V.

Dual Diagnosis: A diagnosis wherein one has an addiction and a psychological-psychiatric condition.

Dysfunctional Family: A family's very ineffective way of interacting with each other and the world.

E

Emotion: An intuitive feeling, based on complex subjective experience from biological, physical, psychological, and social responses to a life situation; influenced by mood, personality, motivation, hormones, and neurotransmitters.

Emotional Bondage: Being caught in cycle of emotional abuse, and feeling unable to break free. Usually inflicted by another person, but can be self-inflicted.

Emotional Flexibility: The ability to experience the full-range of emotions, positive and negative, and express them appropriately, and then let them go.

Emotional Intelligence: The ability to know what you are feeling and how to deal with those feelings.

Emotional Regulation: The ability monitor, evaluate, and modify your emotional reaction, and respond appropriately.

Empathy: The capacity to recognize, feel and ask about another person's emotional experience.

End Stage Addiction: When one's addiction has led them to enough health consequences that they will likely die.

Engagement, The Zone, The Groove: The ability to be totally involved, absorbed, or lost in a challenging activity; can be, but is not always fun.

Enmeshed: Family members drop their boundaries, lose their identity and direction, take on family roles, and help perpetuate the family's addiction.

Environment or Social Trigger: Any person, place, thing, situation, or time that has a past association with using, and that could cause you to feel like using.

Euphoria, High, Intoxication: The emotional brain state of ecstasy, joy, and complete self-satisfaction; usually with change in perception, mood, or consciousness.

Euphoric Recall: Remembering and re-experiencing using as a very positive experience while disregarding the negatives.

F

Facilitator: A person who leads and assists a group in an experience for a common objective.

Faith: Complete trust or belief in a person, thing, teaching or doctrine, not based of proof.

Family System: The way that family members interact with each other, the patterns maintain the roles, rules, orderliness, beliefs, and balance of the family.

Family System (Dysfunctional): An unhealthy style of family relating that is closed to outside influences and discourages communication or change in an attempt to protect the homeostasis (balance) of the system.

Family System (Addicted): See Enmeshed

Feedback System: A way to receive information about your behavior that can guide future actions if you pay attention, examples are other people's reaction to you or your feelings.

Flooding: Becoming emotionally overwhelmed.

G

Genetic Predisposition: A higher level of vulnerability for a condition to develop due to your genetic blueprint.

Gratification: Happiness from engaging in personally satisfying and purposeful activities.

Gratitude: A thankful or appreciative attitude.

Guilt: Inner conflict due to your belief (true or not) that you violated your own standard of conduct, or a moral standard.

H

Half Glass: Half-full is optimistic, half- empty is pessimistic.

Half-life: The time a substance takes to lose ½ of its potency.

Heart Trigger: Your Heart Trigger is the thing that gives you your strongest, emotionally charged motivation to stay clean.

Higher Power (HP): Any spiritual source that you accept as your guide and strength..

Higher Self: Your spiritual self or soul, that connects you to your concept of a higher power or a spiritual reality.

Hyperglycemia: Above normal blood sugar (glucose) level.

Hypoglycemia: Below normal blood sugar (glucose) level.

I

Identified Problem, Identified Patient (IP): As part of the Addicted (Dysfunctional) Family System Model, the IP is the one with the problem, the sick one versus other family members who see themselves as having no problems. The IP takes the pressure off of other members, and keeps balance.

Illusion: Something that appears to be or is interpreted to be real but isn't.

Inherited: Received from your parents, such as genetics or generation habits and beliefs.

Inhibition: A feeling that makes one self-conscious and unable to act in a relaxed and natural way.

Inner Child: A childlike part of one's self that was learned and experienced as a child.

Inner Child Work: The healing of unresolved childhood issues and trauma. Healing your damaged inner child may be essential for your recovery.

Integrate: Merging two or more aspects of yourself, so one functions as a whole.

Intellectualize: To think, reason, or analyze something or someone without awareness of your feelings; not relating on an emotional level to the person or situation. It's often used as a defense.

Intern: A student with scholastic training who is getting experience working directly with clients, fulfilling the requirements for a personal license.

Intimate Others: Anyone you feel comfortable talking with about your personal life. Often, intimate others are part of your support group.

Isolation: Choosing to be physically or emotionally alone, usually to avoid dealing with a difficult issue, person or situation.

J - L

Lapse: After a period of recovery, using briefly, usually less than one day; this is the same for all addictions or addictive behaviors.

Living in the Grays: Living in-between the black and the white, where things are not as clear or precise.

Love Object: A person or thing (such as your addiction) who is the focus of your affection.

M

Maintenance Addiction: A substance or behavior that one chooses to continue to control, because it's necessary, like food, or is very desirable, like an intimate relationship.

Medical Model: A model of addiction as a disease that is best treated by medical professionals.

Minimization: Seeing something or a situation as less significant than it actually is.

Mirroring: Matching or copying another's behavior, non-verbally communicating with each other in the process.

Mirror Neurons: Is a neuron that fires when you act and when you observe the same action performed by another, "mirroring" the behavior of the other person, as though you were performing the action.

Model, Modeling: To watch someone's behavior and practice acting the same way, until it become comfortable.

Mood-Altering, Psychoactive Substance: A substance or behavior that affects the brain, creating intense pleasure and changing one's emotional state.

Motivation: The reasons you act the way they do. There are many factors such as your intensity of desire or need, reward value of the goal, and your or other's expectations.

Multiple Disciplinary Approach: This is the name for a team treatment approach, which can include a psychiatrist, nurse, social worker, counselor, and other professional.

N

Negative Tapes: Negative messages from society are unconsciously accepted as true and are replayed, usually outside of conscious awareness.

Neurons: Brain nerve cells that process and transmit information through chemical signals.

Neuropathways: A path made by many thousands of neurons so that messages can travel in the brain.

Neurotransmitters: The brain chemicals that jump the gap between neurons, causing the completion of neuron transmission and messages to travel throughout the brain.

Normalize: To clarify that something that appears to be abnormal is normal; by showing you that it's more common than you thought that it was.

Nutritional Therapy: A recovery approach that focuses on diet and nutritional supplements.

O

Observing or Observer Self: A mental "self" concept which observes one's thoughts and behaviors, and clarifies what one wants and doesn't want, and motivates one to take desirable actions.

Optimistic: A confident, hopeful, and positive outlook about the future; can be unrealistic.

Orthomolecular Medicine: An alternative medicine that uses diet and nutritional supplements to create an optimum environment in the body and that will fight diseases.

Orthomolecular Psychiatry: The use of orthomolecular medicine to treat mental illness, using unorthodox forms of testing, diagnosis, and treatment.

P

Paradigm Shift: A fundamental change in your approach, assumptions, and thinking, usually a major shift about life.

PAWS (Post Acute Withdrawal Symptoms): A set of persistent impairments that occur after withdrawal from alcohol and drugs, as brain chemistry returns to normal; coming back periodically, usually at milestone times.

Perspective: A point of view or way of looking at things.

Pessimism: Thinking that something is worse than it is.

Pre-agreement: A prearranged agreement about how to act in a difficult situation or what will happen as a result of a negative behavior.

Pre-treatment Stage: The period of decreasing active use and increasing awareness and readiness to start recovery, up to stating recovery.

Primary Addiction(s): The addiction(s) of choice, the most serious one(s), the one(s) which other addictive behaviors lead back to, and the one(s) which cause the most problems.

Process: The experience of exploring an issue and examining the ways it affects your life, and your feelings about it. This normally leads to a decision to deal with the situation.

Process or Behavioral Addiction: An activity, behavior, or process that causes you problems and you continue the behavior, such as compulsive gambling, sex, or work.

Processed Foods: Highly refined food, which have little or no food value, as they are mostly sugars and carbohydrates.

Programming: The learning and integrating of new ways to do things and to live; may or may not be desirable. Desirable: learning lots of valuable things. Negative: losing your ability to think for yourself or learning negative things.

Psychosis: A significant mental break from reality, often indicated by hallucinations and delusions.

Psychotherapist: Someone who has significant training (and usually a private license) in ways of helping resolve a person's problems and initiate positive change, yet they may not have specialized in addiction treatment.

Psychotherapy: License: A state certification to acknowledge at least a minimal level of clinical training. Licenses include: Licensed Clinical Psychologist, Licensed Mental Health Counselor, Licensed Marriage & Family Therapist, Licensed Clinical Social Worker, Board-Certified Psychiatrist.

Psychotropic Medication: Are psychiatric medications that affect the mind and emotions, and one's mood and behavior. Most are used to treat mental illness, some are used and abused recreationally, because of the pleasure they cause.

Pyroluria: A hypothetical blood disorder of excessive levels of pyrroles, resulting from improper hemoglobin synthesis.

R

Reality Testing: Getting feedback from trusted others about the accuracy of your beliefs, perspectives, and thoughts.

Recovery: Stopping your addictive behaviors and lifestyle, and embracing a healthy and growth-oriented lifestyle.

Red Flag: Likely there's a problem or an unsafe situation.

Relapse, Mental-Emotional: Attitudes, feelings, thoughts, and behaviors indicating that you are already mentally and emotionally relapsing. Frequently called Dry Drunk.

Relapse Drift: Mentally or emotionally sliding away from recovery practices toward the behaviors that were indulged in during active addiction.

Relapse Event: Commonly known as relapse, it's when the actual using starts; the using of a substance or the acting out of an addictive behavior, after a period of recovery.

Relapse Symptom: Attitudes, feelings, thoughts and behaviors showing mental-emotional relapse.

Remorse: A feeling of regret, after doing (or not) something, that you believe should not (or should) have done.

Resilient: The ability to quickly bounce back to your normal baseline level of functioning after crisis or misfortune.

Resistance: The declined or refusal to discuss, remember, or think about an important issue or to change your behavior.

Resource Person: Anyone with personal time, recovery wisdom, or other resources that will help you.

Role Model: To behave in a manner that sets a positive example for others.

Rx: Prescription medication.

S

Safe Place: A mental imagery technique wherein you can take yourself to a special, safe place to relax, be emotionally safe, and renew.

Satisficing: Finding a high level approach or solution that is good enough, depending on the situation, someplace between acceptable and perfect.
Savoring: Deeply enjoying a pleasure.

Scope of Practice: The procedures, actions, and processes that are permitted for a specific licensed professional, based on their education, experience, and competency.

Secondary Addiction: A lessor used addiction, yet an issue to be a concerned about; will trigger your primary addiction(s).

Secular: Non-religious.

Self: A concept for describing a pattern that has become so strong that it can be performed unconsciously, such as driver self or addict self.

Self-Report: Responding to a question by only the participant. Often involved in a check-in, survey or questionnaire.

Self-Soothing: Your thoughts and behaviors that cause you to relax, let go, and feel nurtured.

Set Yourself Up For Success: Any behavior that will strengthen your recovery, move you in that direction, or at least cause you to remember (now and in the future) why you really want something, generally recovery.

Social Intelligence: The ability to know what someone else is feeling or care enough to ask (empathy), and how to be helpful to them.

State Learning Disability: Having difficulty recalling information in a sober state that was learned while using.

Stimulus, Stimuli: A change in the environment that you sense and evokes a reaction in you.

Strategic: Skillful and desirable recovery planning.

Stressor: Something external or internal that causes you to feel pressure or even distress, and may be a trigger to use.

Stuck Point: A mental-emotional block that stops the process and progress of your recovery.

Support System: People who care, accept, and support you, most likely people that are themselves in recovery.

Surrendering: Completely letting go of your addiction and accepting recovery and all that comes with it.

T

Temperament: The part of your personality you were born with; it influences the way you respond to the world.

Therapeutic: Something healthy, healing, or beneficial.

Tolerance: The physiological need for an increased amount of a substance in order to feel the desired effect.

Tough Love: Carefronting someone about their addictive behaviors; it includes providing boundaries, setting limits and follow-through on consequences.

Trance State: An external or internal focus and narrowing of vision or mental awareness; many types, like meditation.

Treatment: A professionally run recovery program, with services to assist and encourage clients with changing and growing; includes education classes and process groups; likely some individual support and recovery planning.

Treatment Plan: Your recovery plan set-up by a treatment professional, with your help and agreement.

Trigger, Cue: Any person, place, thing, situation, or time, or internal thought or feelings, that brings up an urge to use. You do not have control over triggers.

Trigger (Hot): A trigger that causes an intense desire to use, every time you experience it.

Trusted Others: Anyone you really trust, based on evidence.

U - Z

Using: Participating in any addiction or addictive activity.

Voice (The), Inner Critic: A negative judge whose strong, consistent, voice, says negative things about you (bad, fat, ugly, stupid, worthless, etc.). Seeing your Critic as an enemy or a misguided ally, make a big difference.

White Flag: Symbolic communication to another to stop whatever is going on and take a break.

Willpower: An inner strength or discipline, built over time through practicing right thinking and behaviors. Everyone has some, but relying heavily on it is a bad idea.

Yellow Flag: Be cautious; there may be a problem.

RECOVERY DEFINITIONS

The following are definitions of words used by recovering individuals:

A - C

A Quart Short: Someone who has not finished with their addition.

Being Sick and Tired of Being Sick and Tired: A general state of acceptance and acknowledgment of hitting bottom.

B.U.D.: Building Up to a Drink. Returning to the negative attitudes and behaviors of someone who is using.

Chasing the High: The pursuit of trying to recapture your best using experience.

Clean: Abstinence from all addictions and addictive behaviors.

Clean & Sober: Abstinent from all addictions and addictive behaviors, and working to improve you character and the quality of your recovery.

Committee: The parts of yourself including your addict self, that try to influence you.

Crutch: Something that is an aid to recovery. It can be positive or negative, but it's often spoke of negatively.

D - F

Dealing with the Wreckage of Addiction of the Past: Damage to yourself, career, family, friends, finances, etc..

Drunk-A-Log, Drug-A-Log: A historical list of your using experiences that ended in negative consequences.

Dry Drunk: Someone who is abstinent, but hasn't done the recovery work to improve their character, and therefore still acts as they did in their addiction.

EGO: Acronym for Edging Out God.

Future Tripping: Obsessive thinking that fears or predicts a future, usually a negative one.

G - H

God Box: A container in which you put your written problems, that seemingly have no solution. Symbolically, this act turns the issue over to God, and you can let go.

Gratitude List: A list of 3 to 5 things that happened that day that you are grateful for.

Guidance: God U and I DANCE.

Half Efforts Avail Us Nothing: Giving less than 100% of your effort to your recovery, is not likely to bring success.

H.A.L.T.: Never get too Hungry, Angry, Lonely, or Tired; to extreme or raw, because these states can trigger a relapse.

Hitting Bottom: A point where you truly accept that you have a problem and you want to change.

Hitting The Wall: A point when you question if recovery is working for you, whether recovery is enough or worth it.

I - L

I'm Doing FINE: Frustrated (F..ked Up), Insecure, Neurotic, Emotional. Translates to: I'm not going to tell you how I'm really doing.

Jail, Institutions, and Death: Where we all will eventually end up if we don't choose recovery.

K.I.S.S.: Keep It Simple, Silly (Stupid).

Leveling: Being direct and totally honest.

Listen for the Pop: The sound of your head coming out of your butt.

M - P

M.O.V.E.: Acronym for: Move and take action; Observe your reality; Visualize anything non-using; positive actions will have a desirable Effect on your recovery.

Normie: A person for whom drinking/using is insignificant.

Pink Cloud: Experienced in the first 60 days of recovery, when one is feeling better and enthusiastic about recovery.

Play The Tape Out...To The End: Mentally playing out and looking at what would happen if you used.

R - T

Restless, Irritable, and Discontent: Being in mental-emotional relapse.

Spin Dry: A brief 28 - 30-day residential treatment program.

Stinkin' Thinkin': Negative thinking, a relapse symptom.

Street Smarts: The ability to understand people, using that knowledge to survive and thrive, similar to Social Intelligence.

Take the Cotton Out of Your Ears and Stick It In Your Month: Listen rather than talk.

Taking Other People's Inventory: Over involvement in, and making judgments about another person's program.

Terminally Unique: Too special to successfully do a recovery program.

Tore-Up From The Floor-Up: Being in bad condition physically, mentally, and emotionally, as a result of addiction.

U - Z

Wall (The): An emotionally charged block; a time for growth and recovery, or relapse.

Walking Your Talk: Doing what you say you will do.

War Story: Sharing and emotionally reliving a using experience and emphasizing the positive; a symptom of relapse.

White Knuckling: Relying only on one's self to stay clean, even though you are emotionally having a hard time.

APPENDIX 5: SOCIAL-EMOTIONAL INTELLIGENCE

Emotions

Emotions are a complex biological, psychological, social, and spiritual feedback system that interprets, arranges, directs, and summarizes the feedback you receive from all your senses and your heart. Accurately identifying your feelings about a situation will help you make accurate, rational decisions and respond with appropriate behaviors.

Recovering Intelligence

Feelings are a feedback system that interprets, summarizes, & directs you!

Emotional Responsibility: Take responsibility for your emotional health by learning to understand and express your emotions. To express your feelings, you need to understand the language of emotions and how to use it to communicate your feelings to others.

Emotional Feelings

Understanding your emotions can broaden your awareness, encourage self-exploration, and build valuable skills to aid in your recovery. By engaging in your emotions, you can develop the ability to release negative feelings and embrace the positive ones.

Recovering Intelligence

Your feelings will help you or hurt you.

Negative feelings can offer you valuable feedback; listen and understand what they are telling you then release them. Hanging onto negative feelings will hurt you by reducing your energy and happiness. You could be left with an intense feeling of emptiness, loss, or loneliness.

Positive feelings enhance life by increasing your health, happiness, and the ability to build quality relationships. Embrace, engage, and experience emotions like excitement, gratitude, hope, joy, and love to become your best self and the ability to release negative feelings, embrace the positive ones and create a sense of well-being.

The Basic Emotions

EMOTION	TRIGGERS	FUNCTION
Anger	Goal blockage Social rule violation Perceived injustice	Remove the block
Disgust	Offensive	Repulsion Eliminate
Fear	Threat of physical or emotional well-being	Avoid Reduce harm
Joy	Goal achievement	Future motivation
Sadness	Loss of valuable object(s)	Call for help
Surprise	Unexpected situation	Increase facts

Emotional Intelligence

Emotional Intelligence is the ability to accurately know what you are feeling, to manage the negative, and to enjoy and use the positive.

Social Intelligence

Social Intelligence, or street smarts, is the ability to know, or the desire to find out, what another person is feeling (empathy), the desire to help them, and the ability to manage your relationships. The socially intelligent person is usually emotionally intelligent.

Social and Emotional Intelligence

Social and Emotional Intelligences are interconnected and difficult to separate. Included are:

- Self-awareness
- Self-management
- Social awareness
- Relationship management

Emotional connection: People are hardwired to want emotional connections with other people, other living things, and The Source. Defending against intimate interactions keeps your relationships emotionally superficial, lacking the depth that emotionally connected people have. Limited involvement or depth yields a pleasant relationship, but with limited gratification. If you want more, you must let go of your fears of being rejected, betrayed, or abandoned. If you can't let go of your fear, it's time for you to do deeper personal work.

Expressing emotions: Learn to share your important feelings about issues, problems, concerns, or hurts as well as appreciations, blessings, joys, and love.

If you don't express your pain, you aren't allowing yourself to be emotionally available or to be known. You can become blocked. That energy builds, and the blockage intensifies until you're filtering your experiences through this built-up pain and blocked energy. You can come to live in emotional bondage, which uses valuable mental energy as you deal with this emotional conflict internally.

Healthy people have emotional flexibility. They can identify a feeling and decide if it's accurate. They choose to look at the situation in a fresh way, causing them to feel differently about it and respond accordingly. They make use of the feedback they get from their emotions. They build and store their positive emotional experiences to call upon when needed at a difficult time. This also broadens their ability to interact and build relationships. They accept responsibility for their feelings and use them constructively.

If someone that you want an ongoing personal relationship with hurts your feelings, tell them directly. They may not respond the way that you'd like them to, but it should help you to release those feelings and clear the air. If they defend or blame you, examine any truth in what they are saying and make use of it. Hopefully, you and this person can talk through the situation and come to an agreement.

Emotional pain and loss: It's natural and healthy to avoid and defend against immediate pain, yet avoiding all emotional pain has negative consequences, especially pain from loss. Learn to manage your fears of:

- Losing someone who loves you, losing their love, or losing your sense of lovability
- Losing control
- Losing self-esteem

The best strategy for dealing with your pain is exploring the original source, facing it, grieving it, and letting go. Facing the pain of an unpleasant truth or even a trauma is hard, yet it's the only healthy way to deal with it. It can be less painful and go quicker than you think with help from a quality psychotherapist who uses an effective approach, or a spiritual guide. To get to the other side, you must go through it.

The more fearful you are of getting hurt, the less likely it is that you'll let yourself be vulnerable. You must open up and risk possible loss to gain the wonderful joy of emotional intimacy. Understand that there will be some pain, as the other person won't match your needs perfectly. You will survive this pain, and you will grow and become healthier and happier. The more that you connect with your inner value and strengths, the easier it will be.

Emotionally Fearful- - -Pleasant- - - Emotionally Engaging
Closed/Disconnected - - Semi-Available- -Open/Vulnerable

Growing Emotionally

If you are early in you emotional growth, expect that you're emotionally younger than your age and that you won't know what you're feeling nor how to handle your emotions.

Practice experiencing your emotional feelings and the physical sensations attached to those feelings. You'll improve. Start by consistently asking yourself, "What am I feeling?" Watch a movie and become a character in the film, and ask yourself, "If I was that character, what would I be feeling?"

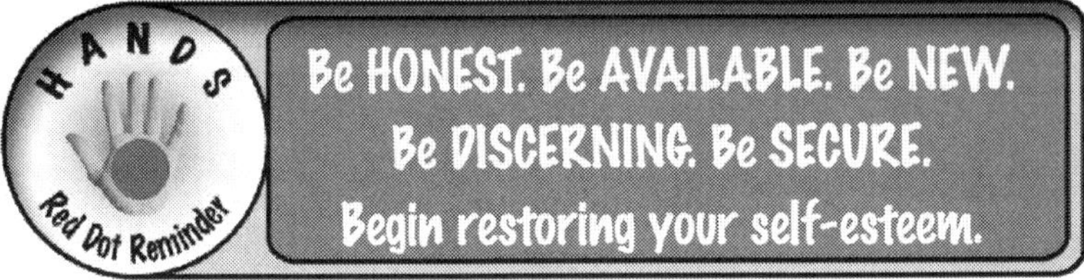

APPENDIX 6: DEVELOPING YOUR RECOVERING FUTURE™

Your Recovering Future™ is the mental picture of your ideal recovery, in the future. A future so desirable, you are compelled to take action to create it and to keep it. You will create this future by:

- Clarifying what you want and don't want.
- Developing a clear and complete mental picture.
- Holding that vision in your mind's eye and reviewing it twice a day, evolving it overtime.
- Doing whatever it takes to create it in reality.

Your vision can be simple. It need only be clear enough to identify it as being yours. Adding details can make it more powerful. Start with the image of you achieving your next recovery milestone. Look as far into the future as is comfortable. If you can't see a future where you are clean, that's an issue.

- Ask yourself why, and pay attention to the answer.
- You may need to develop the skill of visualizing. Start by looking at images that you can picture easily. Close your eyes and picture the room you are in, and then your last vacation.
- Some people just don't visualize:
  - » Can you feel or get a sense of this future?

Develop **Your Recovering Future™** self using all of your five senses – see, hear, feel (both emotions and touch), smell, and taste. Imagine yourself completing a recovery milestone or attaining some other success. Step into your picture and experience it. Experience it as if it's already true – in the future. Then turn around and acknowledge all the steps it took to get there. Practice experiencing this future for at least one minute twice a day.

EXPERIENCING YOUR RECOVERING FUTURE™

Find a comfortable, personal space so you can relax and be alone. Close your eyes and breathe slowly and deeply. Attempt to focus only on creating the intended picture in your mind's eye. Keep breathing deeply and slowly as you ask yourself questions and listen for the answers:

- "What is the next believable recovery milestone I want to achieve?"
  - » Would I like to have 30-days clean? How would it feel to be clean at my next anniversary, or clean at my child's wedding, etc.
- "What would the picture of me achieving this goal look like?"
  - » How would you be rewarding yourself?
- "Would there be a celebration?"
  - » Do you see friends acknowledging and celebrating you, hugs, dancing, a band playing?

- "How does it feel emotionally and physically?"
  - » Exciting, energizing, stimulating, happy, scary?
- "Where does this experience take place?"
  - » The fellowship, home, and group meetings.
- "What would I be doing before, during, and after?"
  - » Meditating, sharing, laughing, and hugging.
- "Who will be there, and what would they be saying?"
  - » Your support group, family, and friends.
- "Who would I be saying helped me?"
  - » "I wish to thank my (mentor) and recognize my (support group) for helping me."

Play the video of the event with you experiencing it, if you can; otherwise, watch or sense it.

- Experience yourself saying things like, "Recovery is a blessing."
  - » "Feel... the handshakes and hugs."
  - » "See... my friends. They're smiling."
  - » "Hear... them saying how proud they are of me."
  - » "Smell... the scent of the food we're eating."
  - » "Taste... the delicious food that friends brought."
- In your mind, turn around, take a deep breath, and look back on your journey. How did you get there? Get a sense of the map of your journey. Let yourself know, believe, or at least hope that it's possible.
  - » "As I take another deep breath and look back to the time when I first created this vision of my future, I'm amazed. I really did it!"

Over time, you'll progress and evolve in your recovery. Adjust to current situations, and achieve new milestones.

Ask yourself:

- "What new milestones do I want to achieve?"
  - » 90 days, 1 year, 5 years clean.
- "What's achievable and what will make me stretch?"
- What additional recovery oriented things do you want to add to your picture?

What you focus on grows, so focus on meeting your needs, wants, and dreams. Doing so will increase your odds of achieving them, and it will decrease the odds of sliding back towards using people, high risk places, and triggering things, and situations.

Having a picture of **Your Recovering Future™** gives your unconscious a clear target to focus on. You need to take action. Build your future in the real world, in the here and now, one step at a time.

Going after what you want can feel scary, even unreal. Breathe and stay focused on what you want. Identify the reasons you think you can't achieve **Your Recovering Future™** then let go of them and move forward into your recovery, until you get it and keep it. Set your next goal before you finish your current goal. You can do this!

Note: You may find it difficult to visualize, and will want to develop this skill. Close your eyes and imagine:

- The room that you're in
- A recent event
- Your last vacation
- Your next significant recovery goal
- Then **Your Recovering Future™**

APPENDIX 7: "IN MY EXPERIENCE... THINGS YOU DON'T WANT."

"In my experience... you don't want a poor connection to your inner and outer resources."

A poor connection to your inner and outer resources will make recovery a struggle, and will undermine your recovery, and your life.

Connecting with your inner resources will help you to feel more relaxed, focused, and clear. Connecting with your outer resources will offer you guidance and support.

The exceptions are:

1. Acknowledging and staying disconnected from your inner negative, critical, or toxic parts that discourage you or tell you to do destructive things. You might hear a voice in your head say, "You're stupid, worthless, a loser, fat; you're not ready yet. You'll always be addicted." Don't believe everything you think.
2. Limit the time you spend with toxic people and situations. Sometimes we have to have contact with people and situations that don't support our recovery. Breathe and learn to deal with the pressure of the situation, and get away from it as soon as possible.

"In my experience... you don't want to avoid, defend against, or resist desirable recovery options."

Resistance to change, new ideas, feedback, and positive recovery options, causes a serious block to quality recovery. When you resist, you block the knowledge and resources you'll need for successful recovery. You can become so defensive and resistant that you won't realize that you're drifting back to old, using behaviors. An example: Formulating a reason why something won't work, just as the person is sharing their suggestion.

In my experience, being unwilling to try new or additional approaches that can be beneficial to health and recovery is unhealthy. Often, this is because you choose to believe that the way you are doing something is the best way, or at least adequate. Remove your ego and fears, reduce your sense of being overwhelmed, and get unstuck.

"In my experience... you don't want to test yourself by putting yourself in risky situations. You don't have to prove anything to anyone!"

Proving anything to your old, using pals that involves showing them you can hang out with them or accompany them to places where you used together, can be a set-up for failure. Unless you absolutely have to, do not engage with your past addiction environment or the people who are still using. Wanting to return to old people, places and habits, is likely just your addict self attempting to manipulate you into familiar experiences or into using. Visiting your using friends and acquaintances to show them how well you're doing in recovery, hanging around a using environment to prove you can be there without using, rationalizing that you can "slip" just once and then you will stop, telling yourself that since you aren't using your addiction of choice, you can try other substances, and participate in highly stimulating activities are all examples of how our addict mind can lead us astray.

"In my experience... you don't want to cling to other secondary addictions or addictive behaviors."

In my experience, your unwillingness to confront or deal with your other secondary addictions, or your addictive behaviors, is choosing to not be in total recovery. Having another active or semi-active addiction is risky. The altered state from these behaviors, or even the craving for it, can trigger your primary addiction and raises the chances of relapsing. Smoking cigarettes, obsessive romantic infatuations, processed sugar, or other "highs" need to be stopped. Take action NOW to do this!

"In my experience... you don't want to be unprepared for sudden or unexpected triggers."

Lack of preparation is a set-up for not being able to deal with problems adequately because triggering events and other crises often happen suddenly or in unexpected ways. they blind side us.

Set yourself up for success by being prepared. Start with knowing your triggers and relapse symptoms and having a plan to deal with them. Practice responding to your triggers and symptoms as well as general negative situations; mental rehearsal and role-playing are very effective for this. As you practice responding, breathe and imagine keeping your boundaries and performing your best recovering behaviors. Notice what you are saying to yourself and how you are feeling. Do this well ahead of time so you are prepared.

"In my experience... you don't want to focus on external power or controlling other people."

Power and control issues are constantly part of our interactions with others. Focusing on external power and trying to control others doesn't work overall and can be destructive. Practice self-awareness to develop self-control and self-empowerment. Stay in control, but don't try to control. Staying in control can include relaxing, focusing inward, and doing nothing external. It can also be about choosing to be playful, going with the flow of what is happening, and allowing your recovery supports to influence you. Learn to be influenced by the wise people you have placed in your life, and their valuable ideas. Focus on being successful through partnership, not controlling.

"In my experience... you don't want poor sleep, extreme stress, and bad nutrition."

Poor sleep can cause fatigue, weight loss or gain, and even hallucinations. Everyone needs a good night's rest to function their best. Eight hours of sleep each night is the standard recommendation.

Uncontrolled stress will wear on your mind, reduce concentration and performance, and cause physical illness. The pressure of life causes many people to have physical symptoms that they don't realize are due to stress. Stress can mimic cravings.

Bad nutrition will undermine your health, your recovery, and shorten your life. A high-quality diet and nutritional supplements are powerful fuel for your brain and body's health and development. A stable blood sugar level, achieved through healthy food, is essential. You are what you eat.

"In my experience... you don't want to over-focus on the negative, your problems, or what you're "losing" by being in recovery."

You tend to get what you focus on, so if you're overly-focused on:

- The negative – you won't see the positive, and you will get more of the negative.
- Your problems – you won't see the solutions or your dreams.
- What you're losing in recovery – you won't fully experience what you're gaining.

Your recovery will be harder, less enjoyable, and less successful if you focus on the negative. For example, if you're preoccupied with not relapsing, you won't be focusing on, nor building, **Your Recovering Future™**.

"In my experience... you don't want to have inaccurate thinking."

Inaccurate thinking always contributes to problems. Your thoughts create your feelings, and both influence your decisions and your behaviors. If your thoughts are inaccurate, your behavior will miss the target.

Accurate thinking increases the chances that you will choose healthy behaviors and achieve your goals. Thinking, "I always overeat at certain times or in certain situations," is very different from, "I have been overeating at certain times and in certain situations, so I'll do (X) and set myself up to successfully change my behavior."

"In my experience... you don't want a relationship goal of being right or getting your way to put off being fulfilled, happy, and successful."

It's very important that you stay clear regarding your relationship goals and that the two of you find one-to-one time to connect and communicate with each other. Without intimate connection and frequent communication, your relationship can get off track and in the ditch quickly. Relationship goals need to benefit both of you in positive ways. Start by attempting to understand what the other person is saying. When you both understand what the other person wants, solutions are easier to find.

Upon acceptance that you have a negative habit, decide how you feel about it and how motivated you are to stop it.

On a scale of 1 to 10, if you are a 6 or higher, you should have enough desire to be successful. Connect with your desire and take action immediately. Decide when you want to start eliminating or reducing your bad habit and by when you will reach your goal. If you use your tools, strategies, and support, you should be successful.

"In my experience... you don't want your emotions to dominate you."

Your emotions can control you. They can control you without you even realizing it. They can dominate you, which is a real problem! As an extreme example, drama junkies are ruled by the regular turbulence of crises, disasters, and even catastrophes. There is always a major problem going on in their life.

Some people consciously ignore their emotions, choosing to believe that they are in total, rational control. This is not true; it is a dysfunctional belief. We all have emotions that need processing.

Many of us receive useful feedback from our emotional feedback system and use it to make better decisions. Yet we are too often compelled to buy the unnecessary item at the checkout stand, order a super-sized meal, or snap at a loved one – all motivated by emotion, not logic. Raise your awareness of your emotions.

"In my experience... you don't want to do anything to strengthen current negative habits or start any new ones."

The moment you realize you are occasionally doing something that you would prefer not to do, acknowledge that you are starting a negative habit. Decide to pay attention. When you realize you are doing that behavior, stop immediately. Validate yourself for stopping. Repeat.

Upon acceptance that you have a negative habit, decide how you feel about it and how motivated you are to stop it. On a scale of 1 to 10, if you are a 6 or higher, you should have enough desire to be successful. Connect with your desire and take action immediately. Decide when you want to start eliminating or reducing your bad habit and by when you will reach your goal. If you use your tools, strategies, and support, you should be successful.

APPENDIX 8:
THE TOP 21 THINKING ERRORS

Applied to Mental-Emotional Relapse Thinking

Inaccurate thinking ("Stinkin Thinkin") about your recovery and your life will cause inaccurate and often negative feelings. Those feelings can lead to decisions and behaviors that are based on false premises. Accurate and balanced thinking will enhance your recovery. Focus on improving one or two thinking errors, then focus on one or two more. Eventually, you will improve the accuracy of your thinking.

The following is a brief introduction of thinking errors:

1. **ASSUMING:** You assume that every part of recovery will be difficult or impossible. You think things like, "This is to hard!" and make a half-hearted attempt or don't even try.
2. **COMPARING (UP/DOWN)** UP: You evaluate yourself as being less able to succeed in recovery compared to those who appear to be doing well. You think things like, "This is too hard!" DOWN: You assess yourself as being more able to succeed in recovery compared to those who are struggling; you then think things like, "This is pretty easy!"
3. **CONFIRMATION BIAS**: To confirm your bias about recovery you scan for things that fit your beliefs, creating a blind spot. You think things like, "I got this recovery thing down pat!"
4. **CONTROL FALLACY**:
   - External: You feel helpless, a victim, not in

control of your recovery. You say things like, "There's not enough support out there to help me to succeed!"

- Internal: You feel powerful and totally in control of your recovery. You think things like, "I can control my behavior in any situation!"

5. **DEFENDING:** You defend your approach to recovery, not listening to important and informed others; you think things like, "I can't" or "It's not true."
6. **DRAMATIZING**: You respond to stressful or triggering situations with exaggerated thinking. You think things like, "This is so outrageous!" or "That's totally unfair!" even when it's not true.
7. **EMOTIONAL LOGIC**: You use your emotions to direct your behavior. You think, "If I feel it, it must be true."
8. **EXTERNAL CHANGE**: You think your recovery would be so much better if others would change; such as your family trusting you again. You think things like, "It's not being fair that they aren't trusting me!"
9. **EXTREME LANGUAGE**: For emphasis or effect, you use extreme words when describing your issues in recovery. You think things like, "That always happens!" or "It never gets easier!"
10. **GENERALIZING**: You draw negative conclusions, about recovery, based on limited evidence. You think things like, "I didn't get anything from that

meeting; these meetings just are not for me."

11. **LIMITING**: You have beliefs about recovery that limit all that it could be for you; you think things like, "Recovery is boring!" Limiting can also be about your self-image or identity; you think things like, "I'm just an addict!"
12. **MANIPULATIVE THINKING**: You attempt to get what you want through manipulation. You think things like, "I need some money so I'll tell my dad that I'm going to my recovery meetings."
13. **MINIMIZING**: You down play or dismiss valued other's opinions about your recovery attitudes and behaviors. You think things like, "I relapsed, it's no big deal!"
14. **MISLABELING**: You attach incorrect, unique, or emotionally loaded labels to yourself and your recovery. You think things like, "People in recovery are squares, and I'm not a square."
15. **PERSONALIZING**: You believe that you are (overly) responsible for other's recovery, especially their failures. You think things like, "If only I'd have been more available, he/she wouldn't have relapsed.
16. **PESSIMISM: :** (glass is half empty): You focus on all of the negatives of your recovery, no matter how much better your life actually is. You think things like, "Recovery will always be hard and boring!"
17. **POLARIZING**: You feel that your father is trying to control your recovery. You tell your mother that his behavior is going to make you relapse, to get her

on your side. You think things like, "I need to get my father off of my back!"

18. **PREDICTING**: : You predict your recovery will go poorly or well, with limited or no evidence. You think things like, "I finished my program so I'll do well in the future!"
19. **REJECTING REALITY**: You reject the truth about your recovery, the good or the bad, and its value in your life. You think things like, "Of course my recovery is solid, even though I relapsed!"
20. **TIME DISTORTION**: You think that the positives of your recovery won't last and the negatives will last forever. You think things like, "Thirty days clean is forever!"
21. **"YES, BUT..."**: You say yes to recovery, appearing to embrace it, but then resist it. You think things like, "Yes, I'll go to meetings, but not yet!"

The moment you realize that you are thinking or speaking inaccurately, stop immediately and correct yourself. Validate yourself for your effort.

APPENDIX 9: INTRODUCTION TO GROUP PROCESS

The focus of an interpersonal group can be:

- Psycho-educational: Learning, solution-oriented processing, goal setting: there could be a theme.
- Process: Usually for deep therapeutic work, but could be solution-oriented; could have specific focus like: Adult Child of Alcoholic, a specific addiction, co-dependency, etc.

Therapeutic Process Groups

Group process or therapy is not an easy experience, yet it can be helpful, cost-effective, and rewarding. It's a microcosm of life. The open and honest sharing of what's going on with group members and how they feel about sharing in a group might be abnormal to you at first, but you'll adjust. Your group will act like a mirror for you, reflecting back what you are experiencing. Learn to breathe deeply, relax, and listen. If you're asked to do something that may feel emotionally difficult, ask for support and guidance.

The group often becomes a place for group members to deal with and even act out their issues. Issues that come up for you in your group, even those between you and other group members or the leader, will be similar to those issues you need to deal with in your recovery and life in general. Take mental or physical notes and address them.

Goal

The goal of all groups is to learn, grow, and change. Depending on the group, you'll likely discuss personal issues and related feelings, and possibly find solutions.

The goal of a therapeutic group is to provide an accepting, trusting, and supportive place for its recovering members to explore, understand, and grow. You will have the opportunity to get to know yourself and the other members on a very real level and to examine your personal style: behaviors, defenses, issues, resources, strengths, etc.

The goal of an educational or coaching group is to provide a supportive learning environment. The structure may also include check-in, goal setting, and results.

Group Interaction

Ideally, the group leader guides members through the interaction process, but it's up to the members to run the group through their participation. When it works, it's an exciting, powerful, and energizing experience for everyone. This format is easy for the leader and helps validate the members. Give it a try; you'll likely be happy that you did.

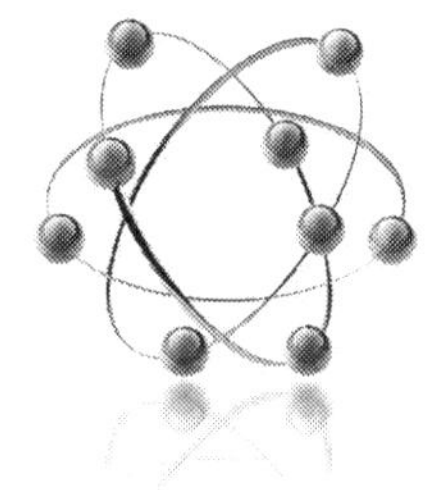

If talking isn't effective, there are other techniques to group interaction that may be used during meetings, depending on the type and amount of training the leader has had. These may include education, mental imagery, and role-playing. One of the benefits of group work is that you can learn from others without doing the work yourself.

Group interaction can be used for any recovery or life issue that concerns you. Avoid being superficial. Get to your real feelings and issues. You will be asked to take action to deal with your concerns. Sometimes, supportive carefrontation is necessary. This is done out of genuine caring.

Note: Not all leaders, also known as facilitators, are well-trained or well-intentioned, so be careful, but also be honest with yourself about whether a desire to leave is just you trying to avoid the group process.

Communication

The key to communication is being open and sharing your feelings appropriately and respectfully. Pay attention to what you are saying, how you are saying it, and your body language:

- Facial expressions
- Body movements and posture
- Gestures
- Eye contact
- Messages: Primary and secondary
- Touch (touching is not advised)
- Space: Placement and use of space, leaning towards or away from someone
- Voice: Tone, pitch, volume, inflection, rhythm, rate

Is your presentation congruent and whole, and not a

mismatch of intentions? Example: You tell the group, "I want to be in recovery," but you don't look him or her in the eyes, you can't stand still, and your teeth are clenched. These are all signs that you really don't want to.

- Clear communication: Use accurate words with specific meanings rather than multiple meanings. Slang or street language may block communication and potentially cause separation with others.
- Direct communication: Talk directly to others rather than about them. Look them in the eye, use their name, and speak clearly and to the point.
- Listen: Really listen to others. Try to create a picture in your mind's eye of what they are describing. This is important, whether the speaker's focus is on you, others, or themselves. If it's about you, take what you can from it. Don't have side conversations!
- Open and honest communication: For the group process to work, members need to be clear and open. Defending, resisting, or lying is destructive and unacceptable, and it will negatively affect others in the group.
- Owning your communication: Take ownership for what you are saying by using "I" instead of "you," "one," "everyone," and other non-personal words.
- Repeating: Say something once. Repeating it is rarely useful and can be annoying.
- Speak for yourself: Tell your own story, and speak your own truth. Take care of yourself, and let others do the same. Allow the leader to take care of others

when they need it, but be supportive.

- Share your position: Be upfront and share your point of view. Avoid asking questions, especially the "why?" ones. If you believe a question would be helpful, use "what?" or "how?" questions.
- Take care of yourself: If you're feeling unsafe, uncomfortable, or stressed out, let the leader know. If your concerns aren't responded to in the moment, talk to the leader after the meeting. If you don't feel heard, check in with another trusted member for feedback. If you still feel uncomfortable, it's okay to change groups. Find a group that works for you.

Feedback

All feedback, from any source, can be helpful. Pay attention and be open.

- Emotional feedback: Feelings are your emotional feedback system and they are real. No one can deny your feelings, though they may try. Addiction and recovery are emotional experiences. You may be out of touch with your real feelings. They need to be uncovered, felt, used, and released. In group, you will feel many emotions. Share your feelings appropriately, with as much care as possible.
- Feedback from your body: Your body will give you information. Physical pain, muscle tension, an upset stomach, or a vague feeling of discomfort is physical feedback that something is wrong.
- Feedback from others: Other group members may

want to give you feedback. Breathe and be open to it. It could be of great value to you. After listening, use what you can and file or let go of the rest.

Relating In Group

- Mental state: Your mental approach to the group will make a big difference in how you relate in it and what you will get from it. Be a curious sponge, and wonder what and how much you will learn.
- Roles: Roles are ways of relating. In groups, it's essential to get past your social mask and onto honest thoughts and feelings. The roles you play in the group will be similar to those you play in your life. The gender mix of the group will encourage different roles.
- All male groups: Issues like playfulness or competitiveness limit the expression of feelings. Men miss the opportunity to receive a female point of view and to process with women.
- Male and female mixed groups: Both sexes have a real chance to learn and grow with each other. Some women have the potential to act girlish, sexy, or motherly, while men may tend to be overly-focused on getting women's attention, both of which interrupt the group process.
- All female groups: Members experience more connection and support, but they miss the opportunity to receive a male point of view and to process with men.

- Be present: Focus on what's going on inside of you. This gives you the gift of knowing what you're thinking and feeling and gives you more control over your experience.
- Avoiding: It's understandable that you may want to avoid issues and feelings. Yet, group interaction is an opportunity to learn and grow. Avoiding your feelings and issues by bringing up a new issue, intellectualizing, making a joke, or responding with, "I don't know," doesn't serve you well. Put avoidance aside, breathe, and ask yourself, "What do I know?" or "Do I want to know?"
- Humor: Sometimes, a humorous comment can help to lighten everyone up, but laughter is often inappropriate, and used to put someone down or to avoid an issue. Making a humorous comment one time can be okay. Doing it repeatedly is not.
- Judging and moralizing: Everyone has personal issues. It's easy to judge others' issues as terrible, stupid, or strange. This has no constructive value and is usually destructive.
- Agreements: Everyone has agreements, both spoken and unspoken. In a group, agreements need to be shared between all parties; the staff should especially know all agreements. Watch out for unspoken agreements that will sabotage your recovery, such as, "If you don't expose me, then I won't expose you."
- Safety: Group has to be a safe place for everyone.

Group members need to limit their interaction to recovery based activities only. There should be no romantic interests, lending or borrowing of money, or trading of business services.

APPENDIX 10: RECOVERY RESOURCES

Resources can be found at
www.thrivingbeyondaddiction.com

- Products:
  - » Books
  - » Healthy living
  - » Tapes
- Resources
  - » Articles
  - » Internet links
  - » Self-help resources
- Services

INDEX

Q

R

ABOUT THE AUTHOR

Dr. Rohrer is the Executive Director of the Addiction Recovery Graduate Programs, which offers education and coaching programs for people after their primary treatment. He is a Life, Performance & Recovery Coach, and Licensed Marriage, & Family Therapist (MFC20325), in private practice in Walnut Creek, CA. Dr. Rohrer works with individuals, couples, and groups, in-person and through video conferencing; he also produces recovery products.

Dr. Rohrer began working in addiction treatment in 1973 and he has worked in many types of programs, with most types of substance and behaviorally addicted clients.

In 1974, Dr. Rohrer completed an Alcoholism Counselor Training Program with the City of Baltimore and John Hopkins University. In 1978, he received his Master of Arts degree, with two specialties, Alcohol Studies and Marriage, Family & Child Counseling from Lone Mountain College (acquired by USF) and University of San Francisco. In 2000, Dr. Rohrer received his Ph.D. from Greenwich University in Psychology, with a specialty in Addiction Treatment.

In the 1990s, Dr. Rohrer produced the Annual San Francisco Bay Area Relapse Prevention Conferences. He has taught at National University, School of Psychology & Human Behavior, and at Relapse Prevention at Cal State E.B.

Personally, Dr. Rohrer has been in recovery since 1985, using many of the resources he presents in this book. He lives with his wife, Dr. Ann Schiebert, in Northern CA. Dr. Rohrer can be contacted at drtom@tomrohrer.com

Made in the USA
San Bernardino, CA
06 July 2016